GUIDE TO FOOD STORAGE

P9-DMP-370

Follow this guide for food storage, and you can be sure that what's in your freezer, refrigerator, and pantry is fresh-tasting and ready to use in recipes.

In the Freezer (at -10° to 0° F)

Dairy and Eggs

Cheese, hard	6 months
Cheese, soft	6 months
Egg substitute, unopened	1 year
Egg whites	1 year
Egg yolks	1 year
Ice cream, sherbet	1 month

Fruits and Vegetables

Commercially frozen fruits	1 year
Commercially frozen vegetables	8 to 12 months

Meats, Poultry, and Seafood
Beef, Lamb, Pork, and Veal

Chops, uncooked	4 to 6 months
Ground and stew meat, uncooked	3 to 4 months
Ham, fully cooked, half	1 to 2 months
Roasts, uncooked	4 to 12 months
Steaks, uncooked	6 to 12 months

Poultry

All cuts, cooked	4 months
Boneless or bone-in pieces, uncooked	9 months

Seafood

Fish, fatty, uncooked	2 to 3 months
Fish, lean, uncooked	6 months

In the Refrigerator (at 34° to 40° F)

Dairy and Eggs

Butter	1 to 3 months
Buttermilk	1 to 2 weeks
Cheese, hard, wedge, opened	6 months
Cheese, semihard, block, opened	3 to 4 weeks
Cream cheese, fat-free, light, and 1/3-less-fat	2 weeks
Egg substitute, opened	3 days
Fresh eggs in shell	3 to 5 weeks

Meats, Poultry, and Seafood
Beef, Lamb, Pork, and Veal

Ground and stew meat, uncooked	1 to 2 days
Roasts, uncooked	3 to 5 days
Steaks and chops, uncooked	3 to 5 days

Chicken, Turkey, and Seafood

All cuts, uncooked	1 to 2 days

Fruits and Vegetables

Apples, beets, cabbage, carrots, celery, citrus fruits, eggplant, and parsnips	2 to 3 weeks
Apricots, asparagus, berries, cauliflower, cucumbers, mushrooms, okra, peaches, pears, peas, peppers, plums, salad greens, and summer squash	2 to 4 days
Corn, husked	1 day

In the Pantry (keep these at room temperature for 6 to 12 months)

Baking and Cooking Staples

Baking powder
Biscuit and baking mixes
Broth, canned
Cooking spray
Honey
Mayonnaise, fat-free, low-fat, and light (unopened)
Milk, canned evaporated fat-free
Milk, nonfat dry powder

Mustard, prepared (unopened)
Oils, olive and vegetable
Pasta, dried
Peanut butter
Rice, instant and regular
Salad dressings, bottled (unopened)
Seasoning sauces, bottled
Tuna, canned

Fruits, Legumes, and Vegetables

Fruits, canned
Legumes (beans, lentils, peas), dried or canned
Tomato products, canned
Vegetables, canned

WeightWatchers®
ANNUAL RECIPES *for* SUCCESS
2011

Oxmoor
House®

©2010 by Time Home Entertainment Inc.
135 West 50th Street, New York, NY 10020

All rights reserved. No part of this book may be reproduced in any form or by any means without the prior written permission of the publisher, excepting brief quotations in connection with reviews written specifically for inclusion in magazines or newspapers, or limited excerpts strictly for personal use.

ISBN-13: 978-0-8487-3329-2
ISBN-10: 0-8487-3329-0
ISSN: 1526-1565
Printed in the United States of America
First Printing 2010

Be sure to check with your health-care provider before making any changes in your diet.
Weight Watchers and **POINTS** are registered trademarks of Weight Watchers International, Inc., and are used under license by Oxmoor House, Inc.

OXMOOR HOUSE
VP, Publishing Director: Jim Childs
Editorial Director: Susan Payne Dobbs
Brand Manager: Victoria Alfonso
Senior Editor: Heather Averett
Managing Editor: Laurie S. Herr

WEIGHT WATCHERS® ANNUAL RECIPES FOR SUCCESS 2011
Editor: Rachel Quinlivan, R.D.
Project Editor: Emily Chappell
Director, Test Kitchens: Elizabeth Tyler Austin
Assistant Director, Test Kitchens: Julie Christopher
Test Kitchens Professionals: Allison E. Cox, Julie Gunter,
   Kathleen Royal Phillips, Catherine Crowell Steele, Ashley T. Strickland
Photography Director: Jim Bathie
Senior Photo Stylist: Kay E. Clarke
Associate Photo Stylist: Katherine Eckert Coyne
Production Manager: Theresa Beste-Farley

CONTRIBUTORS
Designer and Compositor: Carol O. Loria
Copy Editor: Dolores Hydock
Proofreader: Carmine B. Loper
Indexer: Mary Ann Laurens
Interns: Sarah Bélanger, Christine T. Boatwright, Torie Cox, Georgia Dodge,
   Caitlin Watzke
Menu Planner Editor: Carolyn Land Williams, M.Ed., R.D.
Nutritional Analysis: Lauren Page, M.S., R.D.

Cover: Key Lime Cheesecake Parfaits, page 40

To order additional publications, call
1-800-765-6400
or
1-800-491-0551.

For more books to enrich your life, visit
oxmoorhouse.com

To search, savor, and share thousands of recipes, visit
myrecipes.com

WeightWatchers®
ANNUAL RECIPES *for* SUCCESS
2011

contents

Weight Watchers®

At Weight Watchers, weight management is a partnership that combines our knowledge with your efforts. We help you on your weight-loss journey to make positive behavioral changes in your life, inspiring you with our belief in your power to succeed and motivating you every step of the way.

WEIGHT WATCHERS INTERNATIONAL BACKGROUND

SINCE ITS FOUNDING IN 1963, Weight Watchers has helped millions achieve healthy, sustainable weight loss. Weight Watchers International, Inc., is the world's leading provider of weight-management services, operating globally through a network of company-owned and franchise operations. Weight Watchers holds more than 50,000 weekly meetings where members receive group support and learn about healthy eating patterns, behavior modification, and physical activity. **WeightWatchers.com** provides innovative subscription weight-management products over the Internet and is the leading Internet-based weight-management provider in the world. In addition, Weight Watchers offers a wide range of products, publications, and programs for those interested in weight loss and weight control.

For more information about the Weight Watchers program and a meeting near you, call 1-800-651-6000 or visit **www.weightwatchers.com**

THE WEIGHT WATCHERS COMMITMENT TO SCIENCE

Weight Watchers backs up its weight-management plans with a strong commitment to the science of weight loss. The research and conclusions of experts and health organizations worldwide, including the World Health Organization and the National Institutes of Health, are incorporated into the Weight Watchers offerings. Weight Watchers also conducts its own research on weight-loss methods. As scientific findings change, the Weight Watchers plans evolve.

Weight Watchers®
ANNUAL RECIPES FOR SUCCESS 2011

This new cookbook empowers you to make the right food choices every day. There's never been a better time to make a positive change in your health, and you can do it while still enjoying the foods you love. Here's how:

- Over 200 great-tasting recipes that bring pleasure back to mealtime
- A **POINTS**® value per serving for every recipe
- Nutritional analysis with every recipe (see "About Our Recipes" on page 16)
- More than 40 color photographs of delicious recipes
- Step-by-step recipe instructions, prep and cook times, and secrets from our Test Kitchens
- Four seasonal menus, each with a Game Plan for preparing the meal
- Four weeks of 7-Day Menu Planners that incorporate many recipes from the cookbook plus some new ones, too

OUR FAVORITE RECIPES

All of our recipes are rigorously tested to ensure ease of preparation and excellent taste. But some are a cut above the rest. Here are our favorites from this year. We hope you enjoy them just as much.

▶ **FRUITY WHITE SANGRIA**
POINTS value per serving: 2
This traditional cocktail from Spain highlights all the fresh bounty of summer. You can use thawed frozen peach slices if peaches aren't in season. *(page 26)*

▼ **JALAPEÑO RANCH BURGERS**
POINTS value per serving: 7
This burger feels indulgent but it stays lean by using ground sirloin. Jalapeños are mixed into the meat for a subtle kick. The patties are then topped with melty cheese, ranch dressing, and bacon to create one tasty sandwich. *(page 124)*

OUR FAVORITE RECIPES

▶ FRESH PINEAPPLE TART
POINTS value per serving: 6
This showstopping dessert is as delicious as it is beautiful. Caramelizing the pineapple creates a rich and flavorful tart. *(page 44)*

▶▶ FLOURLESS CHOCOLATE COOKIES
POINTS value per serving: 1
These chewy cookies are rich and decadent. It's hard to believe each cookie has a **POINTS** value of only 1. *(page 46)*

▶▶▶ BANANA-NUT MUFFINS WITH PEANUT BUTTER–HONEY DRIZZLE
POINTS value per serving: 4
The peanut butter drizzle takes these muffins from ordinary to extraordinary. The result: A muffin that tastes anything but light. *(page 28)*

▼ TANGERINE-STRAWBERRY SORBET
POINTS value per serving: 2
The flavor and beautiful color of this refreshing sorbet earned it the Test Kitchens' highest rating. *(page 43)*

OUR FAVORITE RECIPES

▶ GRILLED PORTOBELLOS WITH CHEESE GRITS

POINTS value per serving: 5

Rich portobellos top a hearty portion of cheesy, creamy grits spiked with a splash of hot sauce. *(page 78)*

▼ PAN-FRIED TILAPIA WITH CHARD AND PROSCIUTTO

POINTS value per serving: 6

This dish is truly stellar. A mixture of almonds and panko creates a light crust on the delicate white fish, and the crispy prosciutto adds rich, savory flavor to the chard. *(page 72)*

▲ COCONUT–RED CURRY SHRIMP
POINTS value per serving: 7
Serve this dish over basmati rice—you won't want to miss a drop of the flavorful sauce. *(page 76)*

◄ HERBED QUINOA WITH APPLES
POINTS value per serving: 7
Quinoa is a protein-packed grain that, when combined with sweet apple, creamy goat cheese, and fresh thyme, creates a delicious complete meal. *(page 80)*

OUR FAVORITE RECIPES

▶ ITALIAN PINWHEEL STEAKS
POINTS value per serving: 7

This recipe may use an inexpensive cut of meat, but pounding the beef tenderizes it and the rich filling transforms it into a restaurant-quality steak. *(page 90)*

▼ BRAISED CHICKEN WITH PLUM TOMATOES AND FETA
POINTS value per serving: 5

This beautiful entrée was a favorite in our Test Kitchens. Tangy, creamy feta, salty olives, and bright tomatoes are paired with lean chicken breast for a balanced and satisfying meal. *(page 98)*

▲ CHICKEN AND VEGETABLE PAD THAI

POINTS value per serving: 7

There's no need to pick up take-out when you can make your own at home in no time. This version relies on a boxed mix to jump-start this healthier version. *(page 102)*

◄ WATERCRESS AND SWEET PEA SALAD

POINTS value per serving: 1

This bright, fresh salad was a hit in our Test Kitchens. It highlights the fresh taste of tiny spring peas. *(page 172)*

ABOUT OUR RECIPES

Weight Watchers® Annual Recipes for Success 2011 **gives you** the nutrition facts you need to stay on track. Every recipe in this book includes a ***POINTS*®** value per serving. For more information on Weight Watchers, see page 7.

Each recipe has a list of nutrients—including calories, fat, saturated fat (sat), monounsaturated fat (mono), polyunsaturated fat (poly), protein, carbohydrates (Carb), dietary fiber, cholesterol (Chol), iron, sodium, and calcium (Calc)—as well as a serving size and the number of servings. This information makes it easy for you to use the recipes for any weight-loss program that you may choose to follow. Measurements are abbreviated g (grams) and mg (milligrams). Nutritional values used in our calculations either come from The Food Processor, Version 8.9 (ESHA Research), or are provided by food manufacturers.

NUMBERS ARE BASED ON THESE ASSUMPTIONS:

- Unless otherwise indicated, meat, poultry, and fish always refer to skinned, boned, and cooked servings.

- When we give a range for an ingredient (3 to 3½ cups flour, for instance), we calculate using the lesser amount.

- Some alcohol calories evaporate during heating; the analysis reflects this.

- Only the amount of marinade absorbed by the food is used in calculations.

- Garnishes and optional ingredients are not included in an analysis.

Safety Note: Cooking spray should never be used near direct heat. Always remove a pan from heat before spraying it with cooking spray.

A Note on Diabetic Exchanges: You may notice that the nutrient analysis for each recipe does not include Diabetic Exchanges. Most dietitians and diabetes educators are now teaching people with diabetes to count total carbohydrates at each meal and snack, rather than counting exchanges. Almost all of our recipes can be incorporated into a diabetic diet by using the carbohydrate amount in the nutrient analysis and incorporating that into the carbohydrate amount recommended by your physician.

appetizers & beverages

Crostini with Manchego and Honeyed Orange Relish,
page 23

ROASTED VEGETABLE DIP

POINTS value: 2

PREP: 8 minutes ■ **COOK:** 35 minutes

This colorful dip is great with breadsticks or fresh veggies.

- 1 pound carrots, cut into ½-inch slices
- 1 large Vidalia or other sweet onion, cut into 6 wedges
- 1 red bell pepper, cut into 1-inch pieces
- 1 tablespoon olive oil
- 2 tablespoons chili sauce with garlic
- ¼ cup tahini (roasted sesame seed paste)
- ¼ teaspoon salt
- ¼ teaspoon pepper

1. Preheat oven to 450°.
2. Combine first 4 ingredients in a large bowl, and toss well. Place vegetables on a jelly-roll pan. Bake at 450° for 35 minutes or until tender, stirring every 15 minutes.
3. Combine roasted vegetables, chili sauce, and remaining ingredients in a food processor; process until smooth. **YIELD: 9 SERVINGS (SERVING SIZE: ¼ CUP).**

PER SERVING: Calories 86; Fat 5.2g (sat 0.7g, mono 2.4g, poly 1.8g); Protein 1.9g; Carb 9g; Fiber 2.3g; Chol 0mg; Iron 0.6mg; Sodium 115mg; Calc 29mg

 Tahini

A thick paste make from crushed roasted sesame seeds, tahini is used in Middle Eastern cooking as a flavoring for dishes such as hummus. You can find it in Middle Eastern food stores and in some supermarkets.

POBLANO–ROASTED CORN SALSA

POINTS value: 1

PREP: 14 minutes ■ **COOK:** 10 minutes

The heat in poblano chiles varies from mild to spicy-hot. If your peppers are hot, you may want to reduce the amount to ¾ cup. Serve with baked tortilla chips.

- 2 ears corn
- Cooking spray
- 1 cup finely chopped seeded poblano chiles (about 2)
- 1 cup finely chopped tomato
- 2 tablespoons chopped fresh cilantro
- 1 tablespoon chopped fresh chives
- 3 tablespoons fresh lime juice
- 2 teaspoons olive oil
- ¼ teaspoon salt
- 2 garlic cloves, minced

1. Prepare grill.
2. Coat corn with cooking spray. Place corn on grill rack coated with cooking spray. Grill 10 minutes or until tender and slightly charred, turning occasionally.
3. Cut kernels from ears of corn into a medium bowl. Stir in chiles and remaining ingredients. **YIELD: 12 SERVINGS (SERVING SIZE: ¼ CUP).**

PER SERVING: Calories 34; Fat 1.4g (sat 0.1g, mono 0.6g, poly 0.2g); Protein 1.2g; Carb 5.6g; Fiber 1.2g; Chol 0mg; Iron 0.4mg; Sodium 51mg; Calc 5mg

HOW TO SEED A CHILE PEPPER

1. Use a paring knife to cut off the stem and slice the chile in half lengthwise.

2. Cut each half lengthwise to create four separate strips.

3. Lay the strips, skin sides down, and slide the knife against the pepper to cut away the vein and seeds.

COCONUT CREAM SAUCE

POINTS value: 1

PREP: 3 minutes ■ **COOK:** 7 minutes
■ **OTHER:** 20 minutes

This tropical treat makes a delicious dipping sauce for pineapple chunks, sliced banana, and mango pieces. Or spoon it over angel food cake for an easy dessert.

1 (14-ounce) can light coconut milk (such as Thai Kitchen), divided
2 tablespoons cornstarch
⅔ cup sugar
2 tablespoons dark rum
2 teaspoons vanilla extract
Ground cinnamon (optional)

1. Combine ½ cup coconut milk and cornstarch in a medium saucepan; stir with a whisk until cornstarch dissolves. Add remaining coconut milk and sugar, stirring until smooth. Bring to a boil over medium-high heat, and cook 1 minute, stirring frequently. Remove from heat, and cool completely.
2. Stir in rum and vanilla. Sprinkle with cinnamon, if desired. **YIELD: 14 SERVINGS (SERVING SIZE: 2 TABLESPOONS).**

PER SERVING: Calories 63; Fat 1.3g (sat 1.3g, mono 0g, poly 0g); Protein 0.3g; Carb 11.7g; Fiber 0g; Chol 0mg; Iron 0.1mg; Sodium 7mg; Calc 0mg

✳ Light vs. Full-Fat Coconut Milk

Coconut milk is a sweet white liquid pressed from the meat of a mature coconut. The color and rich taste come from the natural oils and sugar found in coconut, but you can bypass some of the fat and calories by choosing light coconut milk when preparing recipes. Light coconut milk has 60 percent less fat and 60 percent fewer calories than the regular version.

EGG SALAD DEVILED EGGS

POINTS value: 2

PREP: 19 minutes

These tasty deviled eggs use only a portion of the egg yolks to keep calories and fat in check. To cook the eggs, place them in a large saucepan. Cover with cool water to 1 inch above eggs; bring just to a rolling boil. Remove them from the heat; cover and let stand 15 minutes. Drain and rinse with cold running water until cool.

12 hard-cooked large eggs
¼ cup drained no-salt-added chickpeas (garbanzo beans)
3 tablespoons light mayonnaise
½ teaspoon dry mustard
¼ teaspoon salt
⅛ teaspoon ground red pepper
3 tablespoons finely chopped celery
1½ tablespoons finely chopped red onion
1 tablespoon finely chopped fresh parsley

1. Cut eggs in half lengthwise; discard 6 yolks or reserve them for another use. Place remaining yolks in a medium bowl. Add chickpeas and next 4 ingredients; mash with a fork until smooth. Stir in celery, onion, and parsley.
2. Spoon egg mixture into a heavy-duty zip-top plastic bag. Seal bag, removing as much air as possible. Snip a small hole in 1 corner of bag. Pipe egg mixture evenly into egg whites. **YIELD: 12 SERVINGS (SERVING SIZE: 2 STUFFED EGG HALVES).**

PER SERVING: Calories 64; Fat 3.6g (sat 1g, mono 1g, poly 0.4g); Protein 5.3g; Carb 2.1g; Fiber 0.3g; Chol 104mg; Iron 0.4mg; Sodium 141mg; Calc 17mg

ASPARAGUS ROLLS WITH HERBED CREAM CHEESE

POINTS value: 1

PREP: 12 minutes ■ **COOK:** 3 minutes
■ **OTHER:** 5 minutes

Select thin asparagus similar in size to a pencil for this dainty hors d'oeuvre. When arranged on a platter with fresh herbs, these rolls make a beautiful addition to a tea or shower menu.

> 1 pound asparagus (about 24 spears), trimmed
> ⅓ cup (2½ ounces) tub light cream cheese with chives and onion (such as Philadelphia)
> ¼ teaspoon dried thyme
> ¼ teaspoon crushed dried rosemary
> ¼ teaspoon freshly ground black pepper
> 1 (10-ounce) package 98% fat-free sliced smoked ham (such as Oscar Mayer)

1. Rinse asparagus, and place in a shallow microwave-safe dish. Microwave at HIGH 3 minutes or until crisp-tender. Plunge asparagus into ice water; let stand 5 minutes. Drain and pat dry with paper towels.
2. Combine cream cheese and next 3 ingredients in a small bowl. Spread about 1 teaspoon cream cheese mixture over each ham slice; cut slices in half. Place 1 asparagus spear on each ham slice half; roll up, pressing to seal. Serve immediately, or chill up to 8 hours. **YIELD: 12 SERVINGS (SERVING SIZE: 2 ROLLS).**

PER SERVING: Calories 42; Fat 1.7g (sat 0.9g, mono 0.4g, poly 0.1g); Protein 5g; Carb 1.9g; Fiber 0.5g; Chol 13mg; Iron 0.8mg; Sodium 229mg; Calc 16mg

HOW TO TRIM ASPARAGUS

Asparagus is at its peak from April through late June. Look for stalks with smooth skin and uniform color. All asparagus should have a dry, compact tip. Fibrous stems and shriveled stalks are signs of age. To prepare the asparagus for cooking, trim the fibrous ends from all the spears.

KITCHEN SHEARS

Our Test Kitchens staff rates a pair of kitchen shears as one of their most indispensable kitchen tools. In this recipe, use shears to chop the tomatoes directly in the can.

CAPONATA CANAPÉS

POINTS value: 1

PREP: 7 minutes ■ **COOK:** 24 minutes
■ **OTHER:** 15 minutes

You can prepare the caponata ahead of time and refrigerate it up to 2 days. You'll want to bring the mixture to room temperature before serving.

> 2 tablespoons olive oil, divided
> 4 cups diced peeled eggplant (1 small)
> ½ cup chopped onion
> 4 garlic cloves, minced
> 1 (14.5-ounce) can stewed tomatoes, undrained and chopped
> 1 tablespoon capers
> 1 tablespoon balsamic vinegar
> ¼ teaspoon crushed red pepper
> ¼ cup chopped fresh basil
> 36 whole-grain crackers

1. Heat 1 tablespoon oil in a large nonstick skillet over medium heat. Add eggplant, onion, and garlic; cook vegetables 5 minutes, stirring often.
2. Stir in tomatoes. Bring to a boil; reduce heat, and simmer 11 minutes or until vegetables are tender, stirring occasionally.
3. Stir in remaining 1 tablespoon oil, capers, vinegar, and red pepper; simmer 5 minutes or until liquid almost evaporates. Remove from heat; stir in basil. Spoon caponata into a bowl; cool to room temperature. Serve with whole-grain crackers. **YIELD: 18 SERVINGS (SERVING SIZE: 2 TABLESPOONS CAPONATA AND 2 CRACKERS).**

PER SERVING: Calories 49; Fat 2.2g (sat 0.4g, mono 1.1g, poly 0.2g); Protein 1.1g; Carb 7.3g; Fiber 1.4g; Chol 0mg; Iron 0.6mg; Sodium 103mg; Calc 17mg

FARMER'S MARKET SLIDERS

POINTS value: 2

PREP: 11 minutes

These small, hand-held sandwiches can offer some variety in the menu at your next party.

- ⅓ **cup refrigerated hummus**
- 1 **teaspoon dried oregano, crumbled**
- 1 **small garlic clove, minced**
- 16 **(¼-inch-thick) slices French bread**
- 3 **tablespoons minced fresh cilantro**
- 8 **(⅛-inch-thick) slices seeded Anaheim chile pepper (about ½ medium)**
- 2 **(0.8-ounce) slices Monterey Jack cheese with jalapeño peppers, cut into fourths**
- 8 **slices plum tomato (1 small)**

1. Combine first 3 ingredients in a small bowl. Spread hummus mixture evenly on bread slices. Layer cilantro, pepper, cheese, and tomato slices evenly over hummus on 8 bread slices. Top with remaining bread slices, hummus sides down, pressing lightly. Serve immediately. **YIELD: 8 SERVINGS (SERVING SIZE: 1 SANDWICH).**

PER SERVING: Calories 121; Fat 2.9g (sat 1g, mono 0.1g, poly 0.2g); Protein 6.1g; Carb 16.6g; Fiber 2g; Chol 5mg; Iron 1mg; Sodium 212mg; Calc 62mg

❋ Anaheim Chiles

Anaheim chiles have a sweet, bell pepper–like flavor with a bit of mild heat. Look for peppers with medium to dark green or greenish-red color and no soft spots, bruises, or shriveled skin.

SMOKED SALMON CROUSTADES

POINTS value: 1

PREP: 22 minutes

Tiny, wafer-thin, crisp shells provide the perfect texture contrast to the creamy salmon filling in this easy appetizer. You can find the shells on the gourmet cracker aisle at your supermarket.

- 1 **(8-ounce) package ⅓-less-fat cream cheese**
- 1 **lemon**
- 2 **tablespoons fat-free milk**
- 1 **(4-ounce) package smoked salmon, coarsely chopped**
- ¼ **cup coarsely chopped red onion**
- 1 **tablespoon chopped fresh dill**
- 1 **tablespoon drained capers**
- 2 **(1.4-ounce) packages baked mini croustades (such as Siljan)**
- **Dill sprigs (optional)**

1. Place cream cheese in a bowl; beat with a mixer at medium speed until smooth. Grate rind and squeeze juice from lemon to measure 1 teaspoon rind and 1 tablespoon juice. Add lemon rind, lemon juice, and milk to cream cheese; beat until well blended.
2. Stir in salmon and next 3 ingredients. Spoon a rounded teaspoonful of salmon mixture into each of 48 croustades. Garnish with dill sprigs, if desired. **YIELD: 24 SERVINGS (SERVING SIZE: 2 CROUSTADES).**

PER SERVING: Calories 47; Fat 3.2g (sat 1.4g, mono 0.1g, poly 0.1g); Protein 2.4g; Carb 2.8g; Fiber 0.1g; Chol 10mg; Iron 0.1mg; Sodium 152mg; Calc 9mg

GREEK NACHOS

POINTS value: 4

(pictured on page 49)

PREP: 16 minutes

This easy, no-cook appetizer comes together quickly, which makes it ideal for preparing food for a crowd.

1 (8-ounce) package baked pita chips (such as Stacy's)
1 (7-ounce) container hummus
1½ cups shredded iceberg lettuce
1½ cups chopped tomato
½ cup (2 ounces) crumbled reduced-fat feta cheese
¼ cup finely chopped red onion
¼ cup chopped pitted kalamata olives

1. Arrange chips in a single layer on a large serving platter. Spoon hummus evenly over chips; top with lettuce and remaining ingredients. **YIELD: 8 SERVINGS (SERVING SIZE: ⅛ OF NACHOS).**

PER SERVING: Calories 209; Fat 9.6g (sat 1.6g, mono 1.9g, poly 1.1g); Protein 7g; Carb 25.5g; Fiber 4.3g; Chol 2mg; Iron 0.8mg; Sodium 540mg; Calc 34mg

✳ Olive Nutrition

Olives like kalamata deliver big flavor in a small package. They're relatively low in calories—five kalamata olives contain about 25 calories—and rich in heart-healthy monounsaturated fats. However, olives can be high in sodium, so you may need to cut back on salty foods elsewhere.

NACHOS GRANDE

POINTS value: 4

PREP: 7 minutes ■ **COOK:** 13 minutes

You can serve this as a fun appetizer or halve the recipe and serve it as a light dinner.

¾ pound ground round
⅓ cup water
2 teaspoons chili powder
1 teaspoon cumin
½ teaspoon garlic salt
1 (16-ounce) can fat-free refried beans
6 ounces light tortilla chips (about 36 chips)
Cooking spray
1 cup (4 ounces) shredded Monterey Jack cheese
1 cup refrigerated fresh salsa
⅓ cup sliced pickled jalapeño peppers (optional)
⅓ cup reduced-fat sour cream
¼ cup chopped fresh cilantro

1. Preheat oven to 425°.
2. Heat a large nonstick skillet over medium-high heat. Add beef; cook 8 minutes or until browned, stirring to crumble. (Drain, if necessary, and return beef to pan.) Stir in ⅓ cup water and next 3 ingredients.
3. Place beans in a medium microwave-safe bowl; microwave at HIGH 2 minutes, stirring once.
4. Arrange chips in a 13 x 9–inch baking dish coated with cooking spray. Spoon beans evenly over chips. Top with beef mixture and sprinkle with cheese. Bake at 425° for 3 minutes or until cheese melts. Top with salsa, jalapeño peppers, if desired, sour cream, and cilantro. Serve immediately. **YIELD: 12 SERVINGS (SERVING SIZE: 1/12 OF NACHOS).**

PER SERVING: Calories 216; Fat 10.1g (sat 4.4g, mono 3.8g, poly 1g); Protein 11.4g; Carb 18.7g; Fiber 3.5g; Chol 31mg; Iron 1.7mg; Sodium 483mg; Calc 123mg

ITALIAN-STYLE GOAT CHEESE–STUFFED MUSHROOMS

POINTS value: 1

PREP: 19 minutes ■ **COOK:** 12 minutes

Clean fresh mushrooms with a mushroom brush or damp paper towel just before using. Never clean them by soaking in water; they're like sponges and will absorb the water and lose their firm texture.

> 18 large button mushrooms
> Olive oil–flavored cooking spray
> ¼ cup (2 ounces) goat cheese
> 2 tablespoons seasoned breadcrumbs
> 2 tablespoons chopped drained oil-packed sun-dried tomato halves
> 2 tablespoons chopped fresh basil

1. Preheat oven to 375°.
2. Remove stems from mushrooms; discard stems or reserve for another use. Place mushroom caps, rounded sides up, on a large baking sheet; coat caps with cooking spray. Turn caps over.
3. Combine goat cheese and next 3 ingredients. Spoon about 1 tablespoon filling into each mushroom cap; gently press filling into mushroom cap. Bake at 375° for 12 minutes or until mushrooms are tender and filling is lightly browned. Serve warm. **YIELD: 9 SERVINGS (SERVING SIZE: 2 MUSHROOMS).**

PER SERVING: Calories 36; Fat 1.7g (sat 1g, mono 0.5g, poly 0.1g); Protein 2.4g; Carb 3g; Fiber 0.4g; Chol 3mg; Iron 0.4mg; Sodium 59mg; Calc 20mg

PEELING SHALLOTS

Shallots differ from onions in that many varieties of shallots produce a cluster of several bulbs to a plant. Shallots also have finer layers and contain less water than onions. Because of the low water content, their flavor is more concentrated than that of onions. When peeling a shallot, remove a couple of the outer layers along with the peel. You might need an extra shallot to make up for the discarded layers, but this method is a lot faster than removing only the thin peel.

CROSTINI WITH MANCHEGO AND HONEYED ORANGE RELISH

POINTS value: 1 *(pictured on page 51)*

PREP: 20 minutes ■ **COOK:** 8 minutes

Manchego cheese is a sheep's milk cheese made in Spain. It has a creamy texture with a taste similar to feta cheese.

> 16 (½-inch-thick) slices diagonally cut French bread baguette
> ½ cup (2 ounces) shredded Manchego cheese
> ½ teaspoon freshly ground black pepper
> 1¼ cups navel orange sections, chopped (about 2 large)
> 2 tablespoons minced shallots (1 medium)
> 2 tablespoons water
> 2 tablespoons honey
> 1½ tablespoons fresh lime juice
> 1 tablespoon chopped fresh basil
> ⅛ teaspoon ground red pepper

1. Preheat oven to 450°.
2. Place baguette slices on a large baking sheet; sprinkle slices evenly with cheese and black pepper. Bake at 450° for 4 minutes or until cheese melts and baguette is lightly toasted.
3. Combine orange sections and next 3 ingredients in a small saucepan; bring to a boil. Remove pan from heat. Remove solids from cooking liquid, using a slotted spoon; place in a small bowl. Stir lime juice, basil, and ground red pepper into orange mixture.
4. Top each toasted baguette slice with about 1 tablespoon orange relish. **YIELD: 16 SERVINGS (SERVING SIZE: 1 CROSTINO).**

PER SERVING: Calories 64; Fat 1.5g (sat 0.9g, mono 0g, poly 0.1g); Protein 2.4g; Carb 10.8g; Fiber 0.7g; Chol 4mg; Iron 0.5mg; Sodium 91mg; Calc 59mg

SOUTHWESTERN EGG ROLLS

POINTS value: 2

PREP: 10 minutes ■ **COOK:** 15 minutes

Corn, black beans, and chipotle seasoning give the traditional egg roll a Southwestern flair. Our baked version is much healthier than deep-fried restaurant versions.

> 1 cup frozen whole-kernel corn, thawed
> ¾ cup canned black beans, rinsed and drained
> ¾ cup refrigerated fresh salsa
> 1 tablespoon chopped fresh cilantro
> 1 tablespoon fresh lime juice
> 1 teaspoon salt-free Southwest chipotle seasoning blend (such as Mrs. Dash)
> 9 egg roll wrappers
> 1 large egg white, lightly beaten
> Cooking spray
> Light sour cream (optional)

1. Preheat oven to 400°.
2. Combine first 6 ingredients in a medium bowl.
3. Working with 1 egg roll wrapper at a time (cover remaining wrappers with a damp towel to keep them from drying), spoon about ¼ cup corn mixture into center of wrapper. Fold lower right corner over corn mixture; fold lower left and top right corners over mixture. Moisten top left corner with egg white; roll up jelly-roll fashion. Repeat procedure with remaining wrappers, corn mixture, and egg white.
4. Coat egg rolls with cooking spray; place, seam sides down, on a baking sheet. Bake at 400° for 15 minutes or until golden. Serve with sour cream, if desired. **YIELD: 9 SERVINGS (SERVING SIZE: 1 EGG ROLL).**

PER SERVING: Calories 113; Fat 0.5g (sat 0g, mono 0g, poly 0.1g); Protein 4.9g; Carb 23.3g; Fiber 2.4g; Chol 0mg; Iron 1.2mg; Sodium 241mg; Calc 9mg

BRITISH BEEF PASTIES

POINTS value: 3

PREP: 17 minutes ■ **COOK:** 24 minutes

These savory pies are a miniature version of the portable British specialty Cornish Pasties. To speed preparation, thaw the vegetables by running under cold water, and drain well.

> 1 (17-ounce) package refrigerated beef pot roast au jus
> 1 (16-ounce) package frozen stew vegetables (such as McKenzie's), thawed
> 2 teaspoons less-sodium soy sauce
> 2 teaspoons no-salt-added tomato paste
> 1 (14.1-ounce) package refrigerated pie dough (such as Pillsbury)
> Butter-flavored cooking spray

1. Preheat oven to 425°.
2. Microwave beef according to package directions. Combine beef, juices, vegetables, soy sauce, and tomato paste in a large deep skillet. Cook over medium-high heat until bubbly, breaking beef and vegetables into pieces with a wooden spoon. Remove from heat, and keep warm.
3. Unroll dough, and roll out into 2 (14-inch) circles. Cut each circle into 30 (2½-inch) circles, re-rolling dough as necessary. Spoon beef mixture evenly into centers of 30 circles; moisten edges of dough with water. Top with remaining 30 circles; pinch edges together. Place pasties on a large baking sheet coated with cooking spray. Crimp edges with a fork to seal.
4. Bake at 425° for 18 minutes or until golden brown. **YIELD: 30 SERVINGS (SERVING SIZE: 1 PASTY).**

PER SERVING: Calories 109; Fat 5.8g (sat 2.4g, mono 1g, poly 0.1g); Protein 5.1g; Carb 8.4g; Fiber 0.1g; Chol 15mg; Iron 0.5mg; Sodium 84mg; Calc 1mg

TURKEY POT STICKERS WITH SPICY DIPPING SAUCE

POINTS value: 2

PREP: 8 minutes ■ **COOK:** 6 minutes

Round, wonton-like gyoza wrappers are sold in Asian markets. If you can't find them, you can substitute wonton wrappers.

   1 garlic clove, peeled
   1 (1-inch) piece peeled fresh ginger
   4 teaspoons less-sodium soy sauce, divided
  ½ pound lean ground turkey breast
   1 green onion, quartered
   1 teaspoon dark sesame oil
 16 gyoza wrappers
    Cooking spray
   6 tablespoons water, divided
  ¼ cup rice vinegar
   2 teaspoons brown sugar
  ¼ teaspoon crushed red pepper

1. Drop garlic through food chute with processor on; process until minced. Drop ginger through food chute, and process until minced. Add 1 teaspoon soy sauce and next 3 ingredients; pulse until onion is finely chopped.
2. Working with 1 gyoza wrapper at a time (cover remaining wrappers with a damp towel to keep them from drying), spoon about 1 teaspoon turkey mixture into center of wrapper. Moisten edges of wrapper with water; gently lift edges over filling and crimp to seal. Repeat procedure with remaining wrappers and turkey mixture.
3. Heat a large nonstick skillet over medium–high heat. Coat pan with cooking spray; add pot stickers. Cook 4 minutes or until browned, turning occasionally. Add ¼ cup water to pan. Cover and steam 2 minutes or until tender.
4. While pot stickers steam, combine remaining 1 tablespoon soy sauce, remaining 2 tablespoons water, vinegar, brown sugar, and red pepper in a small bowl, stirring with a small whisk. Serve sauce with pot stickers. **YIELD: 8 SERVINGS (SERVING SIZE: 2 POT STICKERS AND 1 TABLESPOON SAUCE).**

PER SERVING: Calories 76; Fat 1.1g (sat 0.2g, mono 0g, poly 0g); Protein 8g; Carb 8g; Fiber 0.4g; Chol 13mg; Iron 0.7mg; Sodium 185mg; Calc 9mg

---

HOW TO SHAPE POT STICKERS

1. Working with one gyoza wrapper at a time (cover remaining wrappers with a damp towel to keep them from drying), spoon 1 teaspoon of the filling mixture into the center of each wrapper. Moisten edges of wrapper with water.

2. Gently lift the edges over the filling, and crimp to seal.

HOT SPICED CHOCOLATE

POINTS value: 2

PREP: 4 minutes ■ **COOK:** 17 minutes

Ginger flavor comes through in this warm chocolate treat. You can use fat-free milk if that's what you have on hand.

   4 cups 1% low-fat milk
   3 tablespoons chopped crystallized ginger
   8 whole cloves
   2 (3-inch) cinnamon sticks, broken in half
  ⅓ cup fat-free chocolate syrup (such as Hershey's)

1. Combine first 4 ingredients in a medium saucepan. Bring to a boil; reduce heat, and simmer 12 minutes. Remove from heat.
2. Strain milk mixture through a sieve over a bowl, discarding spices. Return milk to saucepan. Stir in chocolate syrup. Cook over low heat just until thoroughly heated. Serve hot. **YIELD: 6 SERVINGS (SERVING SIZE: ABOUT ¾ CUP).**

PER SERVING: Calories 125; Fat 1.8g (sat 1.1g, mono 0.5g, poly 0.1g); Protein 5.8g; Carb 21.3g; Fiber 0.8g; Chol 7mg; Iron 0.3mg; Sodium 93mg; Calc 209mg

Crystallized Ginger
Crystallized ginger is generally found in supermarket spice sections or in produce departments' specialty areas. Before chopping crystallized ginger, coat your knife with cooking spray to keep the ginger from sticking to it.

STRAWBERRY-LEMONADE COOLER

POINTS value: 0

PREP: 5 minutes

Sugar-free drink mix adds flavor and tartness, but not calories, so this refreshing drink has a **POINTS** value of 0. The **POINTS** value increases to 1 only if you drink all four servings.

> 2 cups coarsely chopped strawberries
> 1½ cups cold water
> 1 (0.3-ounce) tub pink lemonade–flavored sugar-free drink mix (such as Crystal Light)
> 3 cups sparkling water, chilled
> Lemon slices (optional)

1. Place first 3 ingredients in a blender; process until smooth. Pour mixture into 4 tall glasses. Fill each glass with ¾ cup sparkling water. Garnish with lemon slices, if desired. **YIELD: 4 SERVINGS (SERVING SIZE: 1½ CUPS).**

PER SERVING: Calories 27; Fat 0.3g (sat 0g, mono 0g, poly 0.1g); Protein 0.6g; Carb 6.4g; Fiber 1.7g; Chol 0mg; Iron 0.3mg; Sodium 8mg; Calc 42mg

FRUITY WHITE SANGRIA

POINTS value: 2   *(pictured on page 50)*

PREP: 10 minutes

This traditional Spanish cocktail highlights summer's bounty. If peaches aren't in season, use thawed frozen peach slices.

> 1 (750-milliliter) bottle riesling or other slightly sweet white wine, chilled
> 2 cups sliced peeled peaches (about 2 large)
> 1 cup seedless green grapes, halved
> ½ cup fresh raspberries
> ¼ cup frozen lemonade concentrate, thawed
> 2 cups sugar-free ginger ale

1. Combine first 5 ingredients in a large pitcher. Stir in ginger ale just before serving. **YIELD: 8 SERVINGS (SERVING SIZE: 1 CUP).**

PER SERVING: Calories 127; Fat 0.2g (sat 0g, mono 0g, poly 0.1g); Protein 0.7g; Carb 16.4g; Fiber 1.3g; Chol 0mg; Iron 0.3mg; Sodium 16mg; Calc 7mg

HOW TO PEEL STONE FRUIT

Stone fruits, such as plums, apricots, nectarines, and peaches, sometimes require peeling. You can remove the skin using a vegetable peeler or paring knife if the fruit is still firm. If the fruit is soft or your peeling skills aren't up to par, the easiest way to remove the skin is by blanching. Just follow these steps to get skin-free fruit.

1. Cut an X in the bottom of each fruit, carefully cutting just through the skin.

2. Bring a large pot of water to a boil, and drop in the fruit. Cook for 20 seconds to 1 minute. The riper the fruit, the less time it needs.

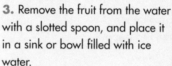

3. Remove the fruit from the water with a slotted spoon, and place it in a sink or bowl filled with ice water.

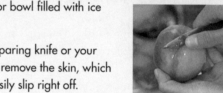

4. Use a paring knife or your fingers to remove the skin, which should easily slip right off.

Wild Mushroom Flatbread, *page 34*

LEMON-GLAZED GINGER MUFFINS

POINTS value: 4

PREP: 7 minutes ■ COOK: 15 minutes
■ OTHER: 2 minutes

Crystallized ginger lends a spicy-sweet punch to everyday poppy seed muffins.

1 (7.6-ounce) package lemon poppy–seed muffin
   mix (such as Martha White)
½ cup fat-free milk
2 tablespoons chopped crystallized ginger,
   divided
Cooking spray
1 lemon
¼ cup powdered sugar

1. Preheat oven to 425°.
2. Prepare muffin mix according to package directions, using ½ cup fat-free milk. Stir in 1½ teaspoons ginger. Spoon batter into 6 muffin cups coated with cooking spray. Bake at 425° for 15 minutes or until lightly browned. Cool muffins in pan 2 minutes; remove to wire racks.
3. Grate rind and squeeze juice from lemon to measure 1 teaspoon rind and 1½ teaspoons juice. Combine lemon rind, lemon juice, and powdered sugar, stirring until smooth. Drizzle over warm muffins, and sprinkle with remaining 1½ tablespoons ginger. **YIELD: 6 SERVINGS (SERVING SIZE: 1 MUFFIN).**

PER SERVING: Calories 196; Fat 4.1g (sat 1g, mono 0g, poly 0g); Protein 2.8g; Carb 36.9g; Fiber 0.6g; Chol 0mg; Iron 1.3mg; Sodium 248mg; Calc 89mg

BANANA-NUT MUFFINS WITH PEANUT BUTTER–HONEY DRIZZLE

POINTS value: 4   *(pictured on page 52)*

PREP: 5 minutes ■ COOK: 16 minutes

Fresh banana and a quick topping of peanut butter and honey give a packaged muffin mix a made-from-scratch flavor.

1 (6.4-ounce) package banana-nut muffin mix
   (such as Betty Crocker)
½ cup water
1 small banana, chopped
Cooking spray
1 tablespoon creamy peanut butter
1 tablespoon honey
½ teaspoon fat-free milk
2 teaspoons finely chopped walnuts, toasted

1. Preheat oven to 400°.
2. Prepare muffin mix according to package directions, using ½ cup water. Stir in banana. Spoon batter into 6 muffin cups coated with cooking spray. Bake at 400° for 16 minutes or until lightly browned. Remove muffins from pan immediately; place on a wire rack.
3. While muffins bake, combine peanut butter, honey, and milk in a 1-cup glass measure. Microwave at HIGH 20 seconds; stir and let stand 2 minutes. Drizzle peanut butter mixture evenly over muffins; sprinkle with walnuts. **YIELD: 6 SERVINGS (SERVING SIZE: 1 MUFFIN).**

PER SERVING: Calories 184; Fat 7.4g (sat 1.7g, mono 0.7g, poly 0.8g); Protein 2.8g; Carb 28.5g; Fiber 1.1g; Chol 0mg; Iron 0.8mg; Sodium 224mg; Calc 40mg

Choosing Peanut Butter

On average, 1 tablespoon of peanut butter contains 100 calories and 8 grams of fat. While that fat count may seem high, the majority of it is good-for-your-heart unsaturated fats. When buying peanut butter, make sure you choose the real, full-fat variety, which offers better flavor and more health benefits. The reduced-fat spreads offer few calorie savings and cost you healthy fats.

RASPBERRY-LEMONADE MUFFINS

POINTS value: 3

PREP: 7 minutes ■ **COOK:** 17 minutes

To keep raspberries fresh as long as possible, store them, unwashed, in the refrigerator in their plastic container. Or if you have room, spread them in a single layer in an airtight container.

    2 cups all-purpose flour
    ½ cup granulated sugar
    2 teaspoons baking powder
    2 teaspoons grated fresh lemon rind
    ½ teaspoon baking soda
    ¼ teaspoon salt
    ¾ cup fresh raspberries
    2 large egg whites
    1 (6-ounce) carton vanilla fat-free yogurt
    ½ cup low-fat buttermilk
    ¼ cup sweetened applesauce
    1 teaspoon vanilla extract
       Butter-flavored cooking spray
    ½ cup powdered sugar
    1 tablespoon fresh lemon juice

1. Preheat oven to 425°.

2. Lightly spoon flour into dry measuring cups; level with a knife. Combine flour and next 5 ingredients in a large bowl, stirring well with a whisk. Gently fold in raspberries until coated. Make a well in center of mixture.

3. Beat egg whites in a medium bowl, stirring with a whisk until foamy. Add yogurt and next 3 ingredients; stir. Add yogurt mixture to flour mixture, stirring gently just until moist. Spoon batter evenly into 12 muffin cups coated with cooking spray; coat batter with cooking spray.

4. Bake at 425° for 17 minutes or until muffins spring back when touched lightly in center. Remove muffins from pan; cool on a wire rack.

5. Combine powdered sugar and lemon juice in a small bowl, stirring with a whisk. Drizzle glaze evenly over warm muffins. **YIELD: 12 SERVINGS (SERVING SIZE: 1 MUFFIN).**

PER SERVING: Calories 158; Fat 0.5g (sat 0.1g, mono 0.1, poly 0.1g); Protein 3.9g; Carb 34.6g; Fiber 1.2g; Chol 1mg; Iron 1.2mg; Sodium 193mg; Calc 100mg

HOW TO MIX MUFFIN BATTER

Muffins are simple to make, but you'll need to measure your ingredients carefully and mix lightly to make sure you get the right result.

1. Lightly spoon flour into dry measuring cups; level with a knife.

2. Combine the dry ingredients in a bowl, and make a well in the center for the wet ingredients.

3. Combine the wet ingredients and add them to the flour mixture.

4. Stir the mixture just until moist.

The secret to tender scones is handling the dough as little as possible.

1. Cut the butter into the flour mixture until it resembles coarse meal. If you don't have a pastry blender, you can use 2 knives (although this takes considerably longer). Or you can pulse the flour mixture and butter in your food processor.

2. After adding the milk mixture, turn the dough out onto a lightly floured surface. With lightly floured hands, gather the dough into a ball. Knead lightly 4 to 5 times. The dough will be sticky, but resist the temptation to add more flour because it will make the scones dry.

3. Pat the dough into an 8-inch circle. Cut the circle into 10 wedges, cutting into but not through dough. This allows the wedges to bake as one large scone, and they will be much more moist than scones baked separately.

WHOLE-GRAIN TOFFEE SCONES
POINTS value: 4

PREP: 11 minutes ■ **COOK:** 21 minutes

These bite-sized scones have the grainy goodness of wheat germ, and the turbinado sugar sprinkled on top adds a crunchy sweetness. Cut these heavenly scones into 8 wedges for a ***POINTS*** value of 6 per serving.

> 1¼ cups all-purpose flour
> ½ cup whole-wheat flour
> ¼ cup toasted wheat germ
> ¼ cup firmly packed light brown sugar
> 2 teaspoons baking powder
> ¼ teaspoon salt
> ¼ teaspoon baking soda
> 6 tablespoons chilled butter, cut into small pieces
> 1 (1.4-ounce) English toffee candy bar, finely chopped (such as Heath or Skor)
> ⅔ cup plus 1 tablespoon fat-free buttermilk
> 2 teaspoons vanilla extract
> Cooking spray
> 1½ teaspoons turbinado sugar

1. Preheat oven to 400°.
2. Lightly spoon flours into dry measuring cups; level with a knife. Combine flours and next 5 ingredients in a large bowl. Cut in butter with a pastry blender or 2 knives until mixture resembles coarse meal. Stir in chopped candy bar. Add buttermilk and vanilla to flour mixture, stirring with a fork just until moist and dough holds together. Knead dough lightly in bowl.
3. Pat dough into a 7-inch circle on a baking sheet coated with cooking spray. Cut dough into 10 wedges, cutting into but not through dough. Coat dough with cooking spray. Sprinkle with turbinado sugar.
4. Bake at 400° for 21 minutes or until browned.
YIELD: 10 SERVINGS (SERVING SIZE: 1 SCONE).

PER SERVING: Calories 203; Fat 8.8g (sat 5.2g, mono 1.8g, poly 0.6); Protein 4.3g; Carb 27g; Fiber 1.7g; Chol 19mg; Iron 1.5mg; Sodium 235mg; Calc 108mg

CHEDDAR-CORNMEAL SCONES

POINTS value: 4

PREP: 10 minutes ■ COOK: 18 minutes
■ OTHER: 10 minutes

When you sink your teeth into these savory cheese scones, you won't believe they're light. Add a bit more kick to them by stirring in a minced seeded jalapeño pepper. It's easiest to knead this soft dough right in the bowl it's mixed in. You'll create less of a mess because you don't have to flour a surface to use for kneading.

1¼ cups all-purpose flour
½ cup yellow cornmeal
1 tablespoon sugar
2 teaspoons baking powder
½ teaspoon salt
¼ teaspoon ground red pepper
¼ cup chilled light stick butter, cut into small pieces
1 cup (4 ounces) reduced-fat finely shredded extra-sharp cheddar cheese
½ cup plus 1 tablespoon low-fat buttermilk
1 large egg
Cooking spray
1 teaspoon yellow cornmeal

1. Preheat oven to 425°.
2. Lightly spoon flour into dry measuring cups; level with a knife. Combine flour and next 5 ingredients in a large bowl; cut in butter with a pastry blender or 2 knives until mixture resembles coarse meal. Add cheese; toss gently. Combine buttermilk and egg in a small bowl, stirring with a whisk. Add buttermilk mixture to flour mixture; stir with a fork just until moist.
3. Knead dough lightly 4 or 5 times in bowl. Pat dough into a 7-inch circle on a baking sheet coated with cooking spray and dusted with 1 teaspoon cornmeal. Cut dough into 8 wedges, cutting into but not through dough. Coat top of dough with cooking spray.
4. Bake at 425° for 18 to 20 minutes or until lightly browned around edges. Remove to a wire rack; cool 10 minutes before serving. **YIELD: 8 SERVINGS (SERVING SIZE: 1 SCONE).**

PER SERVING: Calories 198; Fat 7.7g (sat 4.5g, mono 1.4g, poly 0.4g); Protein 7.8g; Carb 23.9g; Fiber 1.1g; Chol 40mg; Iron 1.7mg; Sodium 512mg; Calc 243mg

STUFFED FRENCH TOAST

POINTS value: 6   (pictured on page 53)

PREP: 10 minutes ■ COOK: 3 minutes

Traditional stuffed French toast recipes are heavy on full-fat cream cheese and half-and-half. Our lightened version delivers the same great taste with a lot fewer calories.

½ cup (4 ounces) ⅓-less-fat cream cheese, softened
2 tablespoons low-sugar apricot preserves
8 (1-ounce) slices whole-grain white bread (such as Wonder)
1 cup egg substitute
½ cup fat-free milk
2 tablespoons granulated sugar
½ teaspoon vanilla extract
Butter-flavored cooking spray
¼ cup sugar-free maple-flavored syrup (such as Mrs. Butterworth's)
¼ cup powdered sugar (optional)

1. Combine cream cheese and preserves in a small bowl. Spread evenly over 4 bread slices; top with remaining bread slices.
2. Combine egg substitute and next 3 ingredients in a shallow dish, stirring well with a whisk. Heat a large nonstick griddle or nonstick skillet over medium heat. Coat pan with cooking spray. Dip bread in egg substitute mixture, and place in pan. Cook 1 to 2 minutes on each side or until browned. Drizzle each serving with 1 tablespoon syrup. Sprinkle with 1 tablespoon powdered sugar, if desired. **YIELD: 4 SERVINGS (SERVING SIZE: 1 STUFFED TOAST AND 1 TABLESPOON SYRUP).**

PER SERVING: Calories 314; Fat 10.4g (sat 5g, mono 0.6g, poly 1.5g); Protein 17.7g; Carb 40.4g; Fiber 4g; Chol 21mg; Iron 3.1mg; Sodium 579mg; Calc 505mg

Preheat your nonstick skillet or griddle, and coat it with cooking spray for easy pancake flipping and removal. To test the surface's heat, sprinkle a few drops of water on the pan. If the drops dance on the surface and evaporate within a few seconds, the pan or griddle is ready.

1. For precision, use about ¼ cup batter for each pancake. Pour the batter into the center of the pan or griddle and let it spread— don't pour it in a circle.

2. Once the edges turn golden and bubbles surface, slide a wide nylon spatula under the pancake—the width will help you lift more, and the nylon won't scratch your pan. Quickly flip the pancake over, and cook 2 minutes.

BLUEBERRY-CORNMEAL PANCAKES

POINTS value: 3

PREP: 15 minutes ■ **COOK:** 12 minutes

You can give a serving of these flavorful pancakes a sweet touch by drizzling it with 1 tablespoon of sugar-free maple syrup and 1 tablespoon of powdered sugar. The ***POINTS*** value will increase to 4. Or, top it with ¼ cup of fresh fruit for a colorful addition to your breakfast meal. The ***POINTS*** value will be 3.

- ¾ **cup all-purpose flour**
- ½ **cup yellow cornmeal**
- 1½ **teaspoons baking powder**
- ¼ **teaspoon baking soda**
- ¼ **teaspoon salt**
- 1 **cup light vanilla soy milk (such as Silk)**
- 2 **teaspoons canola oil**
- 1 **large egg**
- 1 **cup blueberries**
- **Cooking spray**

1. Lightly spoon flour into dry measuring cups; level with a knife. Combine flour and next 4 ingredients in a large bowl, stirring with a whisk.

2. Combine soy milk, oil, and egg, stirring with a whisk until blended; add to flour mixture, stirring just until dry ingredients are moist. Gently fold in blueberries.

3. Pour about ¼ cup batter per pancake onto a hot nonstick griddle or nonstick skillet coated with cooking spray. Cook 2 minutes or until tops are covered with bubbles and edges look cooked. Carefully turn pancakes over; cook 2 minutes or until bottoms are lightly browned. **YIELD: 5 SERVINGS (SERVING SIZE: 2 PANCAKES).**

PER SERVING: Calories 172; Fat 3.8g (sat 0.6g, mono 1.6g, poly 1g); Protein 5.2g; Carb 29.8g; Fiber 2g; Chol 36mg; Iron 2.1mg; Sodium 479mg; Calc 216mg

✳ Soy Milk

Calcium-fortified soy milk is an excellent alternative to cow's milk. Be sure to shake it well before using it; studies have shown that the valuable calcium sinks to the bottom of the carton.

SAVORY HERB POPOVERS

POINTS value: 2

PREP: 13 minutes ■ **COOK:** 29 minutes

Make these airy popovers just before serving. Don't open the oven door during baking or they might collapse. Omit the herbs, garlic, and cheese, and serve with honey for breakfast.

> **Cooking spray**
> ½ **cup all-purpose flour**
> ½ **cup bread flour**
> 1 **cup 2% reduced-fat milk**
> ¼ **cup (1 ounce) shredded Asiago cheese**
> 1 **tablespoon canola oil**
> ½ **teaspoon garlic salt**
> 2 **large eggs**
> 2 **tablespoons minced fresh chives**

1. Preheat oven to 400°.

2. Coat 12 muffin cups with cooking spray, and place in oven while it preheats.

3. Lightly spoon flours into dry measuring cups; level with a knife. Place milk and next 4 ingredients in a blender; add flours. Process 1 minute, scraping sides.

4. Remove muffin cups from oven. Pour batter evenly into prepared cups. Sprinkle batter evenly with chives. Bake at 400° for 29 minutes. Serve immediately.

YIELD: 12 SERVINGS (SERVING SIZE: 1 POPOVER).

PER SERVING: Calories 81; Fat 3.2g (sat 1g, mono 1.3g, poly 0.6g); Protein 3.6g; Carb 9.3g; Fiber 0.3g; Chol 39mg; Iron 0.7mg; Sodium 68mg; Calc 53mg

Although you can make them in muffin cups, popovers are not really quick breads because they're leavened with steam and eggs instead of baking powder or soda. These miniature "bread balloons" are crusty on the outside and almost hollow on the inside.

■ Baking popovers in popover pans produces taller, airier results, but you can use a muffin pan with some minor adjustments.

■ Muffin pan cups are smaller than popover pan cups, so if you'd rather use the popover pan, you'll need 5 minutes more baking time.

■ Whichever pan you use, heat it in the oven for about 3 minutes before adding the batter—this ensures a higher volume because the batter crawls up the heated cups.

■ Popovers should be golden and crispy on the outside and soft and hollow on the inside; undercooked ones are pale on the outside and gummy on the inside. Popovers "deflate" quickly, so serve them immediately.

HERBED PINWHEEL ROLLS

POINTS value: 3

PREP: 18 minutes ■ **COOK:** 28 minutes
■ **OTHER:** 30 minutes

To easily cut the roll of dough into slices, place a long piece of dental floss or string under the roll 1 inch from the end. Cross the ends of the string over the top of the roll, and slowly pull the ends to cut through the dough. To thaw the frozen bread dough, wrap the frozen dough loosely with plastic wrap, and microwave at LOW 5 to 6 minutes or until thawed, rotating the dough a quarter-turn every 2 minutes.

    ¼ cup light butter, softened
    ¼ cup fat-free mayonnaise
    2 tablespoons finely chopped fresh chives
    2 tablespoons finely chopped fresh parsley
    ⅓ cup finely shredded Havarti cheese
    1 (1-pound) loaf frozen bread dough, thawed
    Cooking spray

1. Combine first 4 ingredients in a small bowl; stir well to combine. Remove 1 tablespoon butter mixture, and set aside. Stir cheese into remaining butter mixture.
2. Roll dough into a 10 x 12–inch rectangle on a lightly floured surface. Spread cheese mixture evenly over dough, leaving a ½-inch margin around edges. Roll up dough, jelly-roll fashion, beginning at 1 long edge; pinch seam to seal. Cut roll into 12 equal slices; place slices in muffin cups coated with cooking spray. Cover and let rise in a warm place (85°), free from drafts, 30 minutes or until dough has doubled in size. (Press two fingers into dough. If indention remains, dough has risen enough.)
3. Preheat oven to 350°.
4. Bake at 350° for 28 minutes or until golden. Brush warm rolls with reserved butter mixture. **YIELD: 12 SERVINGS (SERVING SIZE: 1 ROLL).**

PER SERVING: Calories 134; Fat 5.2g (sat 2.2g, mono 1g, poly 0.1g); Protein 5.8g; Carb 18.6g; Fiber 2.5g; Chol 9mg; Iron 1.3mg; Sodium 246mg; Calc 42mg

WILD MUSHROOM FLATBREAD

POINTS value: 2   *(pictured on page 51)*

PREP: 5 minutes ■ **COOK:** 13 minutes

Allowing the liquid to evaporate when cooking the mushrooms allows them to brown and develops a rich flavor. This bread would also make a nice appetizer.

    1 (11-ounce) can refrigerated thin crust pizza
      dough (such as Pillsbury)
    Cooking spray
    2 teaspoons olive oil
    2 tablespoons minced shallots (about 1 large)
    1 (8-ounce) package presliced exotic mushroom
      blend (such as shiitake, cremini, and oyster)
    ¼ teaspoon salt
    ¼ teaspoon freshly ground black pepper
    2 tablespoons dry white wine
    1 cup shredded reduced-fat Italian cheese blend
    1 tablespoon fresh oregano

1. Preheat oven to 425°.
2. Roll dough into a 16 x 12–inch rectangle on a baking sheet coated with cooking spray. Place on bottom rack of oven and bake at 425° for 8 minutes or just until beginning to brown.
3. While crust bakes, heat oil in a large nonstick skillet over medium-high heat. Add shallots and mushrooms; sauté 4 minutes or until tender. Add salt, pepper, and wine; cook 1 to 2 minutes or until liquid evaporates and mushrooms begin to brown.
4. Sprinkle mushroom mixture over crust; sprinkle with cheese. Bake an additional 5 minutes or until crust is golden brown and cheese melts. Sprinkle with oregano just before serving. **YIELD: 15 SERVINGS (SERVING SIZE: 1 PIECE).**

PER SERVING: Calories 93; Fat 3.5g (sat 1.2g, mono 1.3g, poly 0.4g); Protein 4.4g; Carb 11.1g; Fiber 0.5g; Chol 4mg; Iron 0.6mg; Sodium 233mg; Calc 55mg

desserts

Marbled Chocolate Mousse, *page 39*

RASPBERRY UPSIDE-DOWN CUPCAKES

POINTS value: 3

PREP: 7 minutes ■ COOK: 8 minutes
■ OTHER: 15 minutes

Like the fruit in traditional upside-down cakes, the berries in these little cakes sink to the bottom of the muffin cups. If you want a more cakelike texture, toss the berries in a small amount of dry cake mix before folding them into the batter.

1½ cups fresh raspberries
Cooking spray
1 (9-ounce) package lemon cake mix (such as Jiffy)
1 large egg
½ cup reduced-fat sour cream
1½ teaspoons grated lemon rind, divided
½ cup powdered sugar
1 tablespoon fresh lemon juice

1. Preheat oven to 400°.
2. Arrange raspberries evenly in bottoms of 12 muffin cups coated with cooking spray.
3. Combine cake mix, egg, sour cream, and 1 teaspoon lemon rind in a bowl. Beat with a mixer at medium speed 2 minutes. Pour batter evenly over raspberries. Bake at 400° for 8 to 10 minutes or until cupcakes spring back when touched lightly in center. Cool cupcakes in pan on a wire rack 2 minutes. Remove from cups, and place upside down on wire racks; cool 5 minutes. Place cupcakes, upside down, on parchment paper; cool completely.
4. While cupcakes cool, combine ½ teaspoon lemon rind, powdered sugar, and lemon juice in a small bowl, stirring with a whisk. Drizzle glaze over cooled cupcakes. **YIELD: 12 SERVINGS (SERVING SIZE: 1 CUPCAKE).**

PER SERVING: Calories 138; Fat 4g (sat 2g, mono 1.7g, poly 0.3g); Protein 2.4g; Carb 23.7g; Fiber 1g; Chol 19mg; Iron 0.6mg; Sodium 155mg; Calc 25mg

Raspberries

Raspberries have an intense flavor. They're usually available from May through November. You'll want to choose brightly colored, plump berries without hulls. Like blackberries, if the hulls are still attached, the berries are not mature and will be tart. Store raspberries in the refrigerator in a moisture-proof container for two to three days. Because they are fragile, it's best to store them in a single layer if possible.

STRAWBERRY CUPCAKES

POINTS value: 3

PREP: 15 minutes ■ COOK: 20 minutes
■ OTHER: 15 minutes

We recommend using regular ginger ale in this recipe instead of diet ginger ale. Many diet ginger ales contain aspartame, which, when heated, can become toxic.

1 (18.25-ounce) package strawberry cake mix (such as Duncan Hines)
1 (12-ounce) can ginger ale
Cooking spray
½ cup fat-free hot fudge topping (such as Smucker's)
1 (8-ounce) container frozen fat-free whipped topping, thawed
3½ cups strawberries, sliced

1. Preheat oven to 350°.
2. Combine cake mix and ginger ale in a large bowl, stirring until blended. Spoon batter evenly into 24 muffin cups coated with cooking spray. Bake at 350° for 20 minutes or until a wooden pick inserted in center comes out clean. Cool in pans on wire racks 5 minutes. Remove from pans. Cool completely on wire racks.
3. Warm hot fudge topping according to directions on jar. Top cupcakes evenly with dollops of whipped topping. Drizzle cupcakes evenly with hot fudge topping, and top evenly with strawberry slices. **YIELD: 24 SERVINGS (SERVING SIZE: 1 CUPCAKE).**

PER SERVING: Calories 129; Fat 1.6g (sat 0.5g, mono 0.5g, poly 0.5g); Protein 1.3g; Carb 27g; Fiber 0.5g; Chol 0mg; Iron 0.7mg; Sodium 164mg; Calc 44mg

When making shortcakes, biscuits, scones, and other quick breads, you need to cut the butter into the dry ingredients. Butter is best cut into dry ingredients with a pastry blender (see page 30) or 2 knives. Pull the knives through the butter until the mixture resembles coarse meal. It's important that the butter is chilled so that it doesn't melt. The "cutting" action distributes little lumps of butter throughout the dough that melt during baking and keep the bread tender.

BROWN SUGAR SHORTCAKES WITH PAN-ROASTED PLUMS

POINTS value: 6

PREP: 13 minutes ■ **COOK:** 14 minutes

Nectarines also work well in this recipe, or you could use a mixture of plums and nectarines.

> **Butter-flavored cooking spray**
> **1 cup reduced-fat baking mix**
> **3 tablespoons dark brown sugar, divided**
> **2 tablespoons butter, cut into small pieces**
> **⅓ cup nonfat buttermilk**
> **1 tablespoon turbinado sugar**
> **1 pound plums, pitted and cut into ¼-inch slices**
> **¼ cup frozen fat-free whipped topping, thawed**

1. Preheat oven to 425°.

2. Line a baking sheet with foil. Coat foil with cooking spray. Lightly spoon baking mix into a dry measuring cup; level with a knife. Combine baking mix and 2 tablespoons brown sugar in a medium bowl. Cut in butter with a pastry blender or 2 knives until mixture resembles coarse meal. Add buttermilk; stir just until moist.

3. Turn dough out onto a lightly floured surface; knead lightly 5 times. Pat dough into a 5-inch square; cut into 4 (2½-inch) squares. Place on prepared pan. Coat squares with cooking spray; sprinkle evenly with turbinado sugar.

4. Bake at 425° for 10 minutes or until golden. Remove shortcakes from pan; cool on a wire rack.

5. While shortcakes cool, heat a large nonstick skillet over medium-high heat. Coat pan heavily with cooking spray. Add plums and remaining 1 tablespoon brown sugar. Sauté 4 minutes or until plums are tender and caramelized.

6. Split shortcakes in half. Spoon plum mixture evenly over bottom halves of shortcakes. Dollop each serving with 1 tablespoon whipped topping, and top with remaining shortcake halves. **YIELD: 4 SERVINGS (SERVING SIZE: 1 SHORTCAKE).**

PER SERVING: Calories 275; Fat 8.5g (sat 4g, mono 1.9g, poly 0.4g); Protein 4g; Carb 47.4g; Fiber 2.1g; Chol 15mg; Iron 1.3mg; Sodium 412mg; Calc 67mg

✳Turbinado Sugar

This sugar is prized for its coarse, amber-hued crystals. Use it when you want extra crunch—atop shortcakes, like this recipe, or cookies and muffins, or in a crisp or crumble.

1. Once you've prepared the batter, heat a 10-inch crepe pan or nonstick skillet over medium-high heat. Coat the pan with cooking spray. Remove the pan from heat. Pour a scant ¼ cup batter into the pan, and quickly tilt the pan in all directions so the batter covers the pan with a thin film.

2. Cook the batter for about 1 minute, and then carefully lift the edge of the crepe with a spatula to test for doneness.

3. Turn crepe over when it can be shaken loose from the pan and the underside is lightly browned; cook 30 seconds. Place crepe on a towel; cool. Repeat procedure until all of the batter is used.

CHOCOLATE-HAZELNUT CREPES
POINTS value: 3

PREP: 6 minutes ■ **COOK:** 15 minutes

Homemade crepes take the place of flour tortillas, and cream cheese replaces hard cheese in this sweet take on quesadillas. The crepes can be made up to three days in advance and stacked between single layers of wax paper to prevent sticking. Store in a zip-top plastic bag in the refrigerator.

> ½ cup all-purpose flour
> ¾ cup fat-free milk
> 1 tablespoon powdered sugar, divided
> 1 large egg
> Butter-flavored cooking spray
> ¼ cup chocolate-hazelnut spread (such as Nutella)
> 2 tablespoons fat-free cream cheese, softened
> 1 cup thinly sliced strawberries

1. Lightly spoon flour into a dry measuring cup; level with a knife. Place flour in a medium bowl. Combine milk, 2 teaspoons powdered sugar, and egg; add mixture to flour, stirring with a whisk until smooth.
2. Heat a 10-inch crepe pan or nonstick skillet over medium–high heat. Coat pan with cooking spray. Remove pan from heat. Pour a scant ¼ cup batter into pan; quickly tilt pan in all directions so batter covers pan with a thin film. Cook about 1 minute. Carefully lift edge of crepe with a spatula to test for doneness. Turn crepe over when it can be shaken loose from the pan and the underside is lightly browned; cook 30 seconds. Place crepe on a towel; cool. Repeat procedure until all of the batter is used.
3. Place chocolate-hazelnut spread and cream cheese in a bowl; beat with a mixer until smooth. Spread mixture evenly in center of each of 6 crepes. Top evenly with strawberries. Fold crepes in half.
4. Heat a large nonstick skillet over medium–high heat. Coat pan with cooking spray. Add 2 filled crepes; cook 1 minute on each side or until golden brown and cream cheese mixture begins to melt. Dust crepes with remaining 1 teaspoon powdered sugar. **YIELD: 6 SERVINGS (SERVING SIZE: 1 CREPE).**

PER SERVING: Calories 144; Fat 4.7g (sat 1.4g, mono 0.4g, poly 0.2g); Protein 5.1g; Carb 20.8g; Fiber 1.2g; Chol 31mg; Iron 1mg; Sodium 60mg; Calc 64mg

MARBLED CHOCOLATE MOUSSE

POINTS value: 6   (pictured on page 56)

PREP: 9 minutes ■ COOK: 1 minute
■ OTHER: 5 minutes

We used full-fat sweetened condensed milk in this recipe because it yielded a thick, luscious mousse. If we'd used fat-free, the **POINTS** value per serving would have been 5, but the result wouldn't have been as creamy and pleasing. We think the extra **POINTS** value is worth it for the show-stopping flavor and texture of this decadent dessert.

1 (14-ounce) can sweetened condensed milk
1 cup cold water
1 (3.9-ounce) package chocolate instant
   pudding mix
3 ounces semisweet chocolate (such as
   Ghirardelli), melted
2 cups frozen fat-free whipped topping, thawed

1. Place milk and 1 cup cold water in a bowl; beat with a mixer at medium–low speed until blended. Add pudding mix; beat until smooth. Stir in melted chocolate. Cover and chill 5 minutes.

2. Gently fold in whipped topping, leaving large chocolate streaks. Spoon into serving dishes. YIELD: 8 SERVINGS (SERVING SIZE: ABOUT ½ CUP).

PER SERVING: Calories 275; Fat 7.6g (sat 4.7g, mono 1.3g, poly 0.2g); Protein 5g; Carb 47.9g; Fiber 0.5g; Chol 17mg; Iron 0.6mg; Sodium 261mg; Calc 143mg

CHOCOLATE MINT COOKIES 'N' CREAM TORTONI

POINTS value: 2

PREP: 11 minutes ■ OTHER: 2 hours

Tortoni is traditionally a high-fat frozen dessert made with sweetened whipped cream, crumbled macaroons, and nuts. Our version is much lower in calories and fat, but doesn't compromise on richness or creaminess.

1 (1-ounce) package sugar-free, fat-free
   cheesecake instant pudding mix
1½ cups 1% chocolate low-fat milk
¼ teaspoon peppermint extract
1 (5.3-ounce) carton vanilla fat-free Greek yogurt
   (such as Oikos)
½ cup frozen reduced-fat whipped topping,
   thawed
7 reduced-fat cream-filled chocolate sandwich
   cookies (such as reduced-fat Oreos), coarsely
   chopped

1. Place 10 paper muffin cup liners in muffin cups. Combine pudding mix, milk, and peppermint extract, stirring with a whisk 2 minutes. Stir in yogurt; fold in whipped topping until blended. Fold in cookies. Spoon mixture evenly into liners. Freeze 2 hours or until firm. YIELD: 10 SERVINGS (SERVING SIZE: 1 TORTONI).

PER SERVING: Calories 86; Fat 1.8g (sat 0.7g, mono 0.6g, poly 0.2g); Protein 3g; Carb 13.5g; Fiber 0.2g; Chol 3mg; Iron 0.4mg; Sodium 122mg; Calc 54mg

MINI SWEET POTATO CHEESECAKE PARFAITS

POINTS value: 1

PREP: 17 minutes

These miniature parfaits are a perfect small dessert, but the colorful layers and pretty presentation also make them an ideal treat for a crowd.

- ½ (1-ounce) package sugar-free, fat-free cheese-cake instant pudding mix
- 1 cup fat-free milk
- ½ cup refrigerated mashed sweet potatoes (such as Simply Potatoes)
- 12 (1½-ounce) shot glasses
- 1 cup gingersnap crumbs (about 15 cookies)
- 1 cup frozen fat-free whipped topping, thawed
- ¼ teaspoon ground cinnamon

1. Prepare pudding mix according to package directions, using 1 cup fat-free milk. Add sweet potatoes to pudding mixture, stirring with a whisk.
2. Spoon 2 tablespoons pudding mixture into bottom of each shot glass. Top each with 4 teaspoons crumbs and 4 teaspoons whipped topping. Sprinkle evenly with cinnamon. **YIELD: 12 SERVINGS (SERVING SIZE: 1 PARFAIT).**

PER SERVING: Calories 63; Fat 0.9g (sat 0.2g, mono 0.5g, poly 0.1g); Protein 1.5g; Carb 12.1g; Fiber 0.4g; Chol 0mg; Iron 0.7mg; Sodium 92mg; Calc 31mg

KEY LIME CHEESECAKE PARFAITS

POINTS value: 3

(pictured on page 53)

PREP: 13 minutes

We tested with bottled Key lime juice, but feel free to use fresh Key lime juice or regular lime juice.

- 1 (1-ounce) package sugar-free, fat-free cheesecake instant pudding mix
- 1¼ cups 1% low-fat milk
- ¼ cup Key lime juice
- ½ cup light sour cream
- 1 teaspoon grated lime rind
- 4 cinnamon graham cracker sheets, crumbled
- Grated lime rind (optional)

1. Prepare pudding mix according to package directions using milk and lime juice. Add sour cream and 1 teaspoon lime rind, stirring with a whisk.
2. Spoon about 2 tablespoons crumbs into each of 4 parfait glasses. Layer half of pudding mixture evenly over crumbs. Top evenly with remaining crumbs and pudding mixture. Garnish with grated lime rind, if desired. **YIELD: 4 SERVINGS (SERVING SIZE: 1 PARFAIT).**

PER SERVING: Calories 118; Fat 3.1g (sat 2g, mono 0.2g, poly 0g); Protein 3.8g; Carb 18.9g; Fiber 0.2g; Chol 13mg; Iron 0.2mg; Sodium 397mg; Calc 113mg

❋ Key Lime Juice

Key limes grow in south Florida and are very tart with thin, leathery yellow skins and green flesh. You can find them fresh occasionally in specialty produce markets, but quality bottled Key lime juice is readily available in gourmet stores and some supermarkets.

COCONUT-CARAMEL DESSERT BOWLS

POINTS value: 6

PREP: 10 minutes ■ **COOK:** 4 minutes

Waffle bowls provide a crisp edible container for this yummy cream filling topped with toasted coconut and pecans.

> ¾ cup fat-free sweetened condensed milk
> 1 (8-ounce) tub light cream cheese
> 2½ cups frozen fat-free whipped topping, thawed
> Butter-flavored cooking spray
> 3 tablespoons flaked sweetened coconut
> 3 tablespoons chopped pecans
> 8 (0.4-ounce) waffle bowls (such as Keebler)
> 8 teaspoons fat-free caramel topping

1. Combine sweetened condensed milk and cream cheese, stirring with a whisk until smooth. Fold in whipped topping.

2. Heat a small nonstick skillet over medium heat. Coat pan with cooking spray. Add coconut and pecans; sauté 4 minutes or until lightly toasted.

3. Spoon cream cheese mixture evenly into waffle bowls. Spoon 1 teaspoon caramel topping and about 1 tablespoon coconut mixture over each serving. Serve immediately, or cover and chill up to 2 hours. **YIELD: 8 SERVINGS (SERVING SIZE: 1 BOWL).**

PER SERVING: Calories 279; Fat 8g (sat 3.7g, mono 1.2g, poly 0.6g); Protein 6.2g; Carb 43.2g; Fiber 0.4g; Chol 17mg; Iron 1mg; Sodium 222mg; Calc 113mg

HONEY FROZEN YOGURT WITH FRESH FIGS AND GINGERSNAP CRUMBLE

POINTS value: 6

PREP: 7 minutes

Honey, lemon, and peppery ginger steer the adaptable flavor of fresh figs in a spicy, sweet-tart direction in this unique dessert. The tart honey yogurt really makes this dessert sing, but you could also use vanilla frozen yogurt or vanilla light ice cream.

> ½ cup coarsely crushed gingersnap cookies (about 10 cookies)
> ¼ cup chopped almonds, toasted
> ¼ teaspoon grated lemon rind
> 1 tablespoon honey
> 1 tablespoon butter, melted
> 2 cups tart honey light frozen yogurt blend (such as Edy's)
> 6 large figs, quartered

1. Combine first 5 ingredients in a bowl.

2. Place ½ cup frozen yogurt in each of 4 dessert bowls. Top each serving with 6 fig quarters and about 3 tablespoons gingersnap mixture. **YIELD: 4 SERVINGS (SERVING SIZE: 1 BOWL).**

PER SERVING: Calories 319; Fat 9.4g (sat 3.5g, mono 3.7g, poly 1.2g); Protein 5g; Carb 57.4g; Fiber 3.9g; Chol 13mg; Iron 1.8mg; Sodium 176mg; Calc 163mg

✳ Fresh Figs

Although fresh figs are used interchangeably in most recipes, each has a subtle but distinctive profile. Whichever variety you choose, select figs that are plump and heavy for their size and yield slightly with gentle pressure; the skin should be smooth, and the fruit fragrant. Purchase fresh, ripe figs since the fruit doesn't always ripen well once harvested. Figs are extremely perishable, so you should use them soon after they're purchased. Store them in a single layer on paper towels, cover them with plastic wrap, and refrigerate them for up to two days.

PISTACHIO-PINEAPPLE WHIP

POINTS value: 2

PREP: 5 minutes ■ **OTHER:** 3 hours

This retro dessert was a staple at all 1970s potluck dinners. We've lightened this version by using fat-free yogurt and sugar-free pudding mix.

> 2 (6-ounce) cartons vanilla fat-free yogurt
> 1 (8-ounce) can crushed pineapple in juice, undrained
> 1 (1-ounce) package sugar-free pistachio instant pudding mix
> 1 cup plus 6 tablespoons frozen fat-free whipped topping, thawed and divided

1. Combine first 3 ingredients in a large bowl, stirring well with a whisk. Fold in 1 cup whipped topping. Cover and chill 3 hours or until set. Spoon pudding mixture evenly into 6 dishes, and top evenly with remaining 6 tablespoons whipped topping. **YIELD: 6 SERVINGS (SERVING SIZE: ½ CUP PUDDING MIXTURE AND 1 TABLESPOON WHIPPED TOPPING).**

PER SERVING: Calories 101; Fat 0.1g (sat 0.1g, mono 0g, poly 0g); Protein 3.1g; Carb 21.2g; Fiber 0.3g; Chol 1mg; Iron 0.2mg; Sodium 216mg; Calc 106mg

YOGURT PARFAITS WITH MIXED BERRIES, HONEY, AND MINT

POINTS value: 3

PREP: 8 minutes

This easy-to-assemble snack could also double as a healthy breakfast.

> 1½ cups vanilla fat-free Greek yogurt (such as Oikos)
> 2 tablespoons honey
> 1 cup blueberries
> 1 cup strawberries
> 2 tablespoons chopped fresh mint
> ½ cup low-fat granola without raisins (such as Back to Nature)

1. Combine yogurt and honey. Spoon about 3 tablespoons yogurt mixture into each of 4 parfait or wine glasses. Top with half of berries; sprinkle with half of mint and all of granola. Repeat layers, using remaining yogurt mixture, berries, and mint. **YIELD: 4 SERVINGS (SERVING SIZE: 1 PARFAIT).**

PER SERVING: Calories 161; Fat 1g (sat 0.2g, mono 0g, poly 0.1g); Protein 9.1g; Carb 30.7g; Fiber 2.7g; Chol 0mg; Iron 1.1mg; Sodium 63mg; Calc 77mg

Honey

This wonderful, rich golden liquid is a natural sweetener. The color and flavor of the honey depends on the type of flowers the bees collect the nectar from, but in general, lighter-colored honeys have a milder flavor than darker ones. Honey is available year-round, but it's a fantastic treat if you can find a jar of local honey in the summer and fall when it's just been harvested.

MINI VANILLA WAFER ICE CREAM SANDWICHES

POINTS value: 2

PREP: 10 minutes ■ **OTHER:** 10 minutes

Make a batch of these diminutive treats and wrap in pairs in plastic wrap to keep on hand for a quick snack or dessert.

> 1 cup vanilla fat-free frozen yogurt, softened
> 1½ teaspoons finely chopped crystallized ginger
> ¼ teaspoon ground cinnamon
> 32 reduced-fat vanilla wafers
> ¼ cup finely chopped toasted almonds

1. Combine first 3 ingredients in a small bowl. Quickly spread about 1½ teaspoons yogurt mixture on each of 16 cookies. Top with remaining cookies, pressing until yogurt mixture reaches edges. Carefully smooth filling around edge of sandwich with a spatula. Roll edges of sandwiches in almonds. Freeze 10 minutes. **YIELD: 8 SERVINGS (SERVING SIZE: 2 SANDWICHES).**

PER SERVING: Calories 102; Fat 2.5g (sat 0.1g, mono 1g, poly 0.4g); Protein 1.9g; Carb 18.3g; Fiber 0.4g; Chol 0mg; Iron 0.5mg; Sodium 67mg; Calc 39mg

SPARKLING LEMON-BLUEBERRY FLOAT

POINTS value: 2

PREP: 5 minutes

This delightful dessert is as delicious as it is unique. You can also serve it as a pick-me-up on a hot afternoon.

> 2 cups lemon sorbet
> 1 cup blueberries
> 1⅓ cups diet ginger ale
> Lemon slices (optional)

1. Spoon ½ cup sorbet into each of 4 parfait or dessert glasses; top each with ¼ cup blueberries.
2. Pour ⅓ cup ginger ale over each serving; garnish with lemon slices, if desired. Serve immediately. **YIELD: 4 SERVINGS (SERVING SIZE: 1 FLOAT).**

PER SERVING: Calories 111; Fat 0.1g (sat 0g, mono 0g, poly 0.1g); Protein 0.3g; Carb 27.4g; Fiber 0.9g; Chol 0mg; Iron 0.1mg; Sodium 53mg; Calc 2mg

TANGERINE-STRAWBERRY SORBET

POINTS value: 2   *(pictured on page 54)*

PREP: 6 minutes ■ **COOK:** 2 minutes
■ **OTHER:** 1 hour and 40 minutes

This refreshing light dessert earned our Test Kitchens' highest rating. It's delicious with or without the vodka.

> 2 cups tangerine juice (such as Noble), divided
> ½ cup sugar
> 1 tablespoon grated tangerine or orange rind
> 1½ cups coarsely chopped strawberries
> 2 teaspoons fresh lemon juice
> 3 tablespoons vodka (optional)

1. Combine ½ cup tangerine juice, sugar, and tangerine rind in a saucepan. Bring to a boil, stirring until sugar dissolves. Remove from heat. Pour mixture into a large bowl; stir in remaining 1½ cups tangerine juice.
2. Place strawberries and lemon juice in a food processor; process until pureed. Pour strawberry mixture into tangerine mixture; stir in vodka, if desired.
3. Pour mixture into the freezer can of an ice-cream freezer; freeze according to manufacturer's instructions. Spoon sorbet into a freezer-safe container. Cover and freeze 1 hour or until firm. **YIELD: 8 SERVINGS (SERVING SIZE: ½ CUP).**

PER SERVING: Calories 86; Fat 0.2g (sat 0g, mono 0g, poly 0.1g); Protein 0.5g; Carb 21.4g; Fiber 0.8g; Chol 0mg; Iron 0.3mg; Sodium 1mg; Calc 18mg

FRESH PINEAPPLE TART

POINTS value: 6   *(pictured on page 55)*

PREP: 12 minutes ■ **COOK:** 21 minutes

This stunning dessert earned our Test Kitchens' highest rating. Be sure to nicely caramelize the pineapple in the skillet—the result is a richer and more flavorful tart.

- 1 **fresh pineapple, cored and cut into ¼-inch-thick slices**
- **Butter-flavored cooking spray**
- 3 **tablespoons "measures-like-sugar" calorie-free sweetener (such as Splenda)**
- 3 **tablespoons marzipan (almond paste)**
- 2 **tablespoons light butter, softened**
- ¼ **teaspoon vanilla extract**
- 1 **large egg white**
- 1 **tablespoon all-purpose flour**
- ½ **(17.3-ounce) package frozen puff pastry dough, thawed**

1. Preheat oven to 425°.
2. Stack pineapple slices, and cut into quarters.
3. Heat a large nonstick skillet over medium-high heat. Coat pan with cooking spray. Add pineapple to pan, and cook 1 to 2 minutes on each side or until pineapple begins to brown and juice almost evaporates.
4. While pineapple cooks, place sweetener and next 4 ingredients in a food processor; pulse 3 times or just until smooth. Add flour; pulse 2 or 3 times or just until combined.
5. Roll pastry sheet into an 11-inch square on a large baking sheet coated with cooking spray. Cut a ½-inch-wide strip from right and left sides of dough, using a pizza wheel or kitchen shears; set aside.
6. Cut a ½-inch-wide strip from top and bottom of dough. Brush edges of pastry square with water. Place top and bottom strips on top and bottom edges of pastry square, forming a border. Trim ends of reserved side strips to fit between top and bottom strips on edges of dough, discarding excess dough; place on pastry, completing the border.
7. Spread almond mixture in bottom of pastry shell. Arrange pineapple pieces in a single layer over filling.

8. Bake at 425° for 18 minutes or until golden. Cut into 8 squares. **YIELD: 8 SERVINGS (SERVING SIZE: 1 SQUARE).**

PER SERVING: Calories 245; Fat 15g (sat 4.2g, mono 8.1g, poly 1.9g); Protein 3.7g; Carb 24.6g; Fiber 1.6g; Chol 3mg; Iron 1.1mg; Sodium 99mg; Calc 22mg

HOW TO SLICE FRESH PINEAPPLE

The taste of fresh pineapple can't be beat, but the prickly exterior may tempt you to reach for the pricier precut varieties. Don't let its appearance dissuade you. Follow these tips:

1. A sharp chef's knife is key. Lay the pineapple horizontally on a cutting board, and cut off the leafy top (the plume) and the base.

2. Stand the pineapple upright on the cutting board, and cut down the sides to remove the rind. Try to remove as little of the flesh as possible.

3. While the pineapple is upright, cut it into thirds by carefully slicing downward to remove the fibrous core. Discard core. Slice pineapple.

FROZEN PEANUT BUTTER–BANANA POPS

POINTS value: 3

PREP: 8 minutes ■ **COOK:** 30 seconds
■ **OTHER:** 3 hours and 5 minutes

Creamy bananas are dipped in chocolate and sprinkled with crunchy nuts in this frosty treat that will please both kids and adults. You need to place the chocolate mixture in a narrow glass so that when you dip the bananas, the mixture will completely coat them. A wider glass will only coat part of the bananas.

    8 popsicle sticks
    4 medium-sized ripe bananas, peeled and cut
      in half
    ¼ cup fat-free milk
    3 tablespoons semisweet chocolate chips
    2 tablespoons creamy peanut butter
    ¼ cup finely chopped lightly salted peanuts

1. Line a small baking sheet with wax paper. Insert a popsicle stick lengthwise into each banana half. Place bananas on prepared baking sheet; freeze 2 hours or until firm.

2. Place milk, chocolate chips, and peanut butter in a 1-cup glass measure. Microwave at HIGH 30 seconds or until hot. Stir with a whisk until smooth. Pour into a narrow glass. Let cool 5 minutes.

3. Quickly dip bananas in chocolate mixture, turning to coat; return to baking sheet. Sprinkle bananas evenly with peanuts. Freeze 1 hour or until firm. Store in freezer. **YIELD: 8 SERVINGS (SERVING SIZE: 1 POP).**

PER SERVING: Calories 135; Fat 6g (sat 1.7g, mono 2.1g, poly 1.3g); Protein 3.4g; Carb 19.4g; Fiber 2.1g; Chol 0mg; Iron 0.3mg; Sodium 60mg; Calc 15mg

COCONUT MACAROONS

POINTS value: 1

PREP: 5 minutes ■ **COOK:** 25 minutes
■ **OTHER:** 15 minutes

You won't believe these decadent cookies have a ***POINTS*** value of only 1. They have a crisp, waferlike edge with chewy coconut goodness in the middle.

    1 cup flaked sweetened coconut
    ¼ cup fat-free sweetened condensed milk
    1 tablespoon all-purpose flour
    ¼ teaspoon almond extract
    1 large egg white

1. Preheat oven to 325°.

2. Combine first 4 ingredients in a medium bowl. Beat egg white with a mixer at high speed until stiff peaks form; fold into coconut mixture.

3. Drop dough by level tablespoonfuls 2 inches apart onto a baking sheet lined with parchment paper. Bake at 325° for 25 minutes or until edges are golden brown. Cool on pans 5 minutes. Remove cookies from pan; cool completely on a wire rack. **YIELD: 12 SERVINGS (SERVING SIZE: 1 COOKIE).**

PER SERVING: Calories 51; Fat 1.7g (sat 1.6g, mono 0.1g, poly 0g); Protein 1.1g; Carb 7.7g; Fiber 0.6g; Chol 1mg; Iron 0.1mg; Sodium 29mg; Calc 18mg

✳ Almond Extract

Used in baked goods and desserts, almond extract has a strong, sweet flavor. You'll also find it in frostings and fillings. Be sure to use it sparingly though; it has an intense flavor that can be over-powering when too much is used.

1. Separate eggs while they're still cold—the yolks and whites will be more firm and separate more easily. Don't allow any pieces of yolk to mix with the whites or the whites won't beat to maximum volume.

2. Place egg whites in a large bowl. Beat with a mixer at high speed until soft peaks form. The peaks will hold high when you lift the beater.

3. Be careful not to overbeat. Overbeaten egg whites look dry and grainy.

FLOURLESS CHOCOLATE COOKIES

POINTS value: 1   *(pictured on page 57)*

PREP: 24 minutes ■ **COOK:** 26 minutes

You'll get more volume from your egg whites if, before separating them, you place the eggs, still in their shells, in a bowl of warm water for a few minutes until they are room temperature.

    6 ounces bittersweet chocolate, coarsely chopped
    4 large egg whites
  ⅛ teaspoon salt
    2 cups powdered sugar, divided
  ½ cup unsweetened cocoa
    1 tablespoon cornstarch

1. Preheat oven to 400°.
2. Place chocolate in a medium microwave-safe bowl. Microwave at HIGH 1 minute or until chocolate melts, stirring after 30 seconds. Stir until smooth.
3. Place egg whites and salt in a large bowl; beat with a mixer at high speed until foamy. Add 1 cup powdered sugar, 1 tablespoon at a time, beating until stiff peaks form. Combine remaining 1 cup powdered sugar, cocoa, and cornstarch. Gently fold cocoa mixture into egg white mixture until blended. Gently stir in melted chocolate until well blended.
4. Drop dough by tablespoonfuls onto large baking sheets lined with parchment paper. Bake at 400° for 12 to 13 minutes or until tops of cookies look cracked.
YIELD: 27 SERVINGS (SERVING SIZE: 1 COOKIE).

PER SERVING: Calories 73; Fat 2.9g (sat 1.5g, mono 0.1g, poly 0g); Protein 1.3g; Carb 13.2g; Fiber 1g; Chol 0mg; Iron 0.4mg; Sodium 19mg; Calc 2mg

DROP COOKIES

Drop cookies are some of the simplest to make—just spoon mounds of soft dough onto baking sheets. Ensure even baking by dropping the same amount of dough for each cookie. Use a measuring spoon to scoop the dough, and then push it onto the baking sheet with your finger or another spoon. Or you can use a cookie scoop, which looks like a small ice-cream scoop; they come in a variety of sizes and are available at kitchenware stores. Coat whatever you use to scoop the dough with cooking spray first for easy release.

CHOCOLATE-PEPPERMINT COOKIE SANDWICHES

POINTS value: 2

PREP: 15 minutes ■ **OTHER:** 3 hours and 15 minutes

For a more attractive presentation, sift the broken pieces of candy after crushing to eliminate most of the dust.

- 4 ounces ⅓-less-fat cream cheese, softened
- 1 (3.9-ounce) package sugar-free chocolate instant pudding mix
- 1 cup fat-free milk
- 40 chocolate wafers (such as Nabisco's Famous Chocolate Wafers)
- ¼ cup coarsely crushed peppermint candies (about 9 candies)

1. Beat cream cheese with a hand mixer at medium speed until creamy. Add pudding mix, beating at low speed until blended. Gradually add milk, beating until smooth. Cover and chill 5 minutes or until firm.
2. Spoon cream cheese mixture onto flat sides of 20 cookies; top with remaining cookies, flat sides down. Place sandwiches on a baking sheet; freeze 10 minutes. Roll edges of sandwiches in crushed candies. Cover and freeze 3 hours or until ready to serve. **YIELD: 20 SERVINGS (SERVING SIZE: 1 SANDWICH).**

PER SERVING: Calories 89; Fat 2.8g (sat 1.4g, mono 0.6g, poly 0.2g); Protein 1.9g; Carb 14.1g; Fiber 0.4g; Chol 6.2mg; Iron 0.6mg; Sodium 182mg; Calc 17mg

PEANUT BUTTER–BANANA GRAHAM SANDWICHES

POINTS value: 2

PREP: 9 minutes

Make these ahead by wrapping in plastic wrap and freezing for 1 hour or until firm. Thaw 5 minutes before serving.

- ½ cup frozen fat-free whipped topping, thawed
- ¼ cup creamy peanut butter
- 8 chocolate graham crackers, halved
- 1 medium banana, cut into 24 slices
- 8 teaspoons light chocolate syrup (such as Hershey's), divided

1. Combine whipped topping and peanut butter in a small bowl, stirring with a whisk until well blended.
2. Spread peanut butter mixture evenly over 8 graham cracker halves; arrange banana slices evenly over peanut butter mixture. Drizzle each with 1 teaspoon chocolate syrup. Top with remaining graham cracker halves. Serve immediately. **YIELD: 8 SERVINGS (SERVING SIZE: 1 SANDWICH).**

PER SERVING: Calories 90; Fat 4.6g (sat 0.9g, mono 2.1g, poly 1.1g); Protein 2.4g; Carb 11g; Fiber 1g; Chol 0mg; Iron 0.2mg; Sodium 43mg; Calc 4mg

CARAMEL APPLE CRUNCH BARS

POINTS value: 2

PREP: 8 minutes ■ **COOK:** 10 minutes
■ **OTHER:** 15 minutes

These bars keep well for up to three days—that is, if they last that long.

> 3 tablespoons butter
> ½ cup caramel bits (such as Kraft)
> 1 (10.5-ounce) package miniature marshmallows
> 6 cups caramel-flavored fiber cereal (such as Fiber One Caramel Delight), coarsely crushed
> 1 (5-ounce) package dried apples, chopped
> Cooking spray

1. Melt butter in a large Dutch oven over low heat. Add caramel bits and marshmallows, stirring until marshmallows melt. Remove pan from heat. Stir in cereal and apple until thoroughly coated.
2. Press mixture into a 13 x 9–inch pan coated with cooking spray. Let stand until firm. Cut into bars.
YIELD: 24 SERVINGS (SERVING SIZE: 1 BAR).

PER SERVING: Calories 133; Fat 2.5g (sat 1g, mono 0.7g, poly 0.2g); Protein 1.1g; Carb 27.4g; Fiber 2.6g; Chol 4mg; Iron 1.2mg; Sodium 122mg; Calc 40mg

CHEWY APPLE COOKIE SQUARES

POINTS value: 2 *(pictured on page 56)*

PREP: 10 minutes ■ **COOK:** 40 minutes
■ **OTHER:** 1 hour

These decadent apple-flavored squares are dense and moist.

> ½ cup brown sugar blend for baking (such as Splenda)
> ½ cup cinnamon-flavored applesauce
> 1½ cups reduced-fat vanilla wafer crumbs (about 43 cookies)
> ½ teaspoon vanilla extract
> ½ cup chopped pecans, toasted
> ½ cup flaked sweetened coconut (optional)
> Cooking spray

1. Preheat oven to 300°.
2. Place sugar blend and applesauce in a bowl. Beat with a mixer at medium speed 2 minutes or until smooth. Add crumbs; beat until blended. Stir in vanilla, pecans, and, if desired, coconut.
3. Spread batter into an 8-inch square pan coated with cooking spray. Bake at 300° for 40 minutes or until a wooden pick inserted in center comes out clean. Cool in pan on a wire rack. Cut into 16 squares. YIELD: 16 SERVINGS (SERVING SIZE: 1 SQUARE).

PER SERVING: Calories 103; Fat 3.4g (sat 0.2g, mono 1.5g, poly 0.8g); Protein 0.7g; Carb 16.3g; Fiber 0.4g; Chol 0mg; Iron 0.3mg; Sodium 37mg; Calc 3mg

Greek Nachos, *page 22*

Fruity White Sangria,
page 26

Crostini with Manchego
and Honeyed Orange
Relish, *page 23*

Wild Mushroom
Flatbread,
page 34

Banana-Nut Muffins with
Peanut Butter–Honey Drizzle,
page 28

Stuffed French Toast, *page 31*

Key Lime Cheesecake Parfaits, *page 40*

Tangerine-Strawberry
Sorbet, *page 43*

Fresh Pineapple Tart, *page 44*

Marbled Chocolate
Mousse, *page 39*

Chewy Apple Cookie Squares,
page 48

Flourless Chocolate Cookies,
page 46

Baja Fish Soft Tacos, *page 73*

Salmon Cakes with Corn
and Dill Cream, *page 70*

Hazelnut-Crusted Halibut, *page 68*

Coconut–Red Curry
Shrimp, *page 76*

Grilled Polenta and Summer
Vegetables, *page 79*

Grilled Grouper
with Chipotle Crema, *page 66*

Meatless Burger Tostadas with
Avocado Ranch Dressing, *page 85*

Grilled Portobellos with
Cheese Grits, *page 78*

fish & shellfish

Pan-Fried Tilapia with Chard and Prosciutto, *page 72*

SOY NUT–CRUSTED CATFISH

POINTS value: 5

PREP: 8 minutes ■ **COOK:** 12 minutes

Soy nuts are dried soybeans that have been soaked, drained, and then baked or roasted. They develop a nutty flavor and can be used instead of nuts in a variety of recipes.

> ½ cup salted roasted soy nuts
> ¼ cup plain fat-free Greek yogurt (such as Fage)
> 2 tablespoons fresh lime juice
> 1 teaspoon salt-free Southwest chipotle seasoning (such as Mrs. Dash)
> ¼ teaspoon salt
> ¼ teaspoon freshly ground black pepper
> 4 (6-ounce) catfish fillets
> Cooking spray

1. Preheat oven to 400°.
2. Place soy nuts in a large heavy-duty zip-top plastic bag; coarsely crush soy nuts using a rolling pin or meat mallet. Transfer soy nuts to a shallow dish.
3. Combine yogurt and next 4 ingredients. Brush tops of fish with yogurt mixture; dredge in soy nuts.
4. Place fish on a baking sheet coated with cooking spray. Bake at 400° for 12 minutes or until fish flakes easily when tested with a fork. **YIELD: 4 SERVINGS (SERVING SIZE: 1 FILLET).**

PER SERVING: Calories 220; Fat 6.4g (sat 1.6g, mono 1.4g, poly 1.5g); Protein 34g; Carb 5g; Fiber 2.1g; Chol 98mg; Iron 1mg; Sodium 285mg; Calc 59mg

GRILLED GROUPER WITH CHIPOTLE CREMA

POINTS value: 5   *(pictured on page 62)*

PREP: 2 minutes ■ **COOK:** 10 minutes

This fish has a wonderful flavor that would make a tasty filling for fish tacos. Just top with packaged slaw and fold up in warm corn tortillas.

> 4 (6-ounce) grouper fillets (¾ to 1 inch thick)
> 2 teaspoons olive oil
> 2 teaspoons salt-free fiesta lime seasoning (such as Mrs. Dash)
> ¼ teaspoon kosher salt
> Cooking spray
> ½ cup light sour cream
> 1 tablespoon minced chipotle chile, canned in adobo sauce
> 1 teaspoon fresh lime juice
> Lime wedges (optional)
> Fresh cilantro sprigs (optional)

1. Prepare grill.
2. Brush fish with olive oil; sprinkle evenly with lime seasoning and salt.
3. Place fish on grill rack coated with cooking spray. Grill 5 minutes on each side or until fish flakes easily when tested with a fork.
4. While fish cooks, combine sour cream, chipotle chile, and lime juice. Serve Chipotle Crema over grilled fish. Garnish with fresh lime wedges and cilantro sprigs, if desired. **YIELD: 4 SERVINGS (SERVING SIZE: 1 FILLET AND ABOUT 2 TABLESPOONS CREMA).**

PER SERVING: Calories 214; Fat 6g (sat 2.2g, mono 2g, poly 0.8g); Protein 34g; Carb 4.5g; Fiber 0.3g; Chol 73mg; Iron 1.6mg; Sodium 279mg; Calc 46mg

Be sure to wash the oranges thoroughly to remove dirt and wax before you begin.

1. Cut the top and bottom portions from the orange to create a stable cutting surface. Stand the fruit upright, and use a small paring knife to slice downward in a long, slow curve to remove the rind and the white pith.

2. Hold the fruit in your palm over a bowl, and gently follow the natural sections of the fruit with the knife to cut out wedges.

ORANGE-BASIL GROUPER

POINTS value: 5

PREP: 10 minutes ▪ COOK: 10 minutes

  4 (6-ounce) grouper fillets (about 1 inch thick)
½ teaspoon salt
¼ teaspoon freshly ground black pepper
  1 tablespoon light butter
  4 large navel oranges
  Cooking spray
  1 large shallot, cut into thin vertical slices
  1 tablespoon water
  2 tablespoons thinly sliced fresh basil

1. Sprinkle both sides of fish with salt and pepper. Heat butter in a large nonstick skillet over medium-high heat. Add fish; cook 3 minutes on each side or until fish flakes easily when tested with a fork. Remove fish from pan; keep warm.
2. While fish cooks, squeeze juice from 2 oranges to measure ½ cup. Peel and section remaining 2 oranges over a bowl.
3. Coat pan with cooking spray. Add shallot slices; cook over medium heat 1 minute or until tender, adding 1 tablespoon water, if necessary, to deglaze pan. Stir in ½ cup orange juice; cook over medium-high

heat 1 to 2 minutes or until reduced to ⅓ cup. Stir in basil. Return fish to pan; add orange sections, and cook 1 minute or just until thoroughly heated.
YIELD: 4 SERVINGS (SERVING SIZE: 1 FILLET AND ABOUT 1 TABLESPOON SAUCE).

PER SERVING: Calories 266; Fat 3.8g (sat 1.5g, mono 0.9g, poly 0.7g); Protein 35.2g; Carb 23.2g; Fiber 3.4g; Chol 66mg; Iron 2.2mg; Sodium 401mg; Calc 123mg

CARIBBEAN GRILLED HALIBUT WITH PINEAPPLE SAUCE

POINTS value: 6

PREP: 8 minutes ▪ COOK: 10 minutes

To save time, grill the pineapple alongside the fish.

  1½ pounds halibut fillets (about 1 inch thick)
  2 teaspoons minced fresh thyme
  ⅛ teaspoon salt
  ⅛ teaspoon freshly ground black pepper
  Cooking spray
  4 (½-inch-thick) slices fresh pineapple
  ¼ cup pineapple preserves
  2 tablespoons seasoned rice vinegar
  1 teaspoon chopped fresh thyme
  ⅛ teaspoon crushed red pepper
  1 garlic clove, minced

1. Prepare grill.
2. Rinse fish; pat dry. Combine thyme, salt, and pepper; sprinkle fish with herb mixture, and coat with cooking spray.
3. Place fish on grill rack coated with cooking spray. Grill 4 minutes on each side or until fish flakes easily when tested with a fork.
4. While fish grills, coat pineapple slices with cooking spray; place on grill rack coated with cooking spray. Grill 3 to 4 minutes on each side. Cut slices into eighths.
5. Combine pineapple preserves and next 4 ingredients in a small saucepan. Bring to a boil; boil 1 minute. Stir in pineapple. Spoon pineapple mixture evenly over fish. YIELD: 4 SERVINGS (SERVING SIZE: 1 FILLET AND ½ CUP PINEAPPLE).

PER SERVING: Calories 272; Fat 4g (sat 0.6g, mono 1.3g, poly 1.3g); Protein 35.8g; Carb 22g; Fiber 0.9g; Chol 54mg; Iron 1.7mg; Sodium 314mg; Calc 91mg

HAZELNUT-CRUSTED HALIBUT

POINTS value: 7   *(pictured on page 60)*

PREP: 8 minutes ■ **COOK:** 10 minutes

The sweet, nutty crunch of hazelnuts makes this recipe. To jumpstart, we began with purchased chopped nuts.

> 2 tablespoons plain fat-free Greek yogurt
>   (such as Fage)
> ½ teaspoon freshly ground black pepper
> ¼ teaspoon salt
> 2 garlic cloves, minced
> 4 (6-ounce) halibut fillets
> ½ cup chopped hazelnuts, very finely chopped
> 1 tablespoon olive oil

1. Preheat oven to 400°.
2. Combine first 4 ingredients. Brush yogurt mixture over tops of fish. Dredge fish in hazelnuts.
3. Heat a large nonstick skillet over medium-high heat. Add oil to pan. Add fish; reduce heat to medium-low. Cook 3 minutes or just until nuts are golden; turn fish over. Cook 2 minutes. Place pan in oven. Bake at 400° for 5 minutes or until fish flakes easily when tested with a fork. **YIELD: 4 SERVINGS (SERVING SIZE: 1 FILLET).**

PER SERVING: Calories 314; Fat 16g (sat 1.7g, mono 10.3g, poly 2.7g); Protein 38.3g; Carb 3.4g; Fiber 1.5g; Chol 54mg; Iron 2.2mg; Sodium 240mg; Calc 105mg

HOW TO SKIN AND CHOP WHOLE HAZELNUTS

1. With a little extra work, you can easily substitute whole hazelnuts for chopped. You'll first need to remove the skin, though. Spread shelled whole hazelnuts on a baking sheet. (You'll need about ⅔ cup of whole nuts to end up with ½ cup of chopped.)

2. Bake at 350° for 15 minutes, stirring once. Transfer nuts to a colander or dish, and rub briskly

with a towel to remove the skins. Set aside until cool to touch. Use a food processor or knife to finely chop the nuts.

THAWING HALIBUT

You can find frozen halibut fillets in individually wrapped portions in most grocery stores. They are a great alternative if you can't find fresh halibut. For freshest flavor, keep them frozen until just before using; then, place unwrapped portions in a single layer in a large bowl of cold water, turning occasionally. They will thaw in about 15 minutes.

MEDITERRANEAN HALIBUT WITH CRUMB TOPPING

POINTS value: 5

PREP: 10 minutes ■ **COOK:** 10 minutes

Panko is an ideal topping—it doesn't absorb oil as readily as dry breadcrumbs, resists sogginess, and maintains its crispness.

> 4 (6-ounce) fresh or frozen halibut fillets
>   (about 1 inch thick)
> ¼ teaspoon salt
> ¼ teaspoon freshly ground black pepper
> ½ cup Italian-seasoned panko
>   (Japanese breadcrumbs)
> 2 teaspoons grated lemon rind
> 2 tablespoons sun-dried tomato pesto
>   (such as Classico)
> Cooking spray
> 2 tablespoons chopped fresh flat-leaf parsley
> Lemon wedges (optional)

1. Preheat oven to 425°.
2. Rinse fish, and pat dry with paper towels; sprinkle fish with salt and pepper.
3. Combine panko and lemon rind. Spread pesto on tops of fish; sprinkle with panko mixture, pressing lightly to adhere crumbs.
4. Place fish on the rack of a broiler pan coated with cooking spray. Bake at 425° for 10 minutes or until fish flakes easily when tested with a fork. Sprinkle with parsley before serving. Garnish with lemon wedges, if desired. **YIELD: 4 SERVINGS (SERVING SIZE: 1 FILLET).**

PER SERVING: Calories 235; Fat 4.8g (sat 0.7g, mono 1.3g, poly 1.3g); Protein 36.9g; Carb 8.9g; Fiber 1.3g; Chol 54mg; Iron 2.1mg; Sodium 386mg; Calc 84mg

POACHED SALMON WITH LEMON-CAPER SAUCE

POINTS value: 6

PREP: 4 minutes ■ **COOK:** 10 minutes

When poaching salmon, have the cooking liquid at a bare simmer because it requires gentle heat. Serve this buttery entrée with a mound of polenta topped with a fresh tomato sauce.

> 4 (6-ounce) salmon fillets, skinned
> ⅛ teaspoon salt
> 3 sprigs fresh parsley
> 2 sprigs fresh oregano
> ⅓ cup dry white wine
> 3 tablespoons drained capers
> 1 tablespoon light butter
> 2 teaspoons fresh lemon juice

1. Sprinkle fish with salt; place in a large skillet. Add parsley and oregano sprigs and wine. Fill pan with enough water to come halfway up sides of fish. Bring to a boil; reduce heat, and simmer 4 minutes. Turn fish over, and simmer 3 to 4 minutes or until fish flakes easily when tested with a fork. Remove and discard herbs. Transfer fish to a serving plate; keep warm.

2. Add capers to cooking liquid. Bring to a boil; boil 2 minutes or until liquid is reduced to 3 tablespoons. Whisk in butter and lemon juice. Serve with/over fish **YIELD: 4 SERVINGS (SERVING SIZE: 1 FILLET AND ABOUT 1 TABLESPOON SAUCE).**

PER SERVING: Calories 267; Fat 11.4g (sat 2.7g, mono 3.6g, poly 4.2g); Protein 38.7g; Carb 3.2g; Fiber 0.4g; Chol 102mg; Iron 1.3mg; Sodium 379mg; Calc 19mg

CITRUS AND CHILI-RUBBED SALMON

POINTS value: 5

PREP: 3 minutes ■ **COOK:** 9 minutes

> 1 navel orange
> 1 lemon
> 1 tablespoon brown sugar
> 2 teaspoons olive oil
> ½ teaspoon chili powder
> ½ teaspoon ground cumin
> 4 (6-ounce) salmon fillets (1½ inches thick)
> ¼ teaspoon salt
> ¼ teaspoon freshly ground black pepper
> Cooking spray
> Orange wedges (optional)

1. Prepare grill.

2. Grate rind and squeeze juice from orange to equal 1 teaspoon rind and 1 tablespoon juice. Repeat procedure with lemon. Combine rinds, juices, brown sugar, and next 3 ingredients. Sprinkle fillets evenly with salt and pepper; brush citrus mixture evenly over fillets.

3. Place fillets, skin sides down, on grill rack coated with cooking spray; grill 9 to 10 minutes or until desired degree of doneness. Garnish with orange wedges, if desired. **YIELD: 4 SERVINGS (SERVING SIZE: 1 FILLET).**

PER SERVING: Calories 235; Fat 8.2g (sat 1.3g, mono 3.2g, poly 2.5g); Protein 34g; Carb 4.5g; Fiber 0.3g; Chol 88mg; Iron 1.5mg; Sodium 271mg; Calc 30mg

GRILLING SALMON

Removing the skin from raw salmon can be difficult, but there's no need to do that when you're grilling it. Actually, make sure you keep the skin on your salmon when preparing this fish on the grill, as it prevents the salmon from curling and flaking apart. Place the salmon, skin side down, on the grill rack. The skin will release easily from the fish once it's cooked, and there's no worry that the flesh will stick to the grill.

SALMON CAKES WITH CORN AND DILL CREAM

POINTS value: 6   *(pictured on page 59)*

PREP: 15 minutes ■ **COOK:** 4 minutes

Use a scant ¼-cup measure to divide the salmon mixture evenly for shaping into patties.

- 1 (14.75-ounce) can pink salmon, drained and skin and bones discarded
- 1 cup panko (Japanese breadcrumbs)
- 2 tablespoons minced red bell pepper
- 1 tablespoon chopped fresh dill
- 1 tablespoon fresh lemon juice
- 1 tablespoon light mayonnaise
- 1 teaspoon Worcestershire sauce
- 1 large egg, lightly beaten
- Cooking spray
- 2 teaspoons olive oil
- Corn and Dill Cream

1. Combine salmon and next 7 ingredients in a large bowl; mix with hands just until combined. Divide salmon mixture into 8 equal portions, shaping each into a ½-inch-thick patty.
2. Heat a large nonstick skillet over medium-high heat. Coat pan with cooking spray; add oil. Cook patties 2 to 3 minutes on each side or until golden and done. Remove patties from pan. Serve with Corn and Dill Cream. **YIELD: 4 SERVINGS (SERVING SIZE: 2 SALMON PATTIES AND 3 TABLESPOONS CORN AND DILL CREAM).**

PER SERVING: Calories 278; Fat 12.4g (sat 2.7g, mono 2.1g, poly 0.4g); Protein 24.5g; Carb 18.6g; Fiber 0.9g; Chol 114mg; Iron 1mg; Sodium 645mg; Calc 13mg

Corn and Dill Cream

POINTS value: 2

- ½ cup light sour cream
- ¼ cup frozen baby gold and white corn, thawed
- 2 tablespoons chopped green onions
- 2 tablespoons light mayonnaise
- 1 tablespoon chopped fresh dill
- 2 teaspoons fresh lemon juice
- ¼ teaspoon salt
- ¼ teaspoon freshly ground black pepper

1. Combine all ingredients in a blender, and pulse 1 to 2 times just until combined (mixture will not be smooth).
YIELD: 4 SERVINGS (SERVING SIZE: 3 TABLESPOONS).

PER SERVING: Calories 72; Fat 4.6g (sat 1.9g, mono 0g, poly 0g); Protein 1.4g; Carb 7.1g; Fiber 0.3g; Chol 13mg; Iron 0.1mg; Sodium 236mg; Calc 4mg

BROILING

Broiling is a healthy cooking method that is particularly good for relatively small, tender cuts of meat. When you broil, the food is placed on a broiler pan (usually on the top rack of the oven), and the heat source is above the food. As the food cooks, some of the fat cooks out of the meat and drips away from the food into the bottom of the broiler pan.

BLACKENED RED SNAPPER WITH MANGO SALSA

POINTS value: 4

PREP: 1 minute ■ **COOK:** 6 minutes

Broiling eliminates the fumes created by traditional blackening in a cast-iron skillet on the stovetop. Our version still produces that great blackened flavor. The fresh salsa cools the heat of the spicy seasonings. For a quicker salsa, try stirring diced cucumber and fresh cilantro into prepared mango-peach salsa.

- 4 (6-ounce) red snapper or other firm white fish fillets
- 1 teaspoon olive oil
- 2 tablespoons salt-free Cajun seasoning
- ¼ teaspoon salt
- Cooking spray
- ¾ cup diced peeled mango
- ⅓ cup diced English cucumber
- ¼ cup chopped red bell pepper
- 2 tablespoons finely chopped red onion
- 1 tablespoon chopped fresh cilantro
- 2 tablespoons fresh lime juice
- 1 small jalapeño pepper, seeded and minced

1. Preheat broiler.
2. Rub fish with oil; sprinkle evenly with Cajun seasoning and salt. Place fish on a broiler pan coated with

cooking spray. Broil 3 inches from heat 6 minutes or until fish flakes easily when tested with a fork.

3. While fish cooks, combine mango and next 6 ingredients. Serve salsa with fish. **YIELD: 4 SERVINGS (SERVING SIZE: 1 FISH FILLET AND ABOUT ⅓ CUP SALSA).**

PER SERVING: Calories 211; Fat 3.6g (sat 0.7g, mono 1.3g, poly 0.9g); Protein 35.4g; Carb 7.7g; Fiber 1g; Chol 63mg; Iron 0.4mg; Sodium 256mg; Calc 62mg

FISH TACOS WITH FRESH PEACH SALSA
POINTS value: 7

PREP: 7 minutes ■ **COOK:** 8 minutes
■ **OTHER:** 5 minutes

Juicy, sweet summer peaches are a perfect complement to these fish tacos.

Fresh Peach Salsa
1 pound red snapper fillets (1 inch thick)
3 tablespoons fresh lime juice
2 tablespoons vegetable oil
2 teaspoons ancho chile powder
⅛ teaspoon salt
Cooking spray
4 (6-inch) whole-wheat tortillas, warmed
2 cups packaged angel hair slaw

1. Prepare grill.
2. Prepare Fresh Peach Salsa; set aside.
3. Place fish in an 11 x 7–inch baking dish. Combine lime juice and next 3 ingredients; pour over fish, and let stand 5 minutes.
4. Remove fish from marinade, discarding marinade. Place fish on grill rack coated with cooking spray. Grill 4 minutes on each side or until fish flakes easily when tested with a fork.
5. Divide fish into 4 equal portions. Place fish portions evenly in tortillas; top evenly with slaw and salsa. **YIELD: 4 SERVINGS (SERVING SIZE: 1 TORTILLA, 3 OUNCES FISH, ½ CUP SLAW, AND ⅓ CUP SALSA).**

PER SERVING: Calories 351; Fat 10.7g (sat 1.6g, mono 3.3g, poly 3.6g); Protein 28.3g; Carb 34.4g; Fiber 3.7g; Chol 42mg; Iron 0.4mg; Sodium 606mg; Calc 45mg

Fresh Peach Salsa
POINTS value: 0

1¼ cups chopped peeled peaches
(about 2 medium)
3 tablespoons finely chopped red onion
2 tablespoons chopped fresh cilantro
3 tablespoons fresh lime juice
⅛ teaspoon salt

1. Combine all ingredients in a medium bowl. **YIELD: 1⅓ CUPS (SERVING SIZE: ⅓ CUP).**

PER SERVING: Calories 27; Fat 0.2g (sat 0g, mono 0g, poly 0.1g); Protein 0.6g; Carb 6.8g; Fiber 1g; Chol 0mg; Iron 0.2mg; Sodium 73mg; Calc 7mg

✳ Buying Peaches
Peaches are in season from May to late September. Look for fruit that is firm with a taut, unblemished skin. The fruit should have no signs of bruising or wrinkles. If you can smell the peaches when you walk up to the stand, you know they're ripe.

PAN-FRIED TILAPIA WITH CHARD AND PROSCIUTTO

POINTS value: 6   *(pictured on page 12)*

PREP: 6 minutes ■ **COOK:** 11 minutes

Delicate white fish fillets are coated in almonds and breadcrumbs to create a light crust.

> 4 (6-ounce) tilapia fillets
> Cooking spray
> ⅓ cup slivered almonds
> ⅓ cup panko (Japanese breadcrumbs)
> ½ teaspoon onion powder
> ¼ teaspoon salt
> 1 tablespoon olive oil, divided
> 2 ounces prosciutto, diced
> 7 cups chopped trimmed Swiss chard
> 1 tablespoon fresh lemon juice

1. Coat both sides of fish with cooking spray.

2. Process almonds in a food processor until minced; place in a medium bowl. Stir in panko, onion powder, and salt. Dredge fish in almond mixture, pressing to coat.

3. Heat 2 teaspoons oil in a large nonstick skillet over medium-high heat. Add fish to pan; cook 3 minutes on each side or until fish flakes easily when tested with a fork. Remove from pan.

4. Add remaining 1 teaspoon oil to pan. Add prosciutto; sauté 1 minute or until golden. Add chard; reduce heat to medium-low. Cover and cook 3 minutes or until tender, stirring after 2 minutes. Drizzle fish with lemon juice, and top with chard mixture.
YIELD: 4 SERVINGS (SERVING SIZE: 1 FILLET AND ABOUT ½ CUP CHARD MIXTURE).

PER SERVING: Calories 296; Fat 11.9g (sat 2.2g, mono 6.5g, poly 2.2g); Protein 40.9g; Carb 7.8g; Fiber 2.1g; Chol 93.4mg; Iron 2.6mg; Sodium 595mg; Calc 71mg

✳ Swiss Chard

One of several leafy green vegetables referred to as "greens," Swiss chard offers an earthy, slightly salty flavor. It has fanlike leaves and white, red, or yellow stalks that are thick and crunchy. When buying chard, look for crisp leaves with no dark or moist patches, and avoid bunches with cracked or dried stems.

COCONUT-CRUSTED TILAPIA WITH PEPPERY PINEAPPLE

POINTS value: 7

PREP: 15 minutes ■ **COOK:** 26 minutes
■ **OTHER:** 1 hour

> 1 (13.5-ounce) can light coconut milk
> 1 tablespoon curry powder, divided
> ½ teaspoon salt, divided
> 4 (6-ounce) tilapia fillets
> ½ teaspoon ground red pepper, divided
> 20 reduced-fat round buttery crackers
> ½ cup flaked sweetened coconut
> 2 garlic cloves, peeled and halved
> 2 large egg whites
> 1 tablespoon water
> Butter-flavored cooking spray
> 1 garlic clove, minced
> 1 (8-ounce) can crushed pineapple in juice, undrained
> 1 tablespoon honey
> 2 teaspoons grated peeled fresh ginger
> 1 teaspoon white vinegar
> ¼ cup chopped fresh cilantro

1. Combine coconut milk, 2 teaspoons curry powder, and ⅛ teaspoon salt in a large zip-top plastic bag. Add fillets; seal bag, and marinate in refrigerator 1 hour, turning bag occasionally. Remove fillets from bag, reserving ½ cup marinade. Pat fillets dry with paper towels; sprinkle with remaining 1 teaspoon curry powder, remaining ⅜ teaspoon salt, and ¼ teaspoon red pepper.

2. Place crackers, coconut, and 2 garlic cloves in a food processor; pulse to form coarse crumbs. Place crumb mixture in a shallow dish. Combine egg whites and 1 tablespoon water in a shallow bowl; stir well. Dip fillets in egg mixture; dredge in crumb mixture.

3. Heat a large nonstick skillet over medium heat. Coat half of fillets with cooking spray. Add fillets to pan; cook 4 minutes on each side or until golden brown and fish flakes easily when tested with a fork. Remove fillets from pan; keep warm. Repeat procedure with remaining fillets.

4. Coat pan with cooking spray. Add minced garlic, and sauté 1 minute. Stir in reserved ½ cup marinade, remaining ¼ teaspoon red pepper, pineapple, and next 3 ingredients. Bring to a boil; reduce heat to medium, and simmer 5 minutes or until slightly thick and reduced to ¾ cup. Stir in cilantro. Serve over fillets. **YIELD: 4 SERVINGS (SERVING SIZE: 1 FILLET AND 3 TABLE-SPOONS SAUCE).**

PER SERVING: Calories 351; Fat 7.8g (sat 4.3g, mono 0.9g, poly 0.6g); Protein 37.1g; Carb 31.9g; Fiber 1.2g; Chol 66mg; Iron 2.4mg; Sodium 299mg; Calc 128mg

BAJA FISH SOFT TACOS

POINTS value: 6   *(pictured on page 58)*

PREP: 7 minutes ■ **COOK:** 7 minutes

Instead of using the microwave, you can heat the tortillas for these tacos on the grill. Remove them while they are warm, but still pliable.

> 4 (6-ounce) tilapia fillets
> Cooking spray
> ¼ teaspoon ground red pepper
> ¼ teaspoon salt
> 2 cups packaged angel hair slaw
> 3 tablespoons light mayonnaise
> 2 tablespoons chopped fresh cilantro
> ⅛ teaspoon ground red pepper
> 8 (6-inch) corn tortillas
> ½ cup refrigerated pico de gallo

1. Prepare grill.
2. Coat fish with cooking spray. Combine ¼ teaspoon ground red pepper and salt; sprinkle over both sides of fish. Place fish on grill rack coated with cooking spray. Grill 3 to 4 minutes on each side or until fish flakes easily when tested with a fork.
3. While fish grills, combine slaw and next 3 ingredients in a medium bowl, tossing to coat.
4. Quickly flake fish into bite-sized pieces with 2 forks.
5. Wrap tortillas in 2 layers of damp paper towels. Microwave at HIGH 30 to 40 seconds or until thoroughly heated. Divide fish evenly among tortillas; top evenly with slaw mixture and pico de gallo. **YIELD: 4 SERVINGS (SERVING SIZE: 2 TACOS).**

PER SERVING: Calories 298; Fat 7.6g (sat 1.5g, mono 0.9g, poly 1.2g); Protein 37.1g; Carb 22.8g; Fiber 3.3g; Chol 89mg; Iron 1mg; Sodium 420mg; Calc 38mg

PAN-FRIED CRAB CAKES WITH CREOLE SAUCE

POINTS value: 4

PREP: 10 minutes ■ **COOK:** 4 minutes ■ **OTHER:** 15 minutes

Don't be tempted to skip the chilling step here—it helps the crab mixture bind together and makes the crab cakes easier to turn during cooking.

> 1 cup panko (Japanese breadcrumbs), divided
> ⅓ cup light mayonnaise
> 1 teaspoon minced fresh tarragon
> 1 teaspoon Dijon mustard
> 1 pound lump crabmeat, drained and shell pieces removed
> ½ cup light sour cream
> 2 tablespoons plain fat-free yogurt
> 1 tablespoon Creole mustard
> 2 teaspoons drained capers, chopped
> ¼ teaspoon salt-free Cajun Creole seasoning (such as Spice Hunter)
> Cooking spray
> 2 teaspoons olive oil

1. Combine ½ cup panko and next 3 ingredients in a large bowl. Gently stir in crabmeat. Divide crabmeat mixture into 12 equal portions, shaping each into a 1-inch-thick patty. Place remaining ½ cup panko in a shallow dish. Dredge patties in panko, coating all sides. Cover and chill patties 15 minutes.
2. While patties chill, combine sour cream and next 4 ingredients.
3. Heat a large nonstick skillet over medium heat. Coat pan with cooking spray; add oil. Add patties; cook 2 to 3 minutes on each side or until golden brown. Serve crab cakes with Creole sauce. **YIELD: 6 SERVINGS (SERVING SIZE: 2 CRAB CAKES AND ABOUT 2 TABLESPOONS CREOLE SAUCE).**

PER SERVING: Calories 177; Fat 8.9g (sat 1.9g, mono 1.1g, poly 0.2g); Protein 13.2g; Carb 11.4g; Fiber 0.4g; Chol 79mg; Iron 0.5mg; Sodium 662mg; Calc 38mg

SPICY ASIAN MUSSELS
POINTS value: 6

PREP: 4 minutes ▪ **COOK:** 9 minutes

Thai green curry paste is a mixture of clarified butter and ground green chiles. It tends to be sweeter than curry paste made from red chiles.

> 1 (13.5-ounce) can light coconut milk
> ¼ cup fresh lime juice
> ¼ cup mirin (sweet rice wine)
> 1 tablespoon Thai green curry paste
> 1 teaspoon fish sauce
> 70 mussels (about 3 pounds), scrubbed and debearded
> ½ cup chopped fresh cilantro

1. Combine first 5 ingredients in a large Dutch oven. Bring to a boil; boil 2 minutes, stirring occasionally.
2. Add mussels to pan; cover, reduce heat, and simmer 5 minutes or until mussels open. Remove from heat; discard any unopened shells.
3. Using a slotted spoon, spoon mussels evenly into 6 bowls. Pour broth evenly over mussels, and sprinkle with cilantro. **YIELD: 6 SERVINGS (SERVING SIZE: ABOUT 11 MUSSELS AND ⅓ CUP BROTH).**

PER SERVING: Calories 260; Fat 8.5g (sat 4.2g, mono 1.2g, poly 1.4g); Protein 28g; Carb 15.3g; Fiber 0.1g; Chol 64mg; Iron 9.3mg; Sodium 775mg; Calc 62mg

SEARED SCALLOPS WITH WHITE WINE BUTTER SAUCE
POINTS value: 5

PREP: 2 minutes ▪ **COOK:** 10 minutes

To get the best sear on the scallops, purchase dry-packed ones. They are fresher and have a shorter shelf-life, but will create less liquid when cooking.

> 12 large sea scallops (about 1½ pounds)
> ¼ teaspoon salt
> ¼ teaspoon black pepper
> Cooking spray
> 2 tablespoons butter
> 1 large shallot, finely chopped
> 1 tablespoon all-purpose flour
> ½ cup dry white wine
> 2 tablespoons water
> 1 teaspoon fresh thyme leaves

1. Sprinkle scallops evenly with salt and pepper. Heat a large nonstick skillet over medium–high heat. Coat pan with cooking spray. Add scallops; cook 3 minutes on each side or until done. Remove scallops from pan, and keep warm.
2. Melt butter in pan. Add shallots; sauté 1 minute or until tender. Stir in flour; cook, stirring constantly, 1 minute. Stir in wine and 2 tablespoons water; cook, stirring with a whisk, 2 minutes or until sauce thickens. Stir in thyme. Serve sauce over scallops. **YIELD: 4 SERVINGS (SERVING SIZE: 3 TO 4 SCALLOPS AND ABOUT 3 TABLESPOONS BUTTER SAUCE).**

PER SERVING: Calories 231; Fat 7g (sat 3.7g, mono 1.5g, poly 0.7g); Protein 29g; Carb 9.8g; Fiber 0.2g; Chol 71mg; Iron 1mg; Sodium 640mg; Calc 48mg

BUYING SCALLOPS

Avoid "wet-packed" scallops. This variety has been treated with a liquid solution containing sodium tripolyphosphate. The scallops absorb this mixture and plump up, resulting in a heavier weight and higher market price. But when you cook them, the liquid portion will cook out, leaving you with smaller scallops and a higher sodium content. Dry-packed scallops are not chemically treated and are preferable over wet-packed for price and lower sodium content.

SCALLOP KEBABS
WITH SALSA VERDE

POINTS value: 7

PREP: 7 minutes ■ **COOK:** 5 minutes

Skewering scallops not only makes them easier to turn on the grill, but it also makes a beautiful presentation when combined with brightly colored vegetables.

- ¼ **cup coarsely chopped fresh parsley**
- 2 **teaspoons drained capers, coarsely chopped**
- 1 **teaspoon grated lemon rind**
- ¼ **teaspoon freshly ground black pepper**
- ⅛ **teaspoon salt**
- 1 **small garlic clove, minced**
- ¼ **cup extra-virgin olive oil**
- 12 **large sea scallops (about 1½ pounds)**
- 12 **cherry tomatoes**
- 5 **(12-inch) metal skewers**
- 1 **large zucchini, cut into 12 slices**
- **Cooking spray**

1. Prepare grill.
2. Combine first 6 ingredients in a small bowl. Gradually add olive oil, stirring with a whisk.
3. Thread scallops and tomatoes onto 3 skewers. Thread zucchini slices onto remaining 2 skewers. Coat kebabs with cooking spray, and place on grill rack coated with cooking spray. Grill 4 to 5 minutes or until scallops are done; remove from grill. Continue to grill zucchini 1 to 2 minutes or until tender. Drizzle salsa over kebabs before serving. **YIELD: 4 SERVINGS (SERVING SIZE: 3 SCALLOPS, 3 TOMATOES, 3 ZUCCHINI SLICES, AND 4 TEASPOONS SALSA).**

PER SERVING: Calories 297; Fat 15.7g (sat 2.2g, mono 10.1g, poly 2.6g); Protein 30.2g; Carb 9.8g; Fiber 1.7g; Chol 56mg; Iron 1.3mg; Sodium 404mg; Calc 64mg

WOODEN VERSUS METAL SKEWERS

When grilling, you can use either wooden or metal skewers. It's important that you soak wooden skewers in water for at least 30 minutes before using them to prevent burning. Wooden skewers should be discarded after one use. If you grill often, invest in a set of metal skewers. They are reusable and require no soaking, which makes them ideal for the time-crunched cook.

MEDITERRANEAN SHRIMP
WITH RUSTIC BREAD

POINTS value: 5

PREP: 6 minutes ■ **COOK:** 12 minutes

Succulent shrimp bake in the flavors of the Mediterranean in this quick summer dish. Cut the baguette slices on a sharp diagonal to provide more surface area to soak up the piquant juices.

- ½ **cup thin vertical slices red onion**
- ¼ **cup coarsely chopped kalamata olives**
- 2 **tablespoons olive oil**
- 1 **tablespoon drained capers**
- 4 **large garlic cloves, chopped**
- 1½ **pounds large shrimp, peeled and deveined**
- 2 **cups cherry tomatoes, halved**
- 6 **ounces whole-wheat French bread baguette, cut into 12 diagonal slices**
- **Olive oil–flavored cooking spray**
- ¼ **cup balsamic vinegar**
- ¼ **cup chopped fresh basil**

1. Preheat oven to 425°.
2. Combine first 5 ingredients in a large bowl; add shrimp and tomato, stirring to coat. Spoon mixture into a 13 x 9–inch baking dish. Bake at 425° for 6 minutes.
3. While shrimp mixture bakes, coat bread slices with cooking spray. Place on a large baking sheet. Stir shrimp, and place baking sheet on oven rack below shrimp. Bake an additional 6 minutes or until shrimp are done.
4. Drizzle vinegar over shrimp mixture. Place 2 toasts on each of 6 plates. Spoon shrimp mixture over toasts, and sprinkle evenly with basil. **YIELD: 6 SERVINGS (SERVING SIZE: 1 CUP SHRIMP MIXTURE, 2 TOASTS, AND 2 TEASPOONS BASIL).**

PER SERVING: Calories 228; Fat 7.8g (sat 1.2g, mono 4.7g, poly 1.1g); Protein 20.7g; Carb 17.9g; Fiber 1.1g; Chol 169mg; Iron 3.2mg; Sodium 484mg; Calc 50mg

COCONUT–RED CURRY SHRIMP

POINTS value: 7 *(pictured on page 61)*

PREP: 5 minutes ■ **COOK:** 14 minutes

You may want to serve this in a bowl to allow the rice to soak up the sauce.

- 1½ **tablespoons cornstarch**
- 1¼ **pounds peeled and deveined medium shrimp**
  Cooking spray
- 1 **(15-ounce) can light coconut milk**
- 2 **tablespoons lemongrass paste (such as Gourmet Garden)**
- 1 **tablespoon fish sauce**
- 1 **tablespoon minced peeled fresh ginger**
- 1 **teaspoon brown sugar**
- 2 **teaspoons red curry paste**
- 2 **garlic cloves, minced**
- 1 **(8.8-ounce) package microwaveable precooked basmati rice (such as Uncle Ben's Ready Rice)**
  Lime wedges (optional)
  Chopped fresh cilantro (optional)

1. Sprinkle cornstarch over shrimp in a medium bowl, tossing to coat.
2. Heat a large deep skillet over medium-high heat. Coat pan with cooking spray. Add shrimp and cook 1 to 2 minutes; turn shrimp over. Cook 1 to 2 minutes or until shrimp turn pink. Remove shrimp from pan; keep warm.
3. Combine coconut milk and next 6 ingredients in pan. Bring to a boil; reduce heat, and simmer 2 minutes. Add shrimp; cook 4 to 5 minutes or until thoroughly heated and sauce is slightly thickened.
4. While shrimp heats, microwave rice according to package directions. Serve shrimp over rice. Garnish with lime wedges and cilantro, if desired. **YIELD: 4 SERVINGS (SERVING SIZE: ABOUT 1 CUP SHRIMP MIXTURE AND ABOUT ½ CUP RICE).**

PER SERVING: Calories 311; Fat 8.6g (sat 5.2g, mono 0.4g, poly 1g); Protein 31.7g; Carb 25.9g; Fiber 0.3g; Chol 215mg; Iron 4.5mg; Sodium 766mg; Calc 78mg

SHRIMP AND ASPARAGUS RISOTTO

POINTS value: 5

PREP: 2 minutes ■ **COOK:** 18 minutes

Heating the broth in the microwave while the shrimp and vegetables cook is a time-saving strategy. In regular risotto, cooking is continued for 10 minutes or more after the rice is tender to create a creamy texture. Here, a cornstarch slurry, added at the end of cooking, thickens and becomes creamy in 1 to 2 minutes after the rice is tender.

- 1 **tablespoon olive oil**
- 1 **pound fresh asparagus, cut into 1-inch pieces**
- ½ **pound peeled and deveined large shrimp**
- ¾ **cup refrigerated prechopped onion**
- 2 **cups fat-free, less-sodium chicken broth, divided**
  Cooking spray
- 1 **(8.8-ounce) package precooked long-grain rice (such as Uncle Ben's Ready Rice)**
- 2 **teaspoons cornstarch**
- 1 **tablespoon minced fresh dill**
- ½ **cup grated fresh Parmigiano-Reggiano cheese, divided**
- ½ **teaspoon freshly ground black pepper**

1. Heat oil in a large nonstick skillet over medium-high heat. Add asparagus, shrimp, and onion. Cook 4 minutes or until shrimp are lightly browned and asparagus is crisp-tender, stirring often.
2. While asparagus mixture cooks, pour chicken broth into a large glass measure. Microwave, uncovered, at HIGH 1 minute or until broth is hot.
3. Heat a large saucepan over medium-high heat. Coat pan with cooking spray. Add rice; sauté 1 minute. Gradually add 1¾ cups hot broth, ½ cup at a time, stirring constantly until each portion of broth is absorbed before adding the next.
4. Combine ¼ cup broth and cornstarch, stirring with a whisk until smooth. Add to rice, and cook, stirring constantly, 1 minute or until thickened. Stir in asparagus mixture, dill, and ¼ cup cheese. Sprinkle with pepper and remaining ¼ cup cheese. **YIELD: 4 SERVINGS (SERVING SIZE: ABOUT 1 CUP).**

PER SERVING: Calories 255; Fat 8.9g (sat 3.6g, mono 2.6g, poly 0.6g); Protein 19.7g; Carb 25.2g; Fiber 3.4g; Chol 99mg; Iron 3mg; Sodium 556mg; Calc 174mg

meatless main dishes

Herbed Quinoa with Apples, *page 80*

CHIPOTLE BLACK BEANS

POINTS value: 6

PREP: 7 minutes ■ **COOK:** 20 minutes

With more than 11 grams of fiber per serving, this hearty dish has staying power. That's more than one-third of the daily recommendation for fiber.

- 1 tablespoon olive oil
- 1 cup refrigerated prechopped celery, onion, and bell pepper mix
- 1 chipotle chile, canned in adobo sauce, minced
- 2 teaspoons chopped fresh oregano
- 2 (16-ounce) cans black beans, rinsed and drained
- ¾ cup water
- ⅓ cup fresh orange juice
- ¼ teaspoon salt
- 2 cups cooked brown rice
- ¼ cup fat-free sour cream
- ½ cup shredded mozzarella cheese

1. Heat oil in a large nonstick skillet over medium-high heat. Add celery mixture. Reduce heat to medium, and cook 5 minutes or until tender. Add chile and oregano; cook 2 minutes.
2. Stir in beans and next 3 ingredients. Bring to a boil; reduce heat, and simmer, uncovered, 10 minutes, stirring occasionally. Serve beans over rice; top with sour cream and cheese. **YIELD: 4 SERVINGS (SERVING SIZE: ¾ CUP BEAN MIXTURE, ½ CUP RICE, 1 TABLESPOON SOUR CREAM, AND 2 TABLESPOONS CHEESE).**

PER SERVING: Calories 333; Fat 7.5g (sat 2.2g, mono 3.4g, poly 0.7g); Protein 15.4g; Carb 54.7g; Fiber 11.1g; Chol 10mg; Iron 3mg; Sodium 826mg; Calc 186mg

❋ Chipotle Chiles in Adobo Sauce

Chipotle chile peppers in adobo sauce are smoked jalapeños canned in a sauce of tomatoes, onion, garlic, spices, and vinegar. These peppers add a complex, smoky flavor to a dish. If these fiery chiles are new to you, start easy—a little goes a long way. No recipe requires an entire can of chipotles. Leftovers can be refrigerated in a tightly covered container for several months. Or place one chile and some sauce in each compartment of an ice-cube tray, and freeze. Store the cubes in the freezer in a zip-top plastic bag, and use as needed.

GRILLED PORTOBELLOS WITH CHEESE GRITS

POINTS value: 5   (pictured on page 64)

PREP: 9 minutes ■ **COOK:** 12 minutes

This hearty meatless entrée features portobellos splashed with balsamic vinegar and cheese grits spiked with hot sauce. If desired, stir the shredded spinach topping into the hot grits.

- 1½ cups water
- ½ cup 1% low-fat milk
- 1 tablespoon light butter
- ½ teaspoon salt, divided
- ½ cup uncooked quick-cooking grits
- ¾ cup (3 ounces) reduced-fat shredded sharp cheddar cheese
- ½ teaspoon hot sauce
- 5 (4-inch) portobello caps, stems removed
- Olive oil–flavored cooking spray
- ⅓ cup sun-dried tomatoes, packed without oil, chopped
- 1 tablespoon balsamic vinegar
- ¼ teaspoon pepper
- ¾ cup packed spinach leaves, shredded

1. Bring 1½ cups water, milk, butter, and ¼ teaspoon salt to a boil in a medium saucepan. Gradually stir in grits. Reduce heat to medium; cook, stirring constantly, 5 minutes or until thickened. Remove from heat; stir in cheese and hot sauce. Cover and keep warm.
2. Prepare grill.
3. Coat mushrooms with cooking spray; place on grill rack coated with cooking spray. Grill mushrooms 2 minutes on each side. Chop mushrooms into 1-inch pieces; place in a medium bowl. Stir in remaining ¼ teaspoon salt, tomatoes, vinegar, and pepper.
4. Spoon grits evenly onto each of 4 plates; top evenly with mushroom mixture. Sprinkle with spinach. **YIELD: 4 SERVINGS (SERVING SIZE: ¾ CUP MUSHROOM MIXTURE, ABOUT ½ CUP GRITS, AND 3 TABLESPOONS SPINACH).**

PER SERVING: Calories 219; Fat 7.8g (sat 4.6g, mono 0.7g, poly 0.2g); Protein 11.9g; Carb 26.7g; Fiber 2.6g; Chol 21mg; Iron 2.1mg; Sodium 427mg; Calc 223mg

ROASTED CHAYOTE PILAF

POINTS value: 5

PREP: 3 minutes ■ **COOK:** 45 minutes

Chayote, also known as mirliton, resembles a large pear with light green skin and mild-flavored white flesh.

    2 chayote (about 1¼ pounds), halved lengthwise
       and seeded
       Cooking spray
    1 (6.09-ounce) package rice pilaf (such as
       Near East)
    1 tablespoon olive oil
    ½ cup chopped onion
    ½ cup chopped celery
    2 garlic cloves, minced
    1 cup canned kidney beans, rinsed and drained
    ½ teaspoon freshly ground black pepper
    3 tablespoons grated fresh Parmesan cheese

1. Preheat oven to 450°.
2. Place chayote, cut sides down, on a baking sheet coated with cooking spray. Bake at 450° for 40 minutes or until tender. Dice chayote, and set aside.
3. While chayote cooks, prepare rice pilaf according to package directions, omitting salt and fat. Remove 1 cup rice pilaf, and set aside. Reserve remaining rice pilaf for another use.
4. Heat oil in a large nonstick skillet over medium-high heat. Add onion, celery, and garlic; sauté 2 minutes or until tender. Add chayote, 1 cup rice pilaf, beans, and pepper; cook 2 minutes or until thoroughly heated. Divide evenly among 3 plates. Sprinkle each serving with 1 tablespoon cheese. **YIELD: 3 SERVINGS (SERVING SIZE: 1½ CUPS PILAF AND 1 TABLESPOON CHEESE).**

PER SERVING: Calories 270; Fat 9.1g (sat 2.1g, mono 5.1g; poly 1.5g); Protein 10g; Carb 38.8g; Fiber 8.2g; Chol 4mg; Iron 2.7mg; Sodium 401mg; Calc 144mg

GRILLED POLENTA AND SUMMER VEGETABLES

POINTS value: 5 *(pictured on page 61)*

PREP: 6 minutes ■ **COOK:** 19 minutes

This filling dish is a great way to take advantage of summer vegetables and herbs while not heating up the kitchen. For a cheesier dish, double the cheese. The **POINTS** value will be 7.

    1 (18-ounce) tube of sun-dried tomato and
       garlic–flavored polenta (such as San Gennaro),
       cut into 8 (¼-inch-thick) slices
    3 ears shucked corn
    2 large zucchini, halved
    1 large red bell pepper, halved and seeded
    1 medium Vidalia or other sweet onion,
       cut into ½-inch-thick slices
    ¼ cup light balsamic vinaigrette (such as Kraft),
       divided
       Olive oil–flavored cooking spray
    1 (14.5-ounce) can diced tomatoes with basil,
       garlic, and oregano, undrained
    2 tablespoons chopped fresh basil
    ½ cup (2 ounces) shredded fontina cheese

1. Prepare grill.
2. Brush polenta slices, corn, zucchini, bell pepper, and onion with 3 tablespoons vinaigrette. Place polenta and vegetables on grill rack coated with cooking spray. Grill 19 minutes, or until beginning to char, turning occasionally.
3. Cut kernels from ears of corn; coarsely chop zucchini, bell pepper, and onion. Combine vegetables, tomatoes, basil, and remaining 1 tablespoon vinaigrette in a bowl; toss well. Spoon vegetable mixture over polenta slices; sprinkle with cheese. **YIELD: 4 SERVINGS (SERVING SIZE: 2 POLENTA SLICES, 1¼ CUPS VEGETABLES, AND 2 TABLESPOONS CHEESE).**

PER SERVING: Calories 278; Fat 7.6g (sat 3.1g, mono 1.4g; poly 0.8g); Protein 10.4g; Carb 46.8g; Fiber 6.5g; Chol 16mg; Iron 1.4mg; Sodium 935mg; Calc 112mg

VEGETARIAN STUFFED PEPPERS

POINTS value: 6

PREP: 10 minutes ■ **COOK:** 36 minutes

Packed full of zesty rice and meatless crumbles, these stuffed peppers will satisfy a craving for Mexican flavors and provide a filling meal.

- **4 large red or green bell peppers**
- **2 teaspoons olive oil**
- **½ cup finely diced onion**
- **4 garlic cloves, minced**
- **1 (12-ounce) package frozen meatless crumbles (such as Morningstar Farms), thawed**
- **½ teaspoon ground cumin**
- **2 teaspoons less-sodium taco seasoning**
- **1 cup fresh salsa**
- **¾ cup quick-cooking Spanish-style rice (such as Uncle Ben's)**
- **½ cup organic vegetable broth (such as Swanson)**
- **½ cup water**
- **¾ cup (3 ounces) reduced-fat shredded sharp cheddar cheese, divided**

1. Preheat oven to 350°.
2. Slice tops off bell peppers. Remove seeds and veins; rinse and drain peppers. Stand peppers upright in an 11 x 7–inch microwave-safe baking dish. Microwave at HIGH 7 minutes or until crisp-tender.
3. While peppers cook, heat oil in a large nonstick skillet over medium-high heat. Add onion and garlic to pan; sauté 1 minute or until onion is translucent. Add meatless crumbles, cumin, and taco seasoning; cook 8 minutes. Add salsa and next 3 ingredients, and simmer 1 minute. Remove from heat, and stir in ½ cup cheese.
4. Place peppers in an 8-inch square baking dish. Divide rice mixture evenly among peppers; top evenly with remaining ¼ cup cheese. Bake at 350° for 25 minutes. **YIELD: 4 SERVINGS (SERVING SIZE: 1 STUFFED PEPPER).**

PER SERVING: Calories 312; Fat 11.6g (sat 3.6g, mono 2.4g; poly 3.6g); Protein 23.2g; Carb 27.9g; Fiber 7.1g; Chol 15mg; Iron 3.7mg; Sodium 962mg; Calc 208mg

Buying Bells

Sweet peppers, also called "bells," should have brightly colored, glossy skins. They should be free of soft spots and wrinkles, which are signs of aging, and their stems should be firm and green. When you hold a bell pepper in your hand, it should feel heavy for its size—a sign of thick, juicy flesh.

HERBED QUINOA WITH APPLES

POINTS value: 7   *(pictured on page 77)*

PREP: 1 minute ■ **COOK:** 29 minutes

A staple in South American cuisine, quinoa (pronounced "keen-wah") contains more protein than any other grain and has a delicate flavor similar to couscous. Combined with apple, goat cheese, and fresh thyme, this hearty grain creates a delicious complete meal.

- **1 tablespoon olive oil**
- **1½ cups uncooked quinoa, rinsed and drained**
- **2 green onions, sliced**
- **1 tablespoon chopped fresh thyme**
- **¼ teaspoon crushed red pepper**
- **2 cups organic vegetable broth**
- **1 cup water**
- **¼ teaspoon salt**
- **¼ teaspoon freshly ground black pepper**
- **1 medium Braeburn apple, finely chopped**
- **¼ cup (1 ounce) crumbled goat cheese**
- **Fresh thyme sprigs (optional)**

1. Heat a large saucepan over medium-high heat; add oil. Add quinoa and next 3 ingredients. Sauté 5 minutes or until onion is tender and quinoa is fragrant. Add broth and next 3 ingredients. Cover and bring to a boil; reduce heat, and simmer 15 minutes or until quinoa is tender. Stir in apple, and cook 1 to 2 minutes or until liquid is absorbed (do not stir). Sprinkle with goat cheese. Garnish with fresh thyme sprigs, if desired. **YIELD: 4 SERVINGS (SERVING SIZE: 1¼ CUPS QUINOA MIXTURE AND 1 TABLESPOON CHEESE).**

PER SERVING: Calories 337; Fat 9.5g (sat 2.6g, mono 4.7g; poly 2g); Protein 10.5g; Carb 49.5g; Fiber 5.7g; Chol 7mg; Iron 4.6mg; Sodium 497mg; Calc 67mg

HUEVOS RANCHEROS WITH SUMMER SQUASH AND BROWN RICE

POINTS value: 7

PREP: 6 minutes ■ **COOK:** 18 minutes

Traditional Huevos Rancheros, or "country style" eggs, consist of fried eggs served over fried corn tortillas and smothered with salsa. We lighten the dish significantly by serving over whole-grain rice, adding fresh veggies, and poaching the eggs.

2 (8.8-ounce) packages precooked whole-grain brown rice (such as Uncle Ben's Ready Rice)
Cooking spray
2 cups diced yellow squash
½ cup vertically sliced onion
½ cup diced green bell pepper
1 (14.5-ounce) can diced tomatoes with zesty mild green chiles, undrained
⅓ cup water
1 tablespoon tomato paste
⅛ teaspoon salt
⅛ teaspoon freshly ground black pepper
4 large eggs
½ cup (2 ounces) reduced-fat shredded sharp cheddar cheese
1 cup finely shredded iceberg lettuce

1. Prepare rice according to package directions.
2. Heat a large nonstick skillet over medium-high heat. Coat pan with cooking spray. Add squash, onion, and bell pepper; sauté 7 minutes or until lightly browned. Stir in tomatoes and next 4 ingredients; simmer 3 minutes.
3. Break 1 egg into a small custard cup; carefully pour egg onto tomato mixture. Repeat with remaining eggs. Cover and cook 3 minutes or until eggs are done. Sprinkle 2 tablespoons cheese over each egg; cover and cook 1 minute or until cheese melts.
4. Spoon about 1 cup rice, 1 egg, and ¾ cup tomato mixture onto each of 4 plates. Top each with ¼ cup shredded lettuce. **YIELD: 4 SERVINGS.**

PER SERVING: Calories 364; Fat 11g (sat 3.9g, mono 1.9g; poly 0.8g); Protein 16.8g; Carb 49.2g; Fiber 4.2g; Chol 191mg; Iron 2.6mg; Sodium 550mg; Calc 174mg

ROASTED TOMATO PASTA

POINTS value: 4

PREP: 10 minutes ■ **COOK:** 25 minutes

Minimal stirring allows the vegetables to stay in contact with the pan longer and produces richly browned, caramelized results, adding sweetness to both the mushrooms and the roasted tomatoes.

12 plum tomatoes, halved (about 2¼ pounds)
3 large garlic cloves, halved
Cooking spray
1 tablespoon olive oil
½ teaspoon kosher salt
½ teaspoon freshly ground black pepper
¾ cup coarsely chopped onion (about 1 small)
1 (8-ounce) package sliced baby portobello mushrooms
1 teaspoon dried Italian seasoning
6 ounces uncooked multigrain thin spaghetti (such as Barilla Plus)
2 teaspoons balsamic vinegar
½ cup (2 ounces) shredded fresh Parmesan cheese

1. Preheat oven to 475°.
2. Bring water for pasta to a boil.
3. While pasta water comes to a boil, place tomato halves and garlic on a large rimmed baking sheet coated with cooking spray; drizzle with oil, and sprinkle with salt and pepper. Bake at 475° for 25 minutes or until tomatoes are roasted, stirring once after 20 minutes. Pour tomato mixture into a large bowl. Smash tomato mixture with a large spoon until tomatoes lose their shape.
4. While tomato mixture roasts, heat a large nonstick skillet over medium-high heat. Coat pan with cooking spray. Add onion, mushrooms, and Italian seasoning; cook 10 to 12 minutes or until richly browned, stirring after 10 minutes.
5. Cook pasta in boiling water according to package directions, omitting salt and fat. Drain. Add onion mixture and hot pasta to tomato mixture; add balsamic vinegar. Toss well. Sprinkle with Parmesan cheese.
YIELD: 6 SERVINGS (SERVING SIZE: 1⅓ CUPS).

PER SERVING: Calories 215; Fat 6.4g (sat 1.9g, mono 1.7g; poly 0.4g); Protein 9.9g; Carb 29.4g; Fiber 4.3g; Chol 8mg; Iron 0.7mg; Sodium 319mg; Calc 116mg

"BEEFY" MUSHROOM SPAGHETTI

POINTS value: 4

PREP: 2 minutes ▪ **COOK:** 20 minutes

Shirataki are no-carb noodles made from tofu; they are very low in calories and just as satisfying as traditional pasta. Look for them in the produce section along with other meatless products.

>   Olive oil–flavored cooking spray
>   1 (8-ounce) package mushrooms, halved
> ¾ cup matchstick-cut carrots
>   1 (12-ounce) package frozen meatless crumbles (such as Morningstar Farms), thawed
>   1 (24-ounce) jar fire-roasted tomato-garlic pasta sauce (such as Classico)
> ¼ teaspoon crushed red pepper
>   2 (4-ounce) packages tofu shirataki noodles
> ¼ cup (1 ounce) shredded fresh Parmesan cheese (optional)

1. Heat a large nonstick skillet over medium-high heat. Coat pan with cooking spray. Add mushrooms and carrots; sauté 5 minutes or until tender. Add meatless crumbles, pasta sauce, and red pepper. Bring to a boil; reduce heat, and simmer 10 minutes.
2. While sauce simmers, heat noodles in microwave according to package directions. Drain noodles in a colander lined with several layers of paper towels. Place noodles on additional layers of paper towels, and gently pat to absorb additional moisture.
3. Serve sauce over noodles; sprinkle with Parmesan cheese, if desired. **YIELD: 4 SERVINGS (SERVING SIZE: 1⅔ CUPS SAUCE AND ABOUT ⅔ CUP NOODLES).**

PER SERVING: Calories 231; Fat 5.5g (sat 0.5g, mono 0.8g; poly 2.1g); Protein 22g; Carb 23.8g; Fiber 8.6g; Chol 0mg; Iron 4.5mg; Sodium 903mg; Calc 85mg

BAKED PENNE

POINTS value: 8

PREP: 5 minutes ▪ **COOK:** 41 minutes

Reduced-fat pesto delivers the same great flavor as the full-fat version, without the added calories.

>   1 (14.5-ounce) package uncooked whole-grain penne (such as Barilla Plus)
>   1 (24-ounce) jar tomato-basil pasta sauce (such as Classico), divided
>   1 (8-ounce) package shredded reduced-fat Italian cheese blend (such as Sargento), divided
>   1 cup part-skim ricotta cheese
> ¼ cup reduced-fat refrigerated pesto (such as Buitoni)
>   Cooking spray

1. Preheat oven to 400°.
2. Cook pasta according to package directions, omitting salt and fat; drain. Place pasta in a large bowl. Add 2 cups pasta sauce, 1 cup cheese blend, ricotta cheese, and pesto; stir until blended.
3. Spoon pasta mixture into a 13 x 9–inch baking dish coated with cooking spray. Spread remaining pasta sauce over top; sprinkle with remaining 1 cup cheese blend.
4. Bake at 400° for 30 minutes or until cheese melts.
YIELD: 8 SERVINGS (SERVING SIZE: ⅛ OF CASSEROLE).

PER SERVING: Calories 376; Fat 11.8g (sat 5g, mono 0g; poly 0g); Protein 22.7g; Carb 45.3g; Fiber 5.4g; Chol 30mg; Iron 3.1mg; Sodium 648mg; Calc 360mg

✳The Power of Whole Grains

Whole grains are better for you than their refined counterparts such as white bread and pastas. Research has shown that eating just 2½ servings of whole grains per day is enough to lower your risk for heart disease, although more is better since greater whole-grain intake is associated with a reduced risk of obesity, diabetes, high blood pressure, and high cholesterol. All grains start out as whole grains, but they only remain that way if, after processing, they still contain all three whole-grain components: the germ, endosperm, and bran. The bran is full of fiber, while the germ and endosperm have phytonutrients—beneficial chemicals found in plant foods.

CREAMY VEGETABLE PENNE

POINTS value: 8

PREP: 1 minute ∎ **COOK:** 12 minutes

Mixed frozen vegetables take most of the work out of this recipe by eliminating chopping. Quickly thaw them by microwaving at HIGH 1 to 2 minutes.

- **2 cups uncooked multigrain penne (such as Barilla Plus)**
- **1½ cups fat-free milk**
- **1 tablespoon all-purpose flour**
- **½ teaspoon salt**
- **½ teaspoon freshly ground black pepper**
- **½ (8-ounce) tub light garlic-and-herbs spreadable cheese (such as Rondelé)**
- **1 (16-ounce) package frozen broccoli, mushrooms, onions, and peppers, thawed**

1. Cook pasta according to package directions, omitting salt and fat. Drain.
2. While pasta cooks, combine milk and next 3 ingredients in a medium saucepan, stirring with a whisk. Bring to a simmer over medium heat, stirring frequently. Reduce heat to medium–low; simmer 5 minutes or until slightly thickened. Add cheese, stirring with a whisk until cheese melts.
3. Add vegetables to sauce; cook 1 minute or until thoroughly heated. Add pasta, stirring until combined. Serve immediately. **YIELD: 6 SERVINGS (SERVING SIZE: 1 CUP).**

PER SERVING: Calories 397; Fat 9.4g (sat 4.1g, mono 0g; poly 0.1g); Protein 17.8g; Carb 60.7g; Fiber 7.1g; Chol 17mg; Iron 20.4mg; Sodium 348mg; Calc 100mg

ZUCCHINI-TOMATO-RICE FRITTATA

POINTS value: 4

PREP: 9 minutes ∎ **COOK:** 14 minutes

Remember this recipe the next time you have leftover rice. Brown rice gives this dish a hearty, chewy texture that we prefer, but you can substitute white rice or a combination of brown and white rice if that's what you have available. The *POINTS* value remains the same.

- **Butter-flavored cooking spray**
- **2 cups chopped zucchini (about 2 medium)**
- **2 large eggs**
- **2 (8-ounce) cartons egg substitute**
- **¼ cup (1 ounce) preshredded fresh Parmesan cheese, divided**
- **1 cup hot cooked brown rice**
- **1 cup chopped tomato**
- **½ teaspoon salt**
- **¼ teaspoon freshly ground black pepper**
- **3 tablespoons chopped fresh basil**

1. Preheat broiler.
2. Heat a 12-inch ovenproof skillet over medium heat; coat pan with cooking spray. Add zucchini, and coat zucchini with cooking spray. Cook 4 minutes or until crisp-tender, stirring often.
3. Combine eggs, egg substitute, 2 tablespoons cheese, rice, and next 3 ingredients in a medium bowl, stirring with a whisk. Add egg mixture to zucchini; cover and cook 6 minutes or until almost set. Sprinkle with remaining 2 tablespoons cheese. Broil 4 to 5 minutes or until set and cheese melts. Sprinkle with basil. Serve immediately. **YIELD: 4 SERVINGS (SERVING SIZE: 1 WEDGE).**

PER SERVING: Calories 188; Fat 4.7g (sat 1.8g, mono 1.6g, poly 0.6g); Protein 18.5g; Carb 17.7g; Fiber 2.2g; Chol 109mg; Iron 3.2mg; Sodium 652mg; Calc 135mg

GARDEN HARVEST FRITTATA WITH WATERCRESS SALAD

POINTS value: 5

PREP: 5 minutes ■ **COOK:** 17 minutes

A frittata is a protein-packed way to utilize leftover sautéed vegetables. Make this recipe your own by trying different combinations of vegetables, herbs, and cheeses.

    3 tablespoons olive oil, divided
 1½ cups presliced mushrooms
    1 cup (1-inch) sliced asparagus (about 12 thin spears)
  ½ cup chopped onion
    3 large eggs
    4 large egg whites
  ¼ teaspoon salt, divided
  ¼ teaspoon black pepper, divided
  ¼ cup grated Parmesan cheese
 1½ teaspoons finely chopped fresh tarragon
    1 tablespoon sherry vinegar
    2 cups trimmed watercress

1. Preheat broiler.
2. Heat a 9-inch cast-iron skillet over high heat 1 minute. Add 2 tablespoons oil to pan, swirling pan to coat. Reduce heat to medium-high; add mushrooms, asparagus, and onion. Cook 5 minutes or until vegetables are tender, stirring often.
3. While vegetables cook, combine eggs, egg whites, ⅛ teaspoon salt, and ⅛ teaspoon pepper; stir well with a whisk.
4. Pour egg mixture over vegetables in pan; sprinkle with cheese and tarragon. Reduce heat to medium-low; cook 6 minutes or until edges are set.
5. Broil 4 minutes or until set and lightly browned.
6. While frittata broils, combine vinegar, remaining 1 tablespoon oil, remaining ⅛ teaspoon salt, and remaining ⅛ teaspoon pepper in a medium bowl, stirring with a whisk. Add watercress; toss well. Cut frittata into 4 wedges. Mound watercress mixture on wedges, and serve immediately. **YIELD: 4 SERVINGS (SERVING SIZE: 1 WEDGE AND ½ CUP WATERCRESS SALAD).**

PER SERVING: Calories 210; Fat 14.8g (sat 3.2g, mono 9.2g, poly 1.7g); Protein 12.2g; Carb 6.4g; Fiber 1.4g; Chol 139mg; Iron 1.4mg; Sodium 339mg; Calc 113mg

POACHED EGGS FLORENTINE

POINTS value: 6

PREP: 7 minutes ■ **COOK:** 34 minutes

Serve these eggs with assorted fresh fruits for brunch or a light supper. To speed up the preparation of this dish, crack each egg into a custard cup, and gently pierce each yolk with the tip of a knife or a wooden pick. Cover, and microwave at MEDIUM (50% power) 1 to 1½ minutes or until yolks are firm. Toast the bread while the cheese browns under the broiler.

    1 tablespoon butter, divided
  ½ cup finely minced onion
    2 tablespoons all-purpose flour
    2 cups 1% low-fat milk
  ½ teaspoon salt, divided
  ½ cup (2 ounces) grated fresh Parmesan cheese, divided
    1 teaspoon Dijon mustard
    1 (10-ounce) package frozen chopped spinach, thawed, drained, and squeezed dry
    4 large eggs
Cooking spray
    4 slices whole-wheat bread (such as Arnold), toasted

1. Melt 2 teaspoons butter in a medium saucepan over medium heat. Add onion; cook 5 minutes or until soft. Add flour; cook 3 minutes, stirring constantly with a whisk. Add milk and ¼ teaspoon salt. Bring to a boil; reduce heat, and simmer 5 minutes, stirring constantly. Add ⅓ cup Parmesan cheese and mustard; cook 2 minutes or until cheese melts. Set aside.
2. Melt remaining 1 teaspoon butter in a large non-stick skillet over medium heat. Add spinach and remaining ¼ teaspoon salt; sauté 2 minutes or until thoroughly heated. Set aside; keep warm.
3. Preheat broiler.
4. Add water to a large skillet, filling two-thirds full; bring to a boil. Reduce heat; simmer. Break eggs into each of 4 (6-ounce) custard cups coated with cooking spray. Place custard cups in simmering water in pan. Cover pan; cook 6 minutes. Remove custard cups from water; carefully remove eggs from custard cups.
5. Divide spinach evenly into 4 portions in a shallow baking dish coated with cooking spray. Top each with

½ cup sauce, 1 egg, and an additional ¼ cup sauce. Sprinkle evenly with remaining Parmesan cheese.

6. Broil 6 minutes or until cheese browns. Cut each slice of bread into 4 equal triangles, if desired. Serve immediately. **YIELD: 4 SERVINGS (SERVING SIZE: 1 EGG, ¼ OF SPINACH, ¾ CUP SAUCE, AND 1 SLICE TOAST).**

PER SERVING: Calories 296; Fat 14.1g (sat 6.1g, mono 3.9g, poly 1.1g); Protein 21.6g; Carb 23.8g; Fiber 5.6g; Chol 233mg; Iron 3.5mg; Sodium 809mg; Calc 444mg

ASIAN STIR-FRY LETTUCE WRAPS

POINTS value: 3

PREP: 3 minutes ■ **COOK:** 7 minutes

Convenient frozen seasoned vegetable blends combine flavorful sauces and vegetables all in one package.

1 (12-ounce) package frozen broccoli, water chestnuts, and red peppers in orange sesame sauce (such as Green Giant Steamers)
Cooking spray
1 medium red bell pepper, thinly sliced
1 (12-ounce) package frozen meatless crumbles (such as Morningstar Farms), thawed
¼ cup water
1 tablespoon rice vinegar
4 large iceberg lettuce leaves
¼ cup chopped unsalted, dry-roasted peanuts (optional)

1. Microwave frozen vegetables according to package directions.
2. While vegetables cook, heat a large nonstick skillet over medium-high heat; coat pan with cooking spray. Add bell pepper; cook 3 minutes or until tender. Add meatless crumbles; cook 2 minutes or until thoroughly heated. Add vegetables with sauce, ¼ cup water, and vinegar. Cook 1 minute or until thoroughly heated. Spoon evenly into lettuce leaves; sprinkle with peanuts, if desired. **YIELD: 4 SERVINGS (SERVING SIZE: 1 LETTUCE LEAF AND ¾ CUP FILLING).**

PER SERVING: Calories 175; Fat 5.2g (sat 0.4g, mono 0.8g, poly 3.2g); Protein 17.6g; Carb 16.8g; Fiber 5.6g; Chol 0mg; Iron 3.3mg; Sodium 480mg; Calc 55mg

MEATLESS BURGER TOSTADAS WITH AVOCADO RANCH DRESSING

POINTS value: 5 *(pictured on page 63)*

PREP: 1 minute ■ **COOK:** 9 minutes

Here we've used avocado, rich in good monounsaturated fat, to extend the volume of the dressing and give it a satisfying flavor without adding saturated fat.

4 (6-inch) corn tortillas
Cooking spray
1 (12-ounce) package frozen meatless crumbles (such as Morningstar Farms), thawed
⅓ cup water
2 tablespoons less-sodium taco seasoning
2 cups shredded iceberg lettuce
1¼ cups chopped tomato (about 1 medium)
½ avocado, mashed
⅓ cup fat-free ranch dressing
¼ cup sliced green onions (about 2)

1. Preheat oven to 450°.
2. Coat tortillas with cooking spray. Place on a baking sheet. Bake at 450° for 9 minutes or until crisp and lightly browned.
3. While tortillas bake, combine meatless crumbles, ⅓ cup water, and taco seasoning in a large skillet. Cook over medium heat 5 minutes or until thoroughly heated, stirring occasionally.
4. Place ½ cup lettuce and about one-fourth of chopped tomato on each tortilla. Top tomato evenly with meatless crumbles mixture.
5. Combine avocado and dressing, stirring with a whisk until smooth; drizzle evenly over tostadas, and sprinkle with green onions. **YIELD: 4 SERVINGS (SERVING SIZE: 1 TOSTADA).**

PER SERVING: Calories 253; Fat 7.3g (sat 0.4g, mono 2.4g, poly 3.7g); Protein 17.8g; Carb 31.5g; Fiber 6.5g; Chol 0mg; Iron 3.3mg; Sodium 917mg; Calc 64mg

MUSHROOM-TOFU STROGANOFF

POINTS value: 6

PREP: 10 minutes ■ **COOK:** 20 minutes

 4 ounces uncooked egg noodles
 1 tablespoon butter
2½ cups sliced onion (about 2 medium)
 2 garlic cloves, minced
 1 (8-ounce) package mushrooms, halved
 1 (14-ounce) package soft tofu, drained
 3 tablespoons less-sodium soy sauce
 ¼ teaspoon ground ginger
 ½ cup light sour cream
 ¼ cup chopped fresh parsley

1. Cook noodles according to package directions, omitting salt and fat. Drain; set aside.
2. While noodles cook, melt butter in a large nonstick skillet over medium heat. Add onion and garlic; sauté 5 minutes or until tender. Add mushrooms; cook 10 minutes or until mushrooms and onion are golden brown, stirring occasionally.
3. Place tofu, soy sauce, and ginger in a food processor; process 30 seconds or until smooth. Add tofu mixture to pan; heat thoroughly. Remove from heat; stir in sour cream and parsley. Serve over warm egg noodles. **YIELD: 4 SERVINGS (SERVING SIZE: ¾ CUP TOFU MIXTURE AND ½ CUP NOODLES).**

PER SERVING: Calories 276; Fat 9.8g (sat 4.3g, mono 1.5g, poly 2g); Protein 14.2g; Carb 35.9g; Fiber 3.1g; Chol 50mg; Iron 2.6mg; Sodium 526mg; Calc 172mg

Tofu Nutrition

Tofu is low in calories—a 3-ounce serving contains 30 to 65 calories—and it's packed with vitamins and minerals, including folic acid and iron. Tofu can also be a great nondairy source of calcium, but you need to make sure you buy a brand that's made with calcium sulfate—a 3-ounce serving contains 300 milligrams of calcium (nearly one-third of the daily recommendation). Nigari (magnesium chloride) is another coagulating agent that is commonly used, but it contains virtually zero calcium—3 ounces of tofu made with it may contain as little as 20 milligrams of calcium.

TOFU WITH SESAME-GINGER SPINACH

POINTS value: 6

PREP: 1 minute ■ **COOK:** 14 minutes

Draining tofu removes excess moisture, which helps the tofu brown nicely when sautéing or stir-frying. To properly drain tofu, slice it, and lay the slices between paper towels. Place a heavy skillet or cutting board on top, and let sit 10 minutes, pressing occasionally.

 1 (14-ounce) package extra-firm tofu, cut into
    8 slices and drained
 ¼ teaspoon salt
 ⅛ teaspoon black pepper
1½ tablespoons vegetable oil, divided
 1 (9-ounce) package fresh spinach
 1 tablespoon toasted sesame seeds (such as McCormick)
 ¼ cup orange juice
 1 tablespoon less-sodium soy sauce
1½ teaspoons grated peeled fresh ginger
 1 teaspoon dark sesame oil
 1 garlic clove, minced

1. Sprinkle tofu with salt and pepper. Heat 1 tablespoon oil in a large nonstick skillet over medium-high heat. Add tofu; cook 3 to 4 minutes on each side or until browned. Remove from pan; keep warm.
2. Add remaining 1½ teaspoons oil to pan. Add spinach; cook 1 minute or until spinach wilts, stirring occasionally. Stir in sesame seeds. Transfer spinach to a serving platter; top with tofu, and keep warm.
3. Combine orange juice and next 4 ingredients in pan; bring to a boil. Reduce heat, and simmer 1 minute. Pour sauce over tofu and spinach. **YIELD: 2 SERVINGS (SERVING SIZE: 4 SLICES TOFU, ABOUT ⅔ CUP SPINACH, AND 2 TABLESPOONS SAUCE).**

PER SERVING: Calories 279; Fat 18.6g (sat 1.9g, mono 6.3g, poly 6.7g); Protein 17.5g; Carb 14.3g; Fiber 3.5g; Chol 0mg; Iron 5.7mg; Sodium 807mg; Calc 218mg

meats

Pork Chops with Cranberries and Apples, *page 94*

SEARED BEEF FILLETS WITH "MELTED" TOMATOES AND GREEN ONIONS

POINTS value: 5

PREP: 2 minutes ■ **COOK:** 17 minutes

Serve this saucy steak with mashed potatoes or polenta to soak up the flavorful juices.

> 2 teaspoons olive oil
> 4 (4-ounce) beef tenderloin steaks (about ½ inch thick), trimmed
> ½ teaspoon kosher salt
> ¼ teaspoon freshly ground black pepper
> 2 cups cherry tomatoes
> 4 green onions, cut into 2-inch pieces
> ⅓ cup dry red wine

1. Preheat oven to 400°.
2. Heat olive oil in a large cast-iron or ovenproof skillet over medium–high heat. Sprinkle steaks with salt and pepper. Add steaks to pan; cook 2 to 3 minutes on each side or until browned. Remove steaks from pan; keep warm.
3. Add tomatoes and onions to pan; sauté 2 minutes or until tomatoes begin to burst and onion is tender. Add wine, scraping pan to loosen browned bits; cook 1 minute or until juices thicken. Nestle steaks into tomato mixture.
4. Place pan in oven. Bake at 400° for 8 minutes or until desired degree of doneness. **YIELD: 4 SERVINGS (SERVING SIZE: 1 STEAK AND ABOUT ¼ CUP TOMATO MIXTURE).**

PER SERVING: Calories 194; Fat 9.9g (sat 3.1g, mono 4.6g, poly 0.7g); Protein 18.7g; Carb 6.2g; Fiber 1g; Chol 54mg; Iron 3mg; Sodium 402mg; Calc 14mg

✳ Peppercorn Varieties

You may be familiar with black peppercorns, but green and white varieties (all three are from the same plant harvested at various stages of ripeness) are handy, too. Each adds its own distinctive flavor to dishes. Black peppercorns offer spicy heat balanced by a subtly sweet undertone. Green peppercorns have a mild, fresh flavor and a pleasing aroma without the pungency of black peppercorns. White peppercorns contribute an earthy essence and a mild pepper flavor.

PEPPERCORN-CRUSTED FILLETS WITH POMEGRANATE-CABERNET SAUCE

POINTS value: 5

PREP: 1 minute ■ **COOK:** 19 minutes

Fluffy mashed potatoes are the perfect accompaniment to these richly sauced steaks, which received our Test Kitchens' highest rating. Purchase whole mixed peppercorns; place in a heavy-duty zip-top plastic bag, and crush with a meat mallet or rolling pin.

> 1 tablespoon butter
> 3 tablespoons minced shallots (1 large)
> 1 cup cabernet sauvignon or other dry red wine
> 1 cup fat-free, less-sodium beef broth
> ½ cup pomegranate juice
> 2 teaspoons Dijon mustard
> ½ teaspoon salt, divided
> 4 (4-ounce) beef tenderloin steaks, trimmed (about ½ inch thick)
> 3 tablespoons mixed peppercorns, coarsely ground
> Cooking spray

1. Melt butter in a medium saucepan over medium heat; add shallots. Sauté 1 minute or until tender. Add wine, broth, and pomegranate juice. Bring to a boil; reduce heat to medium-low, and simmer 17 minutes or until reduced to ½ cup. Add mustard and ¼ teaspoon salt, stirring with a whisk.
2. While sauce cooks, sprinkle steaks evenly with remaining ¼ teaspoon salt. Press ground mixed peppercorns onto both sides of steaks.
3. Heat a large nonstick skillet over medium–high heat. Coat pan with cooking spray. Add steaks to pan. Cook 4 minutes on each side or until desired degree of doneness. Spoon sauce over steaks. **YIELD: 4 SERVINGS (SERVING SIZE: 1 STEAK AND 2 TABLESPOONS SAUCE).**

PER SERVING: Calories 229; Fat 10.2g (sat 4.5g, mono 3.7g, poly 0.4g); Protein 26g; Carb 7g; Fiber 0.1g; Chol 84mg; Iron 2.2mg; Sodium 554mg; Calc 41mg

HORSERADISH-CRUSTED BEEF TENDERLOIN STEAKS WITH FRESH CITRUS SALAD

POINTS value: 7   *(pictured on page 131)*

PREP: 8 minutes ▪ **COOK:** 10 minutes

We used a 10-inch cast-iron skillet, but if you don't have one, make sure the handle of your nonstick skillet is ovenproof up to 400°.

- ¼ cup prepared horseradish
- 2 tablespoons Dijon mustard, divided
- 4 teaspoons olive oil, divided
- 4 (4-ounce) beef tenderloin steaks, trimmed (about 1 inch thick)
- ⅜ teaspoon kosher salt, divided
- ½ teaspoon freshly ground black pepper, divided
- ½ cup panko (Japanese breadcrumbs)
- 1 (15-ounce) can mandarin oranges in light syrup, undrained
- 1 teaspoon minced shallots
- 6 cups mixed baby salad greens

1. Preheat oven to 400°.
2. Combine horseradish, 1½ tablespoons mustard, and 1 teaspoon oil in a small bowl. Sprinkle steaks with ¼ teaspoon salt and ¼ teaspoon pepper.
3. Place panko in a shallow bowl. Brush horseradish mixture over both sides of steaks; dredge in panko, pressing crumbs onto both sides of steaks.
4. Heat a 10-inch cast-iron skillet over medium-high heat. Add 1 teaspoon oil, swirling to coat. Add steaks; cook 2 to 3 minutes on each side or until crust is lightly browned. Place pan in oven, and bake at 400° for 5 minutes or until desired degree of doneness.
5. While steaks bake, drain oranges, reserving 2 tablespoons syrup. Combine syrup, shallots, remaining 1½ teaspoons mustard, remaining 2 teaspoons oil, remaining ¼ teaspoon pepper, and remaining ⅛ teaspoon salt in a large bowl, stirring with a whisk. Add drained oranges and salad greens; toss well.
6. Divide citrus salad evenly among 4 plates; top with steaks. Serve immediately. **YIELD: 4 SERVINGS (SERVING SIZE: 1 STEAK AND 1½ CUPS CITRUS SALAD).**

PER SERVING: Calories 334; Fat 12.6g (sat 3.4g, mono 6.3g, poly 1g); Protein 28g; Carb 28.2g; Fiber 3.3g; Chol 76mg; Iron 3.4mg; Sodium 516mg; Calc 90mg

HARISSA-RUBBED FLANK STEAK

POINTS value: 5

PREP: 10 minutes ▪ **COOK:** 21 minutes ▪ **OTHER:** 8 hours

Harissa is a hot chile sauce commonly used in the Moroccan kitchen. For a shortcut, use store-bought bottled harissa paste.

- 1 teaspoon coriander seeds
- ½ teaspoon caraway seeds
- ½ teaspoon cumin seeds
- ½ teaspoon crushed red pepper
- 3 garlic cloves, halved
- 1 cup coarsely chopped bottled roasted red bell peppers
- 1 tablespoon extra-virgin olive oil
- 2 teaspoons paprika
- 1 (1-pound) flank steak, trimmed
- Cooking spray
- ¼ teaspoon salt
- ¼ teaspoon freshly ground black pepper
- Lemon wedges (optional)

1. Heat a small nonstick skillet over medium heat. Combine first 4 ingredients in pan; cook 2 minutes or until seeds are golden brown and fragrant, stirring frequently. Place coriander mixture in a spice or coffee grinder; pulse until blended. Add garlic to hot pan; sauté 2 minutes or until golden brown.
2. Combine garlic, coriander mixture, roasted red bell pepper, oil, and paprika in a mini food processor or blender; process 30 seconds. Place flank steak in a large heavy-duty zip-top plastic bag; add bell pepper mixture to bag. Seal bag, turning to coat steak. Chill at least 8 hours or overnight.
3. Prepare grill.
4. Remove steak from marinade, discarding marinade. Place steak on grill rack coated with cooking spray; grill 8 minutes on each side or until desired degree of doneness. Sprinkle steak with salt and black pepper; cut steak diagonally across grain into thin slices. Serve with lemon wedges, if desired. **YIELD: 4 SERVINGS (SERVING SIZE: 3 OUNCES STEAK).**

PER SERVING: Calories 207; Fat 10g (sat 2.8g, mono 4.9g, poly 0.6g); Protein 24.9g; Carb 2.7g; Fiber 0.7g; Chol 38mg; Iron 2.1mg; Sodium 290mg; Calc 38mg

ITALIAN PINWHEEL STEAKS

POINTS value: 7   *(pictured on page 129)*

PREP: 9 minutes ■ **COOK:** 17 minutes

Skirt steak is a cut of beef similar to flank steak and is often used for fajitas. Pounding this economical cut very thin tenderizes it and makes it easier to roll up around the savory filling. Browning the rolled steaks on the stovetop, then finishing them in the oven, produces a succulent result that received our Test Kitchens' highest rating. Serve with steamed broccoli. A 1-cup serving has a **POINTS** value of 0 (2 cups has a **POINTS** value of 1).

  2 (8-ounce) skirt steaks
  ¼ teaspoon salt
  ¼ teaspoon freshly ground black pepper
  ½ cup (4 ounces) ⅓-less-fat cream cheese, softened
  ¼ cup sun-dried tomatoes, packed without oil
  ¼ cup shredded Parmigiano-Reggiano cheese
  2 cups baby spinach
  Cooking spray

1. Preheat oven to 425°.
2. Place steaks between 2 sheets of plastic wrap; pound to ¹⁄₁₆-inch thickness using a meat mallet or small heavy skillet. Sprinkle steaks with salt and pepper.
3. Place cream cheese, sun-dried tomatoes, and Parmigiano-Reggiano cheese in a food processor or blender; process until blended. Spread half of cheese mixture over 1 side of each steak; top with spinach. Roll up steaks; secure with wooden picks. Cut each roll in half crosswise.
4. Heat a large cast-iron skillet over medium-high heat. Coat pan with cooking spray. Add rolls to pan; cook 6 to 7 minutes or until browned, turning frequently.
5. Place pan in oven; bake at 425° for 10 minutes or until desired degree of doneness. **YIELD: 4 SERVINGS (SERVING SIZE: 1 PINWHEEL STEAK).**

PER SERVING: Calories 290; Fat 16.9g (sat 8.5g, mono 5.2g, poly 0.5g); Protein 29.6g; Carb 3.6g; Fiber 0.7g; Chol 88mg; Iron 3.3mg; Sodium 513mg; Calc 108mg

PEANUTTY BEEF PASTA

POINTS value: 7

PREP: 8 minutes ■ **COOK:** 16 minutes
■ **OTHER:** 30 minutes

Dark sesame oil has a strong nutty flavor and is often used in Asian dishes. Store it in a cool, dark place for up to four months.

  1 teaspoon dried oregano
  ½ teaspoon ground turmeric
  ½ teaspoon ground coriander
  ¼ teaspoon salt
  ¼ teaspoon dry mustard
  ¼ teaspoon ground cumin
  1½ pounds boneless top sirloin steak
  1½ cups uncooked whole-wheat linguine
    (about 6 ounces)
  Cooking spray
  1 teaspoon dark sesame oil
  ⅓ cup minced onion
  2 teaspoons grated peeled fresh ginger
  1 large garlic clove, minced
  ½ cup fat-free, less-sodium chicken broth
  ⅓ cup peanut butter
  ¼ cup light coconut milk
  2 tablespoons fresh lime juice
  1 tablespoon honey
  1 tablespoon less-sodium soy sauce
  ½ teaspoon grated lime rind
  ½ teaspoon crushed red pepper
  Chopped fresh cilantro (optional)

1. Combine first 6 ingredients in a small bowl. Rub both sides of meat with spice mixture; cover and chill at least 30 minutes.
2. While meat chills, cook pasta according to package directions, omitting salt and fat. Drain; keep warm.
3. Cut steak crosswise into ¼-inch-thick slices; cut slices into thin strips. Coat steak with cooking spray.
4. Heat ½ teaspoon oil in a large nonstick skillet over medium-high heat. Add half of meat; sauté 4 minutes or until steak is done. Repeat with remaining ½ teaspoon oil and meat. Remove from heat; keep warm. Wipe drippings from pan with paper towels.
5. Coat pan with cooking spray; place over medium-high heat. Add onion, ginger, and garlic, and sauté

3 minutes or until onion is tender. Stir in broth and next 7 ingredients. Cook until mixture is blended, stirring constantly. Return meat to pan; cook 1 to 2 minutes or until thoroughly heated. Spoon meat mixture over pasta. Sprinkle with cilantro, if desired. **YIELD: 6 SERVINGS (SERVING SIZE: ABOUT ⅔ CUP MEAT MIXTURE AND ½ CUP PASTA).**

PER SERVING: Calories 349; Fat 14g (sat 3.2g, mono 2.1g, poly 1.2g); Protein 29.6g; Carb 29.1g; Fiber 4.3g; Chol 42mg; Iron 2.8mg; Sodium 347mg; Calc 36mg

BARBECUE MEAT LOAF

POINTS value: 6

PREP: 5 minutes ■ **COOK:** 1 hour

Oatmeal is the secret ingredient in this recipe. It traps and holds moisture to keep this lean meat loaf juicy.

Cooking spray
⅓ cup Southwestern-style egg substitute
1 cup barbecue sauce (such as Stubb's), divided
⅓ cup grated onion
½ teaspoon salt
½ teaspoon black pepper
2 pounds ground sirloin
⅓ cup uncooked quick-cooking oats

1. Preheat oven to 350°.
2. Line the bottom of a broiler pan with foil; coat rack with cooking spray. Place egg substitute in a large bowl; add ½ cup barbecue sauce and next 3 ingredients, stirring until blended. Add beef and oats. Using hands, gently mix just until blended.
3. Shape meat mixture into an 8 x 4–inch loaf; place on the rack of prepared pan.
4. Bake meat loaf at 350° for 45 minutes. Spread remaining ½ cup barbecue sauce over loaf. Bake an additional 15 minutes or until a thermometer registers 160°. Cut into 8 slices. **YIELD: 8 SERVINGS (SERVING SIZE: 1 SLICE).**

PER SERVING: Calories 237; Fat 11.6g (sat 4.6g, mono 4.9g, poly 0.4g); Protein 25.1g; Carb 8.3g; Fiber 0.5g; Chol 74mg; Iron 3mg; Sodium 460mg; Calc 22mg

LAMB CHOPS WITH HERBED-FETA ORZO

POINTS value: 9

PREP: 4 minutes ■ **COOK:** 10 minutes

Packed with Mediterranean flavor, this complete meal is easy to put together. The lamb chops are flavored with a simple rub and paired with a flavorful orzo mixed with sharp cheese and sweet sun-dried tomatoes.

1 cup uncooked orzo (rice-shaped pasta)
4 garlic cloves, minced
1 tablespoon dried oregano
½ teaspoon salt, divided
½ teaspoon black pepper, divided
8 (4-ounce) lamb loin chops, trimmed
Cooking spray
½ cup crumbled feta cheese with basil and sun-dried tomatoes
2 tablespoons finely chopped drained oil-packed sun-dried tomato halves
1 tablespoon fresh lemon juice
2 teaspoons olive oil

1. Preheat broiler.
2. Cook orzo according to package directions, omitting salt and fat. Drain pasta; place in a medium bowl.
3. While orzo cooks, combine garlic, oregano, ¼ teaspoon salt, and ¼ teaspoon pepper; rub over both sides of lamb chops. Arrange lamb in a single layer on a broiler pan coated with cooking spray; broil 4 minutes on each side or until desired degree of doneness.
4. Add remaining ¼ teaspoon salt and ¼ teaspoon pepper, cheese, and next 3 ingredients to orzo; toss gently. Serve lamb chops over orzo. **YIELD: 4 SERVINGS (SERVING SIZE: 2 LAMB CHOPS AND ½ CUP ORZO).**

PER SERVING: Calories 417; Fat 14.3g (sat 5g, mono 4.9g, poly 1g); Protein 34.9g; Carb 35.8g; Fiber 2.7g; Chol 93mg; Iron 3.1mg; Sodium 574mg; Calc 90mg

✳ Buying Lean Lamb
For the leanest cuts of lamb, look for "loin" or "leg" on the label. Some other lean cuts include the chops, arm chops, and foreshanks.

HONEY BALSAMIC–GLAZED PORK TENDERLOIN

POINTS value: 4

PREP: 4 minutes ■ **COOK:** 24 minutes
■ **OTHER:** 5 minutes

A foil-lined pan will catch any balsamic glaze that drips off during baking. Spoon glaze over pork before serving.

1 (1-pound) pork tenderloin
¼ teaspoon salt
¼ teaspoon freshly ground black pepper
Cooking spray
¼ cup balsamic vinegar
2 tablespoons honey
4 teaspoons hoisin sauce
2 teaspoons chopped fresh rosemary
Rosemary sprigs (optional)

1. Preheat oven to 425°.
2. Sprinkle pork with salt and pepper. Place on a foil-lined jelly-roll pan coated with cooking spray. Bake at 425° for 10 minutes.
3. While pork bakes, combine balsamic vinegar and next 3 ingredients in a small saucepan; bring to a boil. Boil 1 to 2 minutes or until slightly thickened. Brush a small amount of glaze over pork; bake an additional 14 minutes or until a thermometer registers 155° (slightly pink), basting heavily twice with remaining balsamic glaze. Let stand 5 minutes; cut into ¼-inch-thick slices. Garnish with rosemary sprigs, if desired. YIELD: 4 SERVINGS (SERVING SIZE: 3 OUNCES PORK AND ABOUT 1½ TABLESPOONS SAUCE).

PER SERVING: Calories 202; Fat 4.9g (sat 1.5g, mono 1.8g, poly 0.4g); Protein 24g; Carb 13.8g; Fiber 0.1g; Chol 74mg; Iron 1.6mg; Sodium 281mg; Calc 12mg

*Balsamic Vinegar

Balsamic vinegar is a slightly sweet and full-bodied vinegar with a hint of tartness. Prices vary greatly depending on the quality. The highest quality (and most expensive) balsamic vinegars are aged for decades, becoming more concentrated and syrupy over time. However, you can find a good middle-of-the-road variety for everyday use. Look for vinegars labeled *condimento balsamico.* They're aged for shorter periods but are still very tasty and more reasonably priced.

PORK MEDALLIONS WITH PEAR-THYME PAN SAUCE

POINTS value: 5

PREP: 7 minutes ■ **COOK:** 13 minutes

Pear preserves are the star in this sweet and savory sauce served over pork tenderloin medallions.

1 (1-pound) pork tenderloin, cut crosswise into 8 slices
1 tablespoon all-purpose flour
½ teaspoon freshly ground black pepper
¼ teaspoon salt
2 teaspoons olive oil
Butter-flavored cooking spray
¾ cup coarsely chopped Vidalia or other sweet onion
1 cup coarsely chopped peeled Bartlett pear (about 1 large)
¾ cup fat-free, less-sodium chicken broth, divided
½ cup pear preserves (such as Braswell's)
1½ teaspoons chopped fresh thyme

1. Pound pork slices slightly with the heel of your hand or a meat mallet. Sprinkle pork slices with flour, pepper, and salt.
2. Heat oil in a large nonstick skillet over medium-high heat. Add pork; cook 3 minutes on each side or until browned. Remove pork from pan; keep warm.
3. Coat pan with cooking spray; add onion, chopped pear, and 2 tablespoons broth, scraping pan to loosen browned bits. Cook 3 minutes or until onion and pear are lightly browned. Add pear preserves, remaining broth, and thyme. Cook 1 minute or until preserves melt. Add pork, and cook 1 minute or until sauce is slightly thickened. YIELD: 4 SERVINGS (SERVING SIZE: 2 PORK MEDALLIONS AND ABOUT ⅓ CUP SAUCE).

PER SERVING: Calories 264; Fat 6.4g (sat 1.7g, mono 3.4g, poly 0.7g); Protein 24.6g; Carb 25g; Fiber 1.7g; Chol 74mg; Iron 1.6mg; Sodium 288mg; Calc 15mg

PORK PAPRIKASH WITH SOUR CREAM NOODLES

POINTS value: 6

PREP: 5 minutes ■ **COOK:** 14 minutes

This recipe calls for Hungarian paprika, which is widely considered to be the best paprika in the world. It is available in both sweet and hot varieties.

1½ cups uncooked egg noodles
⅓ cup light sour cream
2 tablespoons chopped fresh flat-leaf parsley
½ teaspoon salt, divided
⅜ teaspoon black pepper, divided
1 (1-pound) pork tenderloin, cut into ½-inch-thick slices
Cooking spray
1 (8-ounce) package refrigerated prechopped tricolor bell pepper
1 (24-ounce) jar caramelized onion and roasted garlic pasta sauce (such as Classico)
3 tablespoons Hungarian paprika
3 tablespoons water

1. Cook noodles according to package directions, omitting salt and fat. Drain, reserving 1 tablespoon pasta water. Place noodles in a medium bowl, and immediately stir in reserved pasta water, sour cream, parsley, ¼ teaspoon salt, and ⅛ teaspoon pepper. Cover and keep warm.
2. While noodles cook, cut pork slices in half; sprinkle pork with remaining ¼ teaspoon salt and remaining ¼ teaspoon pepper. Heat a large nonstick skillet over medium–high heat. Coat pan with cooking spray. Add pork; cook 3 minutes. Turn pork over; cook 2 minutes or just until pork is done. Remove pork from pan; keep warm.
3. Coat pan with cooking spray. Add bell pepper; sauté 3 minutes or until tender.
4. Return pork to pan; stir in pasta sauce, paprika, and 3 tablespoons water. Bring to a boil; reduce heat, and simmer 2 minutes or until thoroughly heated. Serve pork mixture over noodles. **YIELD: 4 SERVINGS (SERVING SIZE: ABOUT 1 CUP PORK MIXTURE AND ½ CUP NOODLES).**

PER SERVING: Calories 324; Fat 7.4g (sat 2.6g, mono 1.6g, poly 0.4g); Protein 28.8g; Carb 33.9g; Fiber 4.4g; Chol 99mg; Iron 3.4mg; Sodium 920mg; Calc 133mg

GRILLED PORK CHOPS WITH WARM APPLE CHUTNEY

POINTS value: 7 *(pictured on page 130)*

PREP: 3 minutes ■ **COOK:** 14 minutes
■ **OTHER:** 10 minutes

The easy apple chutney is the secret to this autumn dish's great flavor. You'd never guess it starts with frozen apples. Serve with sautéed or steamed Brussels sprouts.

3 tablespoons less-sodium soy sauce
1½ tablespoons maple syrup
4 (4-ounce) boneless loin pork chops (¾ inch thick)
1 (12-ounce) package frozen baked apples with cinnamon (such as Stouffer's Harvest Apples)
1 tablespoon cider vinegar
2 tablespoons raisins

1. Prepare grill.
2. Combine soy sauce and maple syrup in a large zip-top plastic bag; add pork chops, and let stand 10 minutes.
3. While pork stands, combine frozen apples, vinegar, and raisins in a small saucepan. Cook over medium-high heat 5 minutes or until thoroughly heated, stirring gently.
4. Remove pork from marinade, reserving marinade. Microwave marinade at HIGH 1 minute or until it just begins to boil. Grill pork chops 4 minutes on each side or until done, basting frequently with marinade. Serve with warm apple chutney. **YIELD: 4 SERVINGS (SERVING SIZE: 1 PORK CHOP AND ABOUT ⅓ CUP CHUTNEY).**

PER SERVING: Calories 302; Fat 10.8g (sat 3.6g, mono 4g, poly 0.7g); Protein 18.3g; Carb 31.8g; Fiber 1.4g; Chol 58mg; Iron 1.4mg; Sodium 497mg; Calc 27mg

PORK CHOPS WITH CRANBERRIES AND APPLES

POINTS value: 6

PREP: 1 minute ■ **COOK:** 14 minutes

The spicy aroma of apples and cranberries will remind you of the holidays, but you can enjoy these savory chops any time of year.

> 4 (4-ounce) boneless center-cut loin pork chops (about ½ inch thick)
> ¼ teaspoon salt
> ¼ teaspoon freshly ground black pepper
> 2 teaspoons olive oil
> 1 (15-ounce) can fried apples (such as Luck's)
> ½ cup fat-free, less-sodium chicken broth
> ½ cup sweetened dried cranberries
> ½ teaspoon ground cinnamon

1. Sprinkle pork chops on both sides with salt and pepper.
2. Heat a large nonstick skillet over medium-high heat. Add oil. Add pork chops; cook 2 minutes on each side or until browned. Cover, reduce heat to medium, and cook 6 minutes or until done.
3. While pork cooks, drain apples, reserving juice. When pork is done, remove from pan and keep warm. Add reserved juice, broth, and cranberries to pan; cook until slightly reduced, scraping pan to loosen browned bits. Stir in apples and cinnamon; cook 1 minute. Return pork to pan; cook just until thoroughly heated. **YIELD: 4 SERVINGS (SERVING SIZE: 1 PORK CHOP AND ½ CUP APPLE MIXTURE).**

PER SERVING: Calories 266; Fat 9.9g (sat 3.2g, mono 5.2g, poly 0.9g); Protein 20.4g; Carb 23.6g; Fiber 2.8g; Chol 51mg; Iron 0.9mg; Sodium 244mg; Calc 9mg

CRANBERRY NUTRITION

Whether fresh, dried, cooked, or made into juice, cranberries are full of health benefits. They contain tannins, which help prevent infection. Tannins are also antioxidants, which neutralize harmful free radicals in the body. Plus, cranberries have a high vitamin C content.

BRINED PORK CHOPS WITH APPLES AND SAGE

POINTS value: 6

PREP: 17 minutes ■ **COOK:** 16 minutes
■ **OTHER:** 8 hours

Marinating the chops overnight in a salt solution leaves the cooked pork moist and juicy without tasting overly salty. You can substitute 1 teaspoon of dried sage for the fresh, if you'd like.

> 2½ cups apple juice, divided
> ½ cup packed light brown sugar
> ¼ cup kosher salt
> 4 (4-ounce) boneless center-cut loin pork chops
> ½ teaspoon black pepper, divided
> 2 teaspoons olive oil
> 3 Granny Smith apples (about 1¼ pounds), peeled and sliced
> 1 tablespoon light brown sugar
> 1 tablespoon chopped fresh sage

1. Combine 2 cups apple juice, ½ cup brown sugar, and kosher salt in a large zip-top plastic bag. Add pork chops; seal bag, and marinate in refrigerator 8 hours, turning bag occasionally.
2. Remove pork chops from bag; discard marinade. Pat pork chops dry with paper towels; sprinkle with ¼ teaspoon black pepper.
3. Heat oil in a large nonstick skillet over medium-high heat. Add pork chops, and cook 3 minutes on each side. Reduce heat to medium-low, and cook 1 to 2 minutes on each side or until pork is no longer pink. Place pork chops on a serving platter; cover and keep warm.
4. Place apples in pan, and cook 4 minutes or until lightly browned, stirring frequently. Add remaining ½ cup apple juice, remaining ¼ teaspoon black pepper, 1 tablespoon brown sugar, and sage. Increase heat to medium-high; cook 3 minutes or until apples are soft and most of juice evaporates. Spoon apples over pork chops. **YIELD: 4 SERVINGS (SERVING SIZE: 1 PORK CHOP AND ½ CUP APPLES).**

PER SERVING: Calories 271; Fat 8.7g (sat 2.7g, mono 4.5g, poly 0.7g); Protein 24.4g; Carb 25g; Fiber 1.5g; Chol 65mg; Iron 1.2mg; Sodium 673mg; Calc 41mg

SAUSAGE, SAGE, AND BUTTERNUT SQUASH–STUFFED SHELLS

POINTS value: 8

PREP: 7 minutes ■ COOK: 21 minutes

32 uncooked jumbo pasta shells
Cooking spray
3 cups refrigerated prechopped butternut squash
6 ounces reduced-fat bulk pork sausage (such as Jimmy Dean)
1 (16-ounce) carton 2% low-fat cottage cheese
½ teaspoon salt, divided
½ teaspoon freshly ground black pepper, divided
2 teaspoons chopped fresh sage
¼ teaspoon ground nutmeg
2 cups fat-free milk
3 tablespoons all-purpose flour
¼ cup (1 ounce) freshly grated Parmigiano-Reggiano cheese
2 tablespoons 50/50 non-hydrogenated buttery blend stick spread (such as Smart Balance)

1. Preheat broiler.
2. Cook pasta according to package directions, omitting salt and fat. Drain. Arrange shells in a single layer in a 13 x 9–inch baking dish or 8 individual oval dishes coated with cooking spray.
3. While pasta cooks, place squash in a medium microwave-safe bowl. Cover bowl with plastic wrap; vent. Microwave at HIGH 3 minutes or until tender.
4. While squash cooks, cook sausage in a large skillet over medium-high heat until browned, stirring to crumble. Drain sausage; pat dry with paper towels. Wipe drippings from pan with a paper towel.
5. Place cottage cheese, ¼ teaspoon salt, and ¼ teaspoon pepper in a food processor; process 20 seconds or until smooth. Return sausage to pan. Add cottage cheese mixture and squash; stir in sage and nutmeg. Spoon mixture evenly into cooked pasta shells.
6. Combine milk, flour, remaining ¼ teaspoon salt, and ¼ teaspoon pepper in a medium saucepan, stirring with a whisk. Bring to a boil, whisking constantly. Reduce heat; simmer 3 minutes or until thickened, stirring frequently with a whisk. Add cheese and buttery spread, stirring with a whisk. Pour sauce over stuffed shells.

7. Broil shells 3 minutes or until lightly browned and bubbly. **YIELD: 8 SERVINGS (SERVING SIZE: 4 STUFFED SHELLS).**

PER SERVING: Calories 357; Fat 12.3g (sat 4.5g, mono 1.2g, poly 1g); Protein 21.6g; Carb 39.5g; Fiber 2g; Chol 27mg; Iron 2.1mg; Sodium 888mg; Calc 204mg

QUICK CASSOULET

POINTS value: 5

PREP: 11 minutes ■ COOK: 17 minutes

Traditional French cassoulet involves soaking dried beans and a lengthy baking time in the oven. Our version takes a shortcut by using canned beans and sautéed pork pieces. Be sure to broil on the top rack in the oven for the quickest browning.

2 thick-cut bacon slices, chopped
4 (4-ounce) boneless center-cut loin pork chops, cubed
1½ cups frozen vegetable seasoning blend
1 (14½-ounce) can diced tomatoes with basil, garlic, and oregano, undrained
1 bay leaf
2 teaspoons fresh thyme leaves
2 (15.5-ounce) cans cannellini beans, rinsed and drained
½ cup panko (Japanese breadcrumbs)
Olive oil–flavored cooking spray

1. Preheat broiler.
2. Cook bacon in a large deep cast-iron skillet over medium-high heat until crisp. Remove bacon from pan, reserving drippings in pan. Set bacon aside. Add pork to drippings in pan; cook 4 minutes or until browned, stirring occasionally. Remove from pan; keep warm.
3. Add seasoning blend and tomatoes to pan; cook, stirring constantly, over medium heat 2 minutes. Return bacon and pork to pan; stir in bay leaf and thyme. Spoon beans over pork mixture, and sprinkle with panko. Coat panko with cooking spray.
4. Broil 6 minutes or until crumbs are browned. Discard bay leaf. **YIELD: 6 SERVINGS (SERVING SIZE: ⅙ OF CASSOULET).**

PER SERVING: Calories 251; Fat 7.6g (sat 2.6g, mono 2.9g, poly 0.9g); Protein 21.1g; Carb 22.7g; Fiber 3.9g; Chol 48mg; Iron 2.8mg; Sodium 542mg; Calc 84mg

PORK AND POTATO HASH
POINTS value: 7

PREP: 4 minutes ■ **COOK:** 36 minutes

We call for ground pork loin in this recipe because packaged ground pork is much higher in fat. In some supermarkets, the butcher can grind it for you. Or you can cut the pork loin into 1-inch cubes and process it in your food processor until ground.

Cooking spray
- 1 pound ground pork loin
- ½ cup chopped bottled roasted red bell peppers
- 4 garlic cloves, minced
- 6 center-cut bacon slices
- 2 cups refrigerated diced potatoes and onion (such as Simply Potatoes)
- ½ cup egg substitute
- ½ cup (2 ounces) reduced-fat shredded sharp cheddar cheese
- ¼ cup fat-free milk
- ½ teaspoon salt
- ½ teaspoon black pepper
- Chopped fresh parsley (optional)

1. Heat a large nonstick skillet over medium-high heat. Coat pan with cooking spray. Add pork; cook 6 minutes, stirring to crumble. Add bell pepper; cook, stirring frequently, 3 minutes or until pork is browned. Add garlic; cook 1 minute. Drain. Set aside, and keep warm.
2. Cook bacon in pan over medium heat until crisp. Remove bacon from pan; crumble. Drain drippings from pan, reserving 1 tablespoon in pan. Add diced potatoes and onion to drippings in pan; cook, without stirring, 2 minutes. Stir and cook 2 minutes. Stir in pork mixture. Reduce heat to medium-low, and cook 5 minutes or until potatoes are tender, stirring occasionally.
3. Combine crumbled bacon, egg substitute, next 4 ingredients, and parsley, if desired, in a bowl; pour over potato mixture. Increase heat to medium; cook 5 minutes. **YIELD: 5 SERVINGS (SERVING SIZE: 1 CUP).**

PER SERVING: Calories 309; Fat 15.7g (sat 6.8g, mono 1.4g, poly 0.7g); Protein 28.1g; Carb 13.6g; Fiber 1.3g; Chol 86mg; Iron 0.8mg; Sodium 595mg; Calc 118mg

RUSTIC HAM AND SALAMI PIZZA
POINTS value: 3

PREP: 13 minutes ■ **COOK:** 10 minutes

With meat, vegetables, and cheese, this delicious whole-wheat pizza rivals any franchise brand.

- ½ cup bottled roasted red bell peppers
- ¼ cup pizza sauce
- 1 teaspoon bottled minced garlic
- 1 (10-ounce) Italian cheese–flavored whole-wheat pizza crust (such as Boboli)
- 1 cup sliced cremini, baby portobello, or button mushrooms
- ⅓ cup thinly sliced red onion
- 2 ounces thinly sliced lean ham
- 1 ounce thinly sliced salami
- 2 tablespoons sliced ripe olives
- 1 cup (4 ounces) preshredded reduced-fat 6-cheese Italian blend

1. Preheat oven to 450°.
2. Combine first 3 ingredients in a food processor or blender; process until smooth, scraping down sides, if necessary.
3. Place crust on a baking sheet. Spread red bell pepper sauce evenly over dough, leaving a 1-inch border. Layer evenly with mushrooms and next 4 ingredients. Sprinkle with cheese. Bake at 450° for 10 minutes or until cheese melts. Cut into 8 slices. **YIELD: 8 SERVINGS (SERVING SIZE: 1 SLICE).**

PER SERVING: Calories 165; Fat 5.4g (sat 2.5g, mono 1.5g, poly 0.2g); Protein 11.1g; Carb 1.9g; Fiber 3.5g; Chol 11.2mg; Iron 1mg; Sodium 558mg; Calc 141mg

*Prebaked Pizza Crust
Homemade pizza crust is wonderful, but it isn't always practical for weeknight meals. Instead, premade pizza crusts offer an easy solution. Because you control the toppings, you can create healthy pizza with a low ***POINTS*** value per serving that tastes great and is packed with nutrients. Plus, you can have it on the table in less time than it takes to have one delivered.

Sweet and Spicy Oven-Barbecued Chicken Thighs,
page 103

poultry

BRAISED CHICKEN WITH PLUM TOMATOES AND FETA

POINTS value: 5   (pictured on page 132)

PREP: 3 minutes ■ **COOK:** 17 minutes

This easy-to-prepare entrée earned our Test Kitchens' highest rating. Serve it with orzo to complete the meal.

   6 **(6-ounce) skinless, boneless chicken breast halves**
  ½ **teaspoon freshly ground black pepper**
  ¼ **teaspoon salt**
  3 **tablespoons all-purpose flour**
  1 **teaspoon dried Italian seasoning**
     Cooking spray
  1 **cup fat-free, less-sodium chicken broth**
  1 **tablespoon fresh lemon juice**
  4 **medium plum tomatoes, chopped**
  ¼ **cup halved pitted kalamata olives**
  2 **garlic cloves, minced**
  ½ **cup (2 ounces) crumbled reduced-fat feta cheese with garlic and herbs**
  2 **tablespoons thinly sliced fresh basil**

1. Sprinkle chicken with pepper and salt. Combine flour and Italian seasoning in a medium bowl. Dredge chicken in flour mixture, reserving remaining mixture in bowl.

2. Heat a large nonstick skillet over medium-high heat. Coat pan with cooking spray. Add chicken; cook 3 minutes on each side or until lightly browned. Remove from pan, and keep warm.

3. While chicken cooks, gradually add chicken broth and lemon juice into reserved flour mixture, stirring with a whisk until blended.

4. When chicken is done, add broth mixture to pan, scraping pan to loosen browned bits. Cook over medium-high heat 3 minutes or until sauce is thickened and bubbly.

5. Return chicken to pan. Add tomato, olives, and garlic. Cover and cook 8 minutes or until chicken is done, stirring occasionally.

6. Place a chicken breast half on each of 6 plates. Spoon tomato mixture evenly over chicken; sprinkle evenly with cheese and basil. **YIELD: 6 SERVINGS (SERVING SIZE: 1 CHICKEN BREAST HALF, ¼ CUP SAUCE, 4 TEASPOONS CHEESE, AND 1 TEASPOON BASIL).**

PER SERVING: Calories 253; Fat 7.1g (sat 2g, mono 2.6g, poly 1.1g); Protein 37.9g; Carb 7.5g; Fiber 1.7g; Chol 97mg; Iron 2.6mg; Sodium 499mg; Calc 101mg

PLUM TOMATOES

There are few greater pleasures than a freshly picked, just-chopped, ripe red tomato—especially plum tomatoes. Plum tomatoes, also called Roma or Italian, are an egg-shaped variety that can either be red or yellow. Though not as sweet or acidic as beefsteak or globe varieties, plum tomatoes have a lower water content and fewer seeds, so they're especially good for cooking and canning. Plus, they're the best year-round supermarket tomatoes.

GREEK LEMON-ARTICHOKE CHICKEN

POINTS value: 5

PREP: 3 minutes ■ **COOK:** 15 minutes

Serve this easy skillet chicken with rice or orzo to soak up the juices. You can forgo chopping the artichokes if you're in a hurry.

  4 **(6-ounce) skinless, boneless chicken breast halves**
  2 **teaspoons salt-free Greek seasoning (such as Cavender's), divided**
     Cooking spray
  1 **(14-ounce) can quartered artichoke hearts, drained and coarsely chopped**
  ¼ **cup fresh lemon juice**
  ¼ **cup (1 ounce) crumbled reduced-fat feta cheese**

1. Sprinkle chicken evenly on both sides with 1 teaspoon Greek seasoning. Heat a large nonstick skillet over medium heat. Coat pan with cooking spray. Add chicken, and cook 5 minutes on each side.

2. While chicken cooks, combine artichoke hearts, lemon juice, and remaining 1 teaspoon Greek seasoning in a bowl. Add artichoke mixture to chicken. Reduce heat, and simmer 5 minutes or until chicken is tender and liquid almost evaporates.

3. Place 1 chicken breast half on each of 4 plates. Top chicken evenly with artichoke mixture, and sprinkle with cheese. **YIELD: 4 SERVINGS (SERVING SIZE: 1 CHICKEN BREAST HALF, ¼ CUP ARTICHOKE MIXTURE, AND 1 TABLESPOON CHEESE).**

PER SERVING: Calories 223; Fat 4.9g (sat 1.7g, mono 1.4g, poly 0.9g); Protein 37.3g; Carb 5.3g; Fiber 0.2g; Chol 96mg; Iron 1.9mg; Sodium 331mg; Calc 34mg

PAN-SEARING CHICKEN

For the best results when pan-searing chicken, use a nonstick skillet.

1. Heat a large nonstick skillet over medium-high heat, and coat the pan with cooking spray. Add the seasoned chicken to the pan, and cook 5 minutes on each side or until done. To tell if the chicken is done, pierce it with a fork. If the juices run clear, it's done.

2. Remove the chicken, reserving drippings in pan. Add water, and scrape up the sauce and browned bits thoroughly from the bottom of the pan to get the concentrated flavor left behind by cooking the chicken. This will add lots of flavor to the sauce.

PAN-SEARED CHICKEN WITH FRESH PLUM SAUCE

POINTS value: 6

PREP: 1 minute ■ **COOK:** 20 minutes

Ripe, juicy summer plums provide a sweet contrast to savory chicken in this superquick entrée. This dish is excellent when paired with the Almond-Ginger Rice on page 154. Plums come in an assortment of colors, from golden-hued to purplish-black to bright green. Generally, larger plums are juicier and best for eating out of hand, while smaller, firmer plums work well in recipes. To ripen hard plums, store them in a paper bag at room temperature for a day or two. Refrigerate ripe plums in a plastic bag for three to five days.

> Cooking spray
> 4 (6-ounce) skinless, boneless chicken breast halves
> ¼ teaspoon salt
> ¼ teaspoon freshly ground black pepper
> 1 tablespoon water
> 1 cup chopped red onion
> 1½ pounds very ripe plums, pitted and quartered
> 2 tablespoons red currant jelly

1. Heat a large nonstick skillet over medium-high heat. Coat pan with cooking spray. Sprinkle chicken with salt and pepper; add chicken to pan. Cook 5 minutes on each side or until done. Remove chicken, reserving drippings in pan. Cover and keep warm.

2. Stir 1 tablespoon water into drippings, scraping pan to loosen browned bits. Add onion, and cook 3 minutes or until crisp-tender, stirring frequently. Add plums, and cook 5 minutes or until tender, stirring frequently. Add jelly; cook until jelly melts.

3. Return chicken to pan. Cook until thoroughly heated, turning to coat with sauce. **YIELD: 4 SERVINGS (SERVING SIZE: 1 CHICKEN BREAST HALF AND 1 CUP PLUM SAUCE).**

PER SERVING: Calories 317; Fat 5g (sat 1.2g, mono 2.1g, poly 1.1g); Protein 36.1g; Carb 32.5g; Fiber 3.3g; Chol 94mg; Iron 1.4mg; Sodium 229mg; Calc 33mg

CHICKEN WITH CREAMY TOMATO SAUCE

POINTS value: 6

PREP: 3 minutes ■ **COOK:** 20 minutes

Serve this chicken dish over brown rice to soak up its flavorful tomato sauce.

> 4 (6-ounce) skinless, boneless chicken breast halves
> ¼ teaspoon salt
> ¼ teaspoon freshly ground black pepper
> Cooking spray
> ¼ cup chopped onion
> 1 garlic clove, minced
> 2 cups grape tomatoes, halved
> 1½ teaspoons all-purpose flour
> ½ cup fat-free milk
> 1 (10¾-ounce) can condensed reduced-fat, reduced-sodium tomato soup, undiluted
> ½ teaspoon dried basil
> ½ cup (2 ounces) preshredded part-skim mozzarella cheese

1. Sprinkle chicken evenly with salt and pepper. Heat a large nonstick skillet over medium-high heat. Coat pan with cooking spray. Add chicken. Cook 5 minutes on each side or until done. Remove chicken from pan, and keep warm.
2. Add onion, garlic, and tomato to pan. Cook 2 minutes or until onion is tender, stirring occasionally; add flour. Gradually add milk, stirring with a whisk. Cook 2 minutes or until mixture thickens, stirring constantly with a whisk. Add tomato soup and basil. Reduce heat, and simmer 5 minutes or until thoroughly heated.
3. Place 1 chicken breast on each of 4 plates. Spoon tomato mixture evenly over chicken, and sprinkle with cheese. **YIELD: 4 SERVINGS (SERVING SIZE: 1 CHICKEN BREAST HALF, ¾ CUP SAUCE, AND 2 TABLESPOONS CHEESE).**

PER SERVING: Calories 285; Fat 6.9g (sat 2.3g, mono 1.5g, poly 1.2g); Protein 40.9g; Carb 12.7g; Fiber 1.5g; Chol 99mg; Iron 1.9mg; Sodium 365mg; Calc 173mg

PAN-ROASTED CHICKEN WITH STRAWBERRY-RHUBARB COMPOTE

POINTS value: 5

PREP: 1 minute ■ **COOK:** 16 minutes

This dish celebrates some of spring's freshest produce. We used frozen rhubarb for speed and convenience, but you may substitute fresh rhubarb in season.

> 2 teaspoons olive oil
> 4 (6-ounce) skinless, boneless chicken breast halves
> ¼ teaspoon salt
> ¼ teaspoon freshly ground black pepper
> 1 cup frozen sliced rhubarb
> 3 tablespoons minced shallots (about 1 large)
> 1 cup sliced strawberries
> ¼ cup water
> 2 tablespoons sugar
> 1 tablespoon white balsamic vinegar
> 1 tablespoon grated peeled fresh ginger

1. Heat oil in a large nonstick skillet over medium-high heat. Sprinkle chicken with salt and pepper. Add chicken to pan, and cook 3 minutes on each side or until browned. Remove chicken from pan.
2. Add rhubarb and shallots to pan; sauté 2 minutes or until tender. Add strawberries and next 4 ingredients. Bring to a boil; reduce heat, and simmer, uncovered, 1 minute or until sauce thickens. Nestle chicken in sauce. Cover and cook over medium heat 4 minutes or until chicken is done. Serve sauce over chicken. **YIELD: 4 SERVINGS (SERVING SIZE: 1 CHICKEN BREAST HALF AND ¼ CUP SAUCE).**

PER SERVING: Calories 257; Fat 6.4g (sat 1.5g, mono 3.1g, poly 1.2g); Protein 35.1g; Carb 13.1g; Fiber 1.5g; Chol 94mg; Iron 1.5mg; Sodium 231mg; Calc 54mg

 Fresh Rhubarb

Rhubarb season peaks in the spring. When buying fresh rhubarb, choose thick, firm stalks that have no signs of wrinkling or drying. If there are leaves on the stalks, they should be fresh and unwilted. Before using rhubarb, be sure to remove the leaves—they're inedible—and wash the stalks. Refrigerate fresh rhubarb in a plastic bag for up to three days. You can also chop rhubarb, place in a heavy-duty zip-top plastic bag, and freeze for up to eight months.

HONEY-BALSAMIC GRILLED CHICKEN WITH POMEGRANATE-MANGO SALSA

POINTS value: 7

PREP: 7 minutes ■ **COOK:** 12 minutes

Pomegranate seeds add a splash of color and crunchy bursts of flavor to this fresh salsa. Look for prepackaged seeds in the produce section of your supermarket.

> **4** (6-ounce) skinless, boneless chicken breast halves
> ½ teaspoon salt
> ½ teaspoon freshly ground black pepper
> ¼ cup honey, divided
> **1** tablespoon white balsamic vinegar
> Cooking spray
> **2** tablespoons fresh lime juice
> **1** teaspoon extra-virgin olive oil
> ½ cup diced peeled mango
> ½ cup diced peeled avocado (about 1 small)
> ¼ cup pomegranate seeds
> **2** tablespoons chopped fresh mint

1. Prepare grill.

2. Sprinkle chicken evenly with salt and pepper. Combine 3 tablespoons honey and vinegar in a small bowl. Place chicken on grill rack coated with cooking spray. Brush chicken evenly with honey mixture. Grill 6 to 7 minutes on each side or until chicken is done.

3. While chicken cooks, combine remaining 1 tablespoon honey, lime juice, and olive oil in a medium bowl, stirring with a whisk. Add mango and next 3 ingredients, tossing gently. Serve salsa over chicken.

YIELD: 4 SERVINGS (SERVING SIZE: 1 CHICKEN BREAST HALF AND ABOUT ⅓ CUP SALSA).

PER SERVING: Calories 317; Fat 8g (sat 1.7g, mono 4g, poly 1.4g); Protein 35g; Carb 26.4g; Fiber 1.5g; Chol 94mg; Iron 1.6mg; Sodium 377mg; Calc 27mg

HOW TO SEED A POMEGRANATE

If you can't find prepackaged pomegranate seeds, you can always buy a pomegranate and seed it yourself. Unlike most fruits, the seeds of a pomegranate are the edible portion. Each fruit contains hundreds of tiny seeds, and they can stain. Use a bowl of water to help keep you and your kitchen clean.

1. Place the pomegranate in a bowl of water large enough to fit both the fruit and your hands without overflowing. Under the water, use a knife to carefully slice off the ends of the pomegranate so the seeds are just visible. (Be sure not to slice too deeply.) Then score the pomegranate lengthwise into 1½-inch-wide wedges. Carefully pry the pomegranate apart under the water, and turn each section inside out.

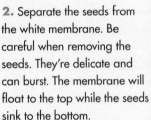

2. Separate the seeds from the white membrane. Be careful when removing the seeds. They're delicate and can burst. The membrane will float to the top while the seeds sink to the bottom.

3. Using a slotted spoon, remove the floating white membrane. Sort through the seeds beneath the water, and discard any stray pieces of the bitter white membrane. Drain the pomegranate seeds in a fine mesh strainer. Use them immediately, or refrigerate for up to one week.

CRISPY BAKED BARBECUE CHICKEN

POINTS value: 8

PREP: 12 minutes ▪ COOK: 13 minutes
▪ OTHER: 10 minutes

This recipe has kid appeal from start to finish. Let little ones squeeze the bag to coat the chicken and then press the tenders into potato chip crumbs. Some children are more likely to clean their plates if they've helped prepare the food.

- 1½ pounds chicken breast tenders
- ½ cup barbecue sauce (such as Stubb's)
- 5 cups barbecue-flavored baked potato chips (such as Lay's), coarsely crushed
- 3 tablespoons instant minced onion
- Cooking spray
- ½ cup (2 ounces) 50% reduced-fat shredded cheddar cheese, divided

1. Preheat oven to 400°.
2. Place chicken in a large heavy-duty zip-top plastic bag. Add barbecue sauce; seal bag, turning to coat chicken. Chill 10 minutes.
3. Combine potato chips and onion in a shallow dish. Remove chicken from bag, discarding sauce. Dredge chicken in potato chip mixture. Place chicken on a large baking sheet coated with cooking spray. Coat tops of chicken with cooking spray.
4. Bake at 400° for 12 minutes or until chicken is done. Sprinkle chicken evenly with cheese. Bake an additional 1 minute or until cheese melts. **YIELD: 4 SERVINGS (SERVING SIZE: ABOUT 3 CHICKEN TENDERS).**

PER SERVING: Calories 391; Fat 11.1g (sat 3.9g, mono 1.4g, poly 0.9g); Protein 40.9g; Carb 29.9g; Fiber 2g; Chol 104mg; Iron 1.6mg; Sodium 572mg; Calc 151mg

CHICKEN AND VEGETABLE PAD THAI

POINTS value: 7 *(pictured on page 131)*

PREP: 2 minutes ▪ COOK: 7 minutes

This take-out favorite is made superquick by starting with a boxed mix. Customize it by substituting fresh shrimp for chicken or adding sliced red bell pepper or matchstick carrots.

- 2 teaspoons dark sesame oil
- 1 pound chicken cutlets, thinly sliced
- ¼ teaspoon salt
- 1 large egg, lightly beaten
- 1 cup fresh bean sprouts
- 2 cups diagonally-cut snow peas
- 3 green onions, diagonally sliced
- 1 (5.75-ounce) package Pad Thai Noodles (such as A Taste of Thai)
- 4 lime wedges
- Fresh cilantro leaves (optional)
- Chopped unsalted, dry-roasted peanuts (optional)

1. Heat oil in a large nonstick skillet over medium-high heat. Sprinkle chicken evenly with salt. Add chicken to pan; sauté 3 to 4 minutes or until browned. Remove from pan; keep warm. Add egg to pan; cook 1 to 2 minutes or until set, stirring constantly. Remove from pan; coarsely chop egg. Keep warm.
2. Add bean sprouts, snow peas, and onions to pan; cook 2 minutes or until tender, stirring frequently.
3. While vegetables cook, prepare noodles according to package stovetop directions. Return chicken and egg to pan; add cooked noodles, and stir to combine. Top with chopped peanuts from package. Serve with lime wedges, and garnish with fresh cilantro and additional chopped peanuts, if desired. **YIELD: 4 SERVINGS (SERVING SIZE: 1½ CUPS).**

PER SERVING: Calories 315; Fat 8.3g (sat 1.7g, mono 1.4g, poly 0.8g); Protein 28.3g; Carb 31.2g; Fiber 2.1g; Chol 116mg; Iron 2.2mg; Sodium 367mg; Calc 55mg

✳ Chicken Cutlets

Cutlets are the skinless, boneless portion of the chicken breast that has been cut thin and tenderized. This cut is ideal for quick cooking methods like sautéing, stir-frying, and pan-frying.

SWEET AND SPICY OVEN-BARBECUED CHICKEN THIGHS

POINTS value: 8   *(pictured on page 132)*

PREP: 3 minutes ■ COOK: 33 minutes

This delicious dish received our Test Kitchens' highest rating. Once the thighs are cooked, let the sauce stand in the dish for a few minutes—it'll thicken and make a tasty addition to hot cooked brown rice or roasted squash and zucchini.

> 8 (3-ounce) skinless, boneless chicken thighs
> Cooking spray
> ¼ teaspoon salt
> ¼ teaspoon freshly ground black pepper
> ½ cup spicy barbecue sauce (such as Stubb's)
> ¼ cup low-sugar orange marmalade (such as Smucker's)
> 1 large garlic clove, pressed
> ½ teaspoon grated peeled fresh ginger

1. Preheat oven to 375°.
2. Coat chicken with cooking spray; sprinkle with salt and pepper. Heat a large nonstick skillet over medium-high heat. Coat pan with cooking spray. Add chicken, and cook 3 minutes on each side or until browned. Place chicken in an 11 x 7–inch baking dish coated with cooking spray.
3. Combine barbecue sauce and next 3 ingredients in a small bowl. Pour sauce over chicken. Bake, uncovered, at 375° for 26 to 28 minutes or until chicken is done. YIELD: 4 SERVINGS (SERVING SIZE: 2 CHICKEN THIGHS AND 3 TABLESPOONS SAUCE).

PER SERVING: Calories 332; Fat 12.8g (sat 3.6g, mono 4.9g, poly 2.9g); Protein 30.5g; Carb 19.4g; Fiber 0.1g; Chol 112mg; Iron 1.9mg; Sodium 639mg; Calc 16mg

HOW TO PREPARE FRESH GINGER

Ginger's warm, slightly woody flavor makes it one of the world's favorite spices. Virtually all of the plant possesses ginger's signature spicy fragrance, although cooks look solely to the pungent root for their purposes. Fresh ginger, with its gnarled root and papery brown skin, is available in almost any grocery's produce department. Chopped or grated, fresh ginger gives subtle sweetness to many dishes. When buying, choose fresh, young-looking ginger. Old ginger is fibrous, tough, and flavorless. Store it tightly wrapped in plastic wrap in the vegetable crisper section of your refrigerator for up to three weeks.

1. Use a vegetable peeler to remove the tough skin and reveal the yellow flesh.

2. For grated ginger, rub a peeled piece of ginger across a fine grater, such as a microplane.

APPLE BUTTER–GLAZED CHICKEN THIGHS

POINTS value: 6

PREP: 8 minutes ■ **COOK:** 6 minutes

This family-friendly dish is easy to prepare and ready in minutes.

½ cup apple butter
1 tablespoon spicy brown mustard (such as Grey Poupon)
1½ teaspoons Worcestershire sauce
1½ teaspoons honey
8 (3-ounce) skinless, boneless chicken thighs
¼ teaspoon salt
¼ teaspoon freshly ground black pepper
Cooking spray

1. Prepare grill.
2. Combine first 4 ingredients in a small bowl.
3. Trim excess fat from chicken thighs. Sprinkle chicken evenly with salt and pepper. Brush half of apple butter mixture evenly over chicken. Place chicken on grill rack coated with cooking spray. Grill 3 to 4 minutes; turn chicken over, and brush with remaining apple butter mixture. Grill 3 to 4 minutes or until done. **YIELD: 4 SERVINGS (SERVING SIZE: 2 CHICKEN THIGHS).**

PER SERVING: Calories 278; Fat 6.7g (sat 1.7g, mono 2.1g, poly 1.7g); Protein 33.6g; Carb 18.1g; Fiber 0.6g; Chol 141mg; Iron 2mg; Sodium 355mg; Calc 25mg

✳ Chicken Thighs

Chicken thighs are higher in fat than breast meat and have a succulent and hearty flavor. The dark meat is dark simply because those muscles are used more frequently and have more myoglobin proteins. In non-flying birds, like chickens and turkeys, the legs become dark while the breast meat stays light.

CHICKEN, ARUGULA, AND ROASTED RED PEPPER PIZZA

POINTS value: 7

PREP: 2 minutes ■ **COOK:** 11 minutes

We've given store-bought pizza a makeover with top-shelf ingredients that take it from ordinary to extraordinary.

1 (11.9-ounce) frozen thin crust margherita pizza (such as Kashi)
1½ cups shredded cooked chicken breast
1 cup thinly sliced red bell pepper
3 cups baby arugula
¼ teaspoon freshly ground black pepper
1 tablespoon extra-virgin olive oil

1. Preheat oven to 400°.
2. Top pizza with chicken and bell pepper. Place pizza directly on bottom oven rack. Bake at 400° for 11 minutes or until golden and cheese melts.
3. Transfer pizza to a serving platter. Top with arugula; sprinkle with black pepper, and drizzle with olive oil. Cut pizza into 8 slices. **YIELD: 4 SERVINGS (SERVING SIZE: 2 SLICES).**

PER SERVING: Calories 322; Fat 12.3g (sat 4g, mono 3.4g, poly 0.8g); Protein 27.4g; Carb 23.7g; Fiber 3.7g; Chol 45mg; Iron 1.9mg; Sodium 514mg; Calc 213mg

BUYING AND STORING ARUGULA

The flavor of arugula is often likened to peppery mustard, making it somewhat stronger than most lettuces. You'll find it as loose leaves in bags and plastic bins, or sometimes it's bundled with the stems attached. Whatever way it comes, look for firm, fresh, uniformly green leaves without yellow or brown spots. Arugula is highly perishable and may only last about two days after purchase. Store it in the refrigerator in a perforated plastic bag. Rinse it thoroughly, and dry before using.

GRILLED CORN–CHICKEN TOSTADAS

POINTS value: 7

PREP: 15 minutes ■ **COOK:** 12 minutes

For additional flavor, grill the chicken alongside the corn, or just pick up a rotisserie chicken from the deli.

 4 (7-inch) flour tortillas
 Cooking spray
 2 ears shucked yellow corn
 1½ cups chopped tomato
 1 small peeled avocado, chopped
 3 tablespoons fresh lime juice
 ¼ teaspoon salt
 3 cups shredded cooked chicken breast
 ¼ cup reduced-fat sour cream
 2 tablespoons chopped fresh cilantro

1. Prepare grill.
2. Coat tortillas with cooking spray. Place tortillas and corn on grill rack coated with cooking spray; grill 1 minute. Turn tortillas over; grill an additional 1 minute or until toasted. Remove tortillas from grill. Grill corn an additional 10 minutes or until tender, turning frequently.
3. While corn cooks, combine tomato and next 3 ingredients, tossing gently.
4. Cut kernels from ears of corn. Add corn and chicken to tomato mixture, tossing gently. Top each tortilla with about 1 cup chicken mixture, 1 tablespoon sour cream, and 1½ teaspoons cilantro. Serve immediately. **YIELD: 4 SERVINGS (SERVING SIZE: 1 TOSTADA).**

PER SERVING: Calories 363; Fat 11.5g (sat 3.1g, mono 4.4g, poly 1.6g); Protein 37.6g; Carb 28.4g; Fiber 4.7g; Chol 95mg; Iron 2.5mg; Sodium 402mg; Calc 44mg

HOW TO PREPARE AVOCADOS

Although avocados are high in fat, the majority of it is heart-healthy monounsaturated fat. To easily chop them, use a chef's knife.

1. Insert the chef's knife into the top where the stem was, and gently press down until you reach the pit. Holding the knife steady, rotate the fruit so the knife moves around the pit, cutting the entire avocado.

2. Remove the knife; slowly and gently twist the two sides away from each other to separate.

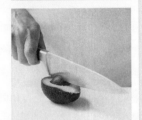

3. Strike the pit, and pierce it with the blade. Then twist and remove the knife; the pit will come with it.

4. Use the knife's tip to cut the flesh in horizontal and vertical rows. Be careful not to cut through the skin.

5. Remove the flesh gently with a spoon.

Egg noodles differ from regular pasta in that they contain whole eggs, egg yolks, or just egg whites. Regular egg noodles that contain the yolks are slightly higher in fat than other noodles, but the variety made without yolks is similar in fat content to other noodles. Egg noodles are usually short and flat, but they may come in the form of fettuccine, tagliatelle, or other shapes. Because of their sturdy texture, they're often used in soups and casseroles or paired with cream or meat sauces. Look for egg noodles in the pasta section of the supermarket. Store them, unopened, in a cool, dry pantry for six to eight months.

CHICKEN AND BUTTERMILK DUMPLINGS

POINTS value: 4

PREP: 10 minutes ■ **COOK:** 17 minutes

Give these dumplings a few minutes to dry and firm up before dropping them in the simmering soup.

Cooking spray
1 cup refrigerated prechopped onion
2 celery stalks with leaves, chopped
2 carrots, chopped
2 cups shredded cooked chicken breast
1 cup water
½ teaspoon poultry seasoning
¼ teaspoon freshly ground black pepper
1 (32-ounce) container fat-free, less-sodium chicken broth
1 cup low-fat baking mix
⅛ teaspoon salt
⅓ cup nonfat buttermilk
Chopped fresh flat-leaf parsley (optional)

1. Heat a Dutch oven over medium heat; coat pan with cooking spray. Add onion, celery, and carrot; sauté 5 minutes or just until tender. Add chicken and next 4 ingredients; cover and bring to a boil over medium-high heat.

2. While chicken mixture comes to a boil, combine baking mix, salt, and buttermilk. Stir with a fork until a soft dough forms. Turn dough out onto a lightly floured surface; knead 12 times. Roll dough to ⅛-inch thickness. Cut into 2 x 1½–inch strips. Let stand until ready to cook.

3. Drop strips, 1 at a time, into boiling broth. Return to a boil; reduce heat, cover, and simmer 12 minutes or until dumplings are done. Garnish with parsley, if desired. **YIELD: 5 SERVINGS (SERVING SIZE: 1½ CUPS).**

PER SERVING: Calories 222; Fat 4g (sat 0.6g, mono 1.6g, poly 0.8g); Protein 21.2g; Carb 24.4g; Fiber 2g; Chol 48mg; Iron 1.7mg; Sodium 858mg; Calc 145mg

BACON RANCH CHICKEN PASTA

POINTS value: 5

PREP: 4 minutes ■ **COOK:** 12 minutes

Ranch dressing lovers will like this creamy, kid-friendly, one-dish meal.

3 cups uncooked medium yolk-free egg noodles
1 tablespoon light butter
1 (12-ounce) package fresh broccoli florets
Cooking spray
2 cups chopped cooked chicken breast
1 cup nonfat buttermilk
½ cup reduced-fat sour cream
2 tablespoons dry ranch dressing mix
6 tablespoons real bacon pieces (such as Oscar Mayer)
¼ cup (1 ounce) shredded fresh Parmesan cheese
¼ teaspoon freshly ground black pepper

1. Cook noodles according to package directions, omitting salt and fat; drain. Add butter, and stir to combine; keep warm.

2. While noodles cook, microwave broccoli according to package directions. Heat a large nonstick skillet over medium-high heat. Coat pan with cooking spray. Add chicken, and cook 2 to 3 minutes or until lightly browned.

3. Combine buttermilk, sour cream, and dressing mix in a large bowl, stirring with a whisk until smooth. Add noodles, broccoli, and chicken. Toss

until noodles are coated. Sprinkle with bacon, cheese, and pepper. **YIELD: 6 SERVINGS (SERVING SIZE: 1½ CUPS).**

PER SERVING: Calories 252; Fat 8.6g (sat 4.6g, mono 1.6g, poly 0.6g); Protein 25.7g; Carb 18g; Fiber 2g; Chol 59mg; Iron 1.2mg; Sodium 742mg; Calc 160mg

CHICKEN AND SPINACH ENCHILADA CASSEROLE

POINTS value: 7

PREP: 20 minutes ■ **COOK:** 55 minutes

In Mexican cuisine, masa refers to "corn dough." Masa harina is made from drying fresh masa and grinding it into a fine powder. Traditionally it is used to make corn tortillas, but we use it to thicken the sauce and lend an authentic corn flavor. Look for it in the Mexican/Latin section of the grocery store.

> Cooking spray
> 1 cup chopped onion
> 2 garlic cloves, minced
> 1 teaspoon ground cumin
> 1 (14-ounce) can fat-free, less-sodium chicken broth
> 1½ tablespoons masa harina
> ½ cup (4 ounces) ⅓-less-fat cream cheese
> ½ cup light sour cream
> 1 (10-ounce) package frozen chopped spinach, thawed and drained
> 1 (4-ounce) can chopped green chiles, undrained
> ¼ cup chopped fresh cilantro
> ½ teaspoon salt
> ¼ teaspoon black pepper
> 2½ cups shredded rotisserie chicken
> 8 (6-inch) corn tortillas, torn in half
> 1 cup (4 ounces) shredded reduced-fat colby-Jack cheese, divided
> Fresh salsa (optional)

1. Preheat oven to 350°.
2. Heat a large nonstick skillet over medium-high heat. Coat pan with cooking spray. Add onion and garlic; sauté 3 minutes. Add cumin; sauté 1 minute. Combine broth and masa harina, stirring until masa harina dissolves; add to pan. Stir in cream cheese and next 6 ingredients; bring to a boil. Reduce heat,

and simmer 2 to 3 minutes or until cream cheese melts, stirring occasionally. Stir in shredded chicken.
3. Arrange half of torn tortillas in an 11 x 7–inch baking dish coated with cooking spray; top with half of chicken mixture and ⅓ cup colby-Jack cheese. Top with remaining half of torn tortillas, remaining half of chicken mixture, and remaining ⅔ cup cheese; cover with foil coated with cooking spray.
4. Bake at 350° for 25 minutes; uncover and bake an additional 20 minutes or until lightly browned and bubbly. Serve with salsa, if desired. **YIELD: 6 SERVINGS (SERVING SIZE: ⅙ OF CASSEROLE).**

PER SERVING: Calories 318; Fat 12.9g (sat 6.8g, mono 0.8g, poly 0.9g); Protein 31g; Carb 23.7g; Fiber 3.6g; Chol 70mg; Iron 1.9mg; Sodium 789mg; Calc 311mg

CHOPPING FRESH CILANTRO

Also called coriander or Chinese parsley, cilantro has a pungent flavor. The leaves are often mistaken for flat-leaf parsley, so read the label to verify that you're purchasing the correct herb. You don't need to worry about removing the stems when using cilantro—the stems are tender and can be chopped and used with the leaves. Simply place the bunch on a cutting board, and chop using a sharp knife.

POBLANO CHICKEN TORTILLA BAKE

POINTS value: 7

PREP: 5 minutes ■ **COOK:** 14 minutes

Poblano chiles range in color from dark green to almost black. The darkest ones have the richest flavor.

Cooking spray
½ cup coarsely chopped seeded poblano chile
4 (6-inch) corn tortillas
2 cups shredded skinless, boneless rotisserie chicken breast
1½ cups fresh salsa
¾ cup (3 ounces) preshredded reduced-fat Mexican blend cheese
½ cup light sour cream
2 tablespoons finely chopped fresh cilantro
1 teaspoon grated lime rind
1 tablespoon fresh lime juice
½ teaspoon ground cumin

1. Preheat oven to 425°.
2. Heat a large nonstick skillet over medium-high heat. Coat pan with cooking spray. Add chile peppers; sauté 3 minutes or until tender.
3. Arrange tortillas in an 8-inch square baking dish, overlapping slightly. Top tortillas with chicken, peppers, salsa, and cheese. Bake at 425° for 10 minutes or until thoroughly heated.
4. While casserole bakes, combine sour cream and next 4 ingredients in a small bowl.
5. Remove casserole from oven; serve with sour cream mixture. **YIELD: 4 SERVINGS (SERVING SIZE: ¼ OF CASSEROLE AND 2 TABLESPOONS SOUR CREAM MIXTURE).**

PER SERVING: Calories 299; Fat 10.4g (sat 5.6g, mono 0.9g, poly 0.8g); Protein 28.7g; Carb 19.1g; Fiber 1.5g; Chol 85mg; Iron 1.1mg; Sodium 542mg; Calc 220mg

CHICKEN SAUSAGE AND SPINACH PENNE ALFREDO

POINTS value: 8

PREP: 2 minutes ■ **COOK:** 12 minutes

Creamy and colorful, this satisfying pasta is a quick weeknight meal solution.

1½ cups uncooked multigrain penne pasta (such as Barilla Plus)
1 (6-ounce) package baby spinach
Cooking spray
3 (2.75-ounce) links chicken sausage with spinach and feta, sliced
1 cup chopped red bell pepper
1 (8-ounce) package sliced cremini mushrooms
1 (10-ounce) container light Alfredo sauce (such as Buitoni)
¼ cup (1 ounce) grated fresh Parmesan cheese
¼ teaspoon freshly ground black pepper

1. Cook pasta according to package directions, omitting salt and fat. Add spinach to pasta water during last minute of cooking time. Drain.
2. While pasta cooks, heat a large nonstick skillet over medium-high heat. Coat pan with cooking spray. Add sausage, and sauté 5 minutes or until lightly browned. Add bell pepper and mushrooms; sauté 5 minutes. Stir in Alfredo sauce, and cook until thoroughly heated. Stir in pasta, spinach, and cheese. Serve in pasta bowls; sprinkle evenly with black pepper.
YIELD: 6 SERVINGS (SERVING SIZE: 1 CUP).

PER SERVING: Calories 387; Fat 12.3g (sat 4.8g, mono 0g, poly 0.1g); Protein 23.6g; Carb 46g; Fiber 5.4g; Chol 46mg; Iron 16.2mg; Sodium 734mg; Calc 183mg

TURKEY MOLE

POINTS value: 5

PREP: 3 minutes ▪ **COOK:** 12 minutes

This flavorful adaptation of the Mexican specialty, which combines chiles, onion, garlic, and cinnamon-scented Mexican chocolate, takes a fraction of the time it takes to make the traditional version.

> 1 tablespoon canola oil
> 2 (¾-pound) turkey tenderloins
> ½ cup finely chopped onion
> 1 garlic clove, minced
> 1 cup fat-free, less-sodium chicken broth
> 1 tablespoon unsweetened cocoa
> 1 tablespoon chopped chipotle chile, canned in adobo sauce
> 1 tablespoon tomato paste
> 1 teaspoon ground cumin
> ¼ teaspoon salt
> Chopped fresh cilantro (optional)

1. Heat oil in a large nonstick skillet over medium-high heat. Add turkey, and cook 3 minutes on each side or until browned. Remove turkey from pan, and keep warm. Add onion and garlic to pan; sauté 2 minutes or until tender. Stir in broth and next 5 ingredients.

2. Nestle turkey into broth mixture; turn to coat. Cover and bring to a boil; reduce heat, and simmer 3 to 4 minutes or until a thermometer registers 165°.

3. Remove turkey from pan, and cut diagonally into ½-inch-thick slices. Serve turkey with sauce. Sprinkle with cilantro, if desired. **YIELD: 4 SERVINGS (SERVING SIZE: ABOUT 5 OUNCES TURKEY AND ¼ CUP SAUCE).**

PER SERVING: Calories 235; Fat 6.3g (sat 0.4g, mono 2.1g, poly 1.1g); Protein 43.1g; Carb 4.5g; Fiber 1.4g; Chol 68mg; Iron 2.8mg; Sodium 443mg; Calc 13mg

TURKEY FLORENTINE SKILLET LASAGNA

POINTS value: 5 *(pictured on page 133)*

PREP: 5 minutes ▪ **COOK:** 14 minutes
▪ **OTHER:** 5 minutes

This easy skillet supper received our Test Kitchens' highest rating. We used packaged precooked lasagna noodles to speed prep time and allow the flavors of the sauce to soak into them while they cook.

> Cooking spray
> ¾ pound ground turkey breast
> 1 cup chopped onion
> 1 (16-ounce) carton 2% low-fat cottage cheese
> 1 (10-ounce) package frozen chopped spinach, thawed, drained, and squeezed dry
> 4 cups tomato-basil pasta sauce, divided
> 10 packaged precooked lasagna noodles (such as Barilla)
> 1½ cups (6 ounces) preshredded reduced-fat 6-cheese Italian blend

1. Heat a large deep skillet over medium-high heat. Coat pan with cooking spray. Add turkey and onion to pan; cook 4 minutes or until turkey is browned and onion is tender, stirring frequently to crumble turkey.

2. While turkey and onion cook, place cottage cheese in a food processor or blender; process until smooth.

3. Add spinach and 3 cups pasta sauce to turkey mixture. Cook 1 minute or until thoroughly heated, stirring constantly. Remove from pan, and keep warm.

4. Add remaining 1 cup pasta sauce to pan. Top with 5 noodles, half of turkey mixture, half of cottage cheese, and half of cheese blend. Repeat with remaining noodles, turkey mixture, cottage cheese, and cheese blend. Cover and cook on medium heat 8 minutes or until noodles are tender. Remove from heat; let stand 5 minutes before serving. **YIELD: 8 SERVINGS (SERVING SIZE: ⅛ OF CASSEROLE).**

PER SERVING: Calories 277; Fat 8.1g (sat 3.3g, mono 0g, poly 0.1g); Protein 21.3g; Carb 30.2g; Fiber 4.3g; Chol 38mg; Iron 1.9mg; Sodium 612mg; Calc 305mg

PENNE AND PEPPERS WITH TURKEY SAUSAGE

POINTS value: 6

PREP: 4 minutes ■ **COOK:** 11 minutes

The Greek seasoning used in this pasta dish is a leafy herb blend in a bottle; don't look for powdered seasoning. The bottled variety lifts the flavors of this simple skillet dinner.

6 ounces uncooked multigrain penne pasta (such as Barilla Plus)
8 ounces reduced-fat smoked turkey sausage (such as Oscar Mayer), cut into ¼-inch slices
Cooking spray
2 cups refrigerated presliced green, yellow, and red bell pepper mix
2 teaspoons Greek seasoning (such as McCormick)
¼ teaspoon salt
¼ teaspoon black pepper
2 tablespoons water
⅓ cup (1.3 ounces) preshredded fresh Parmesan cheese

1. Cook pasta according to package directions, omitting salt and fat; drain.
2. While pasta cooks, cook sausage in a large nonstick skillet over medium-high heat 6 minutes or until browned; drain. Wipe drippings from pan with a paper towel. Coat pan with cooking spray. Add bell pepper mix and next 3 ingredients. Sauté 4 minutes or until crisp-tender. Add 2 tablespoons water, stirring to loosen browned bits.
3. Stir in pasta and sausage; add cheese, and toss gently. Serve immediately. **YIELD: 4 SERVINGS (SERVING SIZE: 1½ CUPS).**

PER SERVING: Calories 315; Fat 10.4g (sat 3.6g, mono 0g, poly 0.1g); Protein 19.4g; Carb 37.3g; Fiber 4.5g; Chol 39mg; Iron 2.4mg; Sodium 956mg; Calc 124mg

APRICOT-CHIPOTLE–GLAZED CORNISH HENS

POINTS value: 4

PREP: 4 minutes ■ **COOK:** 47 minutes

Removing the calorie-laden skin of the hens allows the sweet and spicy glaze to cook into the hens and provides more flavor.

2 (1¼-pound) Cornish hens
Cooking spray
¼ teaspoon salt
¼ teaspoon freshly ground black pepper
½ cup low-sugar apricot preserves (such as Smucker's)
2 tablespoons chopped green onions
1 tablespoon minced chipotle chile, canned in adobo sauce
1½ teaspoons less-sodium soy sauce

1. Preheat oven to 350°.
2. Remove and discard giblets and necks from hens. Rinse hens with cold water; pat dry. Remove skin; trim excess fat. Split hens in half lengthwise. Place hen halves, meaty sides up, in a shallow roasting pan coated with cooking spray. Sprinkle hen halves evenly with salt and pepper.
3. Combine preserves and next 3 ingredients in a small saucepan. Cook 2 minutes over medium-low heat or until preserves melt. Brush hen halves with half of glaze.
4. Bake at 350° for 45 minutes or until a thermometer registers 170°, basting occasionally with remaining glaze. **YIELD: 4 SERVINGS (SERVING SIZE: 1 HEN HALF).**

PER SERVING: Calories 196; Fat 4.1g (sat 1g, mono 1.3g, poly 1g); Protein 24.6g; Carb 12.9g; Fiber 0.5g; Chol 111mg; Iron 1mg; Sodium 346mg; Calc 18mg

salads

Watermelon and Red Onion Salad with Feta,
page 112

MARINATED BERRY SALAD

POINTS value: 1

PREP: 5 minutes

To save time, look for packages of mixed berries in the produce section of your supermarket. Adding the optional rum to this fruit salad doesn't change the **POINTS** value per serving.

- 1 large lime
- ¼ cup water
- 1 tablespoon chopped mint
- 2 tablespoons honey
- 2 tablespoons light rum (optional)
- 1 cup sliced strawberries
- ½ cup raspberries
- ½ cup blueberries
- ½ cup blackberries

1. Grate 1 teaspoon rind and squeeze 1½ tablespoons juice from lime. Place rind and juice in a medium bowl. Add ¼ cup water, mint, honey, and rum, if desired, stirring with a whisk until blended. Add berries, and toss gently to coat. YIELD: 4 SERVINGS (SERVING SIZE: ABOUT ⅔ CUP).

PER SERVING: Calories 74; Fat 0.4g (sat 0g, mono 0.1g, poly 0.2g); Protein 0.9g; Carb 18.8g; Fiber 3.3g; Chol 0mg; Iron 0.5mg; Sodium 2mg; Calc 20mg

WATERMELON AND RED ONION SALAD WITH FETA

POINTS value: 2

PREP: 8 minutes

This unique salad contains the powerful antioxidant lycopene—it's found in the watermelon.

- 2 tablespoons white wine vinegar
- 1 tablespoon honey
- 2 teaspoons extra-virgin olive oil
- ¼ teaspoon salt
- ¼ teaspoon freshly ground black pepper
- 4 cups mixed salad greens
- 2 cups cubed watermelon
- ⅓ cup thinly sliced red onion
- ¼ cup (1 ounce) crumbled feta cheese

1. Combine first 5 ingredients in a medium bowl, stirring with a whisk. Add greens and remaining ingredients; toss gently to coat. Serve immediately. YIELD: 4 SERVINGS (SERVING SIZE: ABOUT 1½ CUPS).

PER SERVING: Calories 100; Fat 4.6g (sat 1.8g, mono 2.3g, poly 0.4g); Protein 2.9g; Carb 13.5g; Fiber 1.8g; Chol 8mg; Iron 1mg; Sodium 265mg; Calc 86mg

A GOOD USE FOR A SERRATED KNIFE

Cutting the bread into cubes in this recipe is easy if you use a serrated knife. With its scalloped, toothlike edge similar to a saw, this knife cuts cleanly through foods with a hard exterior and a softer interior, such as a loaf of crusty bread or toasted bread slices.

GRILLED VEGETABLE PANZANELLA

POINTS value: 3   *(pictured on page 135)*

PREP: 9 minutes ■ **COOK:** 12 minutes

This beautiful salad earned our Test Kitchens' highest rating. You can prepare the vegetables a day in advance. Place them in a zip-top plastic bag; seal bag, and store in the refrigerator until ready to grill. Grill the bread during the last few minutes of vegetable grill time.

- 1 yellow bell pepper
- 3 plum tomatoes
- 2 zucchini, cut in half lengthwise
- 1 large red onion, cut into 4 slices
- Olive oil–flavored cooking spray
- ½ (16-ounce) loaf sourdough bread, cut into 1-inch slices
- 2 tablespoons drained capers
- ⅓ cup light balsamic vinaigrette
- 1 tablespoon fresh lemon juice
- ⅛ teaspoon freshly ground black pepper
- 3 tablespoons chopped fresh basil or small fresh basil leaves (optional)

1. Prepare grill.
2. Cut bell pepper in half lengthwise; discard seeds and membranes. Coat bell pepper, tomatoes, zucchini, and onion slices with cooking spray. Place vegetables on grill rack coated with cooking spray; grill 12 to 15 minutes or until vegetables are slightly charred,

turning twice. Remove vegetables from grill. Cut vegetables into large chunks.

3. While vegetables grill, coat bread slices with cooking spray. Place bread slices on grill rack; grill 2 to 3 minutes on each side. Cut bread into 1-inch cubes to measure 4½ cups.

4. Combine vegetables, bread cubes, and capers in a large bowl. Combine vinaigrette and lemon juice; pour over vegetable mixture, and toss well. Sprinkle with freshly ground black pepper and, if desired, basil. **YIELD: 6 SERVINGS (SERVING SIZE: 1½ CUPS).**

PER SERVING: Calories 155; Fat 3.1g (sat 0.3g, mono 0g, poly 0.4g); Protein 5.3g; Carb 28.7g; Fiber 3.2g; Chol 0mg; Iron 2.2mg; Sodium 520mg; Calc 60mg

FRESH MOZZARELLA AND ARUGULA SALAD WITH PROSCIUTTO

POINTS value: 4

PREP: 7 minutes

Ciliegine mozzarella is a cherry tomato–shaped fresh mozzarella found in the specialty cheese section of most supermarkets.

  2 tablespoons sherry vinegar
  1 tablespoon minced shallots
1½ teaspoons Dijon mustard
  ⅛ teaspoon salt
  ⅛ teaspoon freshly ground black pepper
  2 tablespoons olive oil
  1 (5-ounce) package arugula
 12 balls (4.5 ounces) ciliegine mozzarella cheese, halved
 12 grape tomatoes, halved
  2 ounces thinly sliced prosciutto (4 slices)

1. Combine first 5 ingredients in a small bowl, stirring with a whisk. Add oil, stirring to combine.

2. Divide arugula among 4 plates. Top evenly with cheese, tomato, and prosciutto. Drizzle salads with dressing. **YIELD: 4 SERVINGS (SERVING SIZE: 1½ CUPS ARUGULA, 6 TOMATO HALVES, 6 CHEESE BALL HALVES, 1 SLICE PROSCIUTTO, AND 1½ TABLESPOONS VINAIGRETTE).**

PER SERVING: Calories 177; Fat 13.4g (sat 4.3g, mono 5.6g, poly 1g); Protein 11.4g; Carb 4.1g; Fiber 1.3g; Chol 8mg; Iron 0.8mg; Sodium 371mg; Calc 204mg

CREAMY CUCUMBER AND OLIVE SALAD

POINTS value: 1

PREP: 8 minutes

To make prep time even shorter, use English cucumbers in this recipe. They have thinner skins that don't require peeling, and their seeds are so tiny you won't have to seed them either. You'll need 2½ cups of slices.

  ⅓ cup plain fat-free Greek yogurt
  1 tablespoon chopped fresh mint
  1 teaspoon grated lemon rind
  1 tablespoon fresh lemon juice
  ¼ teaspoon sugar
  ¼ teaspoon salt
  ¼ teaspoon freshly ground black pepper
  2 medium cucumbers, peeled, halved lengthwise, and seeded
  ¼ cup thinly sliced red onion
  ¼ cup halved pitted kalamata olives

1. Combine first 7 ingredients in a medium bowl, stirring with a whisk. Cut cucumber halves crosswise into ¼-inch-thick slices; add to dressing. Add onion and olives, tossing to coat. **YIELD: 4 SERVINGS (SERVING SIZE: ¾ CUP).**

PER SERVING: Calories 53; Fat 2.5g (sat 0.3g, mono 1.8g, poly 0.3g); Protein 2.5g; Carb 5.3g; Fiber 1g; Chol 0mg; Iron 0.3mg; Sodium 299mg; Calc 34mg

HOW TO SEED A CUCUMBER

When purchasing cucumbers, remember that the smaller the cucumber, the smaller the seeds and the better the flavor. To seed a cucumber, simply cut it in half lengthwise and scrape out the seeds with a spoon.

GREEK SLAW

POINTS value: 1

PREP: 3 minutes ■ **OTHER:** 10 minutes

Stuff this fresh-tasting slaw in half a pita pocket atop grilled chicken for a tasty sandwich.

2½ cups packaged angel hair slaw
⅓ cup (1.3 ounces) crumbled feta cheese
3 tablespoons fat-free Greek dressing (such as Maple Grove Farms)
2 tablespoons chopped pitted kalamata olives
½ teaspoon chopped fresh oregano
¼ teaspoon freshly ground black pepper

1. Combine all ingredients in a medium bowl; toss well. Let stand 10 minutes or until ready to serve. **YIELD: 4 SERVINGS (SERVING SIZE:** ½ **CUP).**

PER SERVING: Calories 62; Fat 3.8g (sat 2g, mono 1.5g, poly 0.2g); Protein 2.3g; Carb 4.2g; Fiber 1.1g; Chol 11mg; Iron 0.1mg; Sodium 310mg; Calc 64mg

BLUE CHEESE–BACON SLAW

POINTS value: 1

PREP: 5 minutes ■ **COOK:** 2 minutes

The cooling combination of buttermilk and blue cheese makes this a great partner for spicy barbecue or hot wings. You can make it up to 2 hours ahead. Just cover and chill until ready to serve.

½ cup nonfat buttermilk
3 tablespoons low-fat mayonnaise
¼ teaspoon salt
¼ teaspoon freshly ground black pepper
1 (16-ounce) package shredded coleslaw mix
⅓ cup (1.3 ounces) crumbled blue cheese
3 center-cut bacon slices, cooked and crumbled

1. Combine first 4 ingredients in a large bowl, stirring with a spoon until smooth. Add coleslaw mix and cheese, stirring well to coat. Sprinkle with crumbled bacon. **YIELD: 8 SERVINGS (SERVING SIZE: ABOUT** ⅔ **CUP).**

PER SERVING: Calories 56; Fat 2.5g (sat 1.2g, mono 0.4g, poly 0.2g); Protein 3.2g; Carb 5.1g; Fiber 1.4g; Chol 6mg; Iron 0.3mg; Sodium 257mg; Calc 75mg

CENTER-CUT BACON NUTRITION

Because it's cut from closer to the bone, center-cut bacon has approximately 20 percent less saturated fat than regular bacon with the same satisfying, smoky flavor. It's also modest in calories—three pieces contain about 70 calories total.

"FRESH" CORN SALAD

POINTS value: 2

PREP: 5 minutes ■ **COOK:** 1 minute

Frozen baby corn tastes sweeter than regular frozen whole-kernel corn and is the next best thing to fresh corn cut from the cob. This fresh-tasting salad is delicious next to a piece of grilled fish or chicken.

1 (16-ounce) package frozen baby white and yellow corn
¼ cup white wine vinegar
2 tablespoons olive oil
2 teaspoons sugar
¼ teaspoon salt
¼ teaspoon freshly ground black pepper
1 (8-ounce) package refrigerated prechopped tricolor bell pepper
⅓ cup sliced green onions (about 3 small)
¼ cup chopped fresh basil (optional)

1. Place corn in a medium bowl. Microwave at HIGH 1 to 2 minutes or just until thawed. Combine vinegar and next 4 ingredients in another medium bowl. Stir in corn, bell pepper, onions, and, if desired, basil. **YIELD: 8 SERVINGS (SERVING SIZE:** ½ **CUP).**

PER SERVING: Calories 103; Fat 4.1g (sat 0.5g, mono 2.5g, poly 0.4g); Protein 2.1g; Carb 15.1g; Fiber 1.9g; Chol 0mg; Iron 0.4mg; Sodium 75mg; Calc 6mg

DIJON ROASTED POTATO SALAD

POINTS value: 2

PREP: 6 minutes ■ **COOK:** 20 minutes

Roasting the potatoes instead of boiling them brings a new flavor dimension to standard potato salad.

 1 pound small red potatoes, quartered
 2 teaspoons olive oil
 ¼ teaspoon salt
 ¼ teaspoon black pepper
 ¼ cup low-fat mayonnaise
 3 tablespoons white wine vinegar
 1 teaspoon sugar
 1 teaspoon Dijon mustard
 1 garlic clove, pressed
 ½ cup chopped red bell pepper
 ½ cup chopped celery
 ¼ cup chopped green onions

1. Preheat oven to 450°.
2. Combine first 4 ingredients on a large, rimmed baking sheet; toss to coat potatoes. Bake at 450° for 20 minutes or until lightly browned and tender, stirring after 15 minutes.
3. While potatoes roast, combine mayonnaise and next 4 ingredients in a large bowl, stirring with a whisk. Add bell pepper, celery, onions, and roasted potatoes; toss well. **YIELD: 6 SERVINGS (SERVING SIZE: ½ CUP).**

PER SERVING: Calories 87; Fat 2.3g (sat 0.2g, mono 1.1g, poly 0.6g); Protein 1.7g; Carb 15.9g; Fiber 1.9g; Chol 0mg; Iron 0.7mg; Sodium 218mg; Calc 17mg

ROASTING

Roasting may be one of the easiest cooking techniques because your oven does all the work for you. This cooking method involves cooking food in an uncovered pan in the oven. Dry, hot air surrounds the food, cooking it evenly on all sides. Roasting is ideal for cooking dense vegetables, like potatoes, beets, and winter squash, because it concentrates the vegetables' natural sugars and intensifies their flavor while creating a nice browned surface.

WHITE BEAN AND BULGUR SALAD

POINTS value: 3

PREP: 3 minutes ■ **COOK:** 15 minutes

Bulgur, fresh veggies, and white beans make this a filling meatless salad.

 2 cups water
 ¾ teaspoon salt, divided
 1 cup quick-cooking bulgur
 1 large lemon
 1 tablespoon olive oil
 ⅛ teaspoon black pepper
 2½ cups chopped tomato (1 large)
 1 cup chopped peeled cucumber (1 medium)
 ¼ cup chopped fresh flat-leaf parsley
 ¼ cup minced red onion
 1 (15.5-ounce) can cannellini beans, rinsed and drained
 ½ cup (2 ounces) crumbled reduced-fat feta cheese

1. Place 2 cups water and ½ teaspoon salt in a medium saucepan; bring to a boil. Stir in bulgur; cover, reduce heat to medium, and simmer 12 minutes or until tender. Drain well.
2. While bulgur cooks, grate 2 teaspoons rind and squeeze ¼ cup juice from lemon. Place rind and juice in a large bowl. Add olive oil, remaining ¼ teaspoon salt, and pepper, stirring with a whisk. Stir in bulgur, tomato, and next 4 ingredients. Sprinkle with feta cheese; toss gently. **YIELD: 7 SERVINGS (SERVING SIZE: 1 CUP).**

PER SERVING: Calories 163; Fat 3.8g (sat 1.2g, mono 1.4g, poly 0.4g); Protein 7g; Carb 26.7g; Fiber 6.6g; Chol 3mg; Iron 1.5mg; Sodium 318mg; Calc 60mg

Bulgur

Bulgur comes from the kernels of wheat, known as wheat berries, that have been steamed, dried, and then cracked. You can find bulgur at most supermarkets or in Middle Eastern markets and natural-food stores.

ISRAELI COUSCOUS AND VEGETABLE SALAD

POINTS value: 8

PREP: 7 minutes ■ COOK: 11 minutes

For the mixed herbs in the vinaigrette, we used a combination of 2 tablespoons chopped fresh chives and 1 tablespoon, each, chopped fresh parsley, basil, and mint.

1½ cups Israeli couscous
2½ cups fat-free, less-sodium chicken broth
1 cup diced cucumber
1 cup diced seeded plum tomato
Lemon-Herb Vinaigrette
Freshly ground black pepper (optional)

1. Cook couscous in a large deep skillet over medium-high heat 2 minutes or until toasted; stir in broth. Bring to a boil; reduce heat, and simmer 8 minutes or until broth is absorbed, stirring occasionally. Remove from heat; stir in cucumber, tomato, and Lemon-Herb Vinaigrette. Serve warm or at room temperature with freshly ground black pepper, if desired. **YIELD: 5 SERVINGS (SERVING SIZE: 1 CUP).**

PER SERVING: Calories 366; Fat 12.1g (sat 3g, mono 6.5g, poly 0.8g); Protein 12.5g; Carb 51.9g; Fiber 3.5g; Chol 6mg; Iron 0.3mg; Sodium 676mg; Calc 60mg

Lemon-Herb Vinaigrette

POINTS value: 1

3 tablespoons extra-virgin olive oil
2 tablespoons fresh lemon juice
½ teaspoon freshly ground black pepper
¼ teaspoon salt
¾ cup (3 ounces) crumbled reduced-fat feta cheese
5 tablespoons chopped mixed fresh herbs

1. Combine first 4 ingredients in a medium bowl, stirring with a whisk. Stir in cheese and herbs. **YIELD: ¾ CUP (SERVING SIZE: 1 TABLESPOON).**

PER SERVING: Calories 50; Fat 4.6g (sat 1.2g, mono 2.7g, poly 0.3g); Protein 1.8g; Carb 0.6g; Fiber 0.2g; Chol 3mg; Iron 0.1mg; Sodium 166mg; Calc 22mg

GRILLED STEAK AND APPLE SALAD WITH BLUE CHEESE VINAIGRETTE

POINTS value: 8

PREP: 8 minutes ■ COOK: 16 minutes
■ OTHER: 5 minutes

Creamy blue cheese vinaigrette gives a tangy bite to this salad topped with crunchy apples and tender slices of flank steak.

1 teaspoon freshly ground black pepper, divided
1 teaspoon chopped fresh thyme
¼ teaspoon salt
1 (1-pound) flank steak, trimmed
Cooking spray
1 large Granny Smith apple, cut into 4 wedges
8 cups arugula
Blue Cheese Vinaigrette

1. Prepare grill.
2. Combine first 3 ingredients; rub mixture over both sides of steak. Coat steak with cooking spray.
3. Place steak on grill rack coated with cooking spray. Grill 8 minutes on each side or until desired degree of doneness, adding apple to grill rack after 2 minutes. Grill apple 3 minutes on each side. Remove steak and apple from grill; loosely cover steak with foil, and let stand 5 minutes. Cut apple into thin slices.
4. Cut steak diagonally across grain into thin slices. Divide arugula evenly among 4 plates. Arrange steak and apple evenly over arugula; drizzle with Blue Cheese Vinaigrette. **YIELD: 4 SERVINGS (SERVING SIZE: 2 CUPS ARUGULA, 3 OUNCES STEAK, ¼ OF APPLE, AND 2 TABLESPOONS VINAIGRETTE).**

PER SERVING: Calories 317; Fat 18.5g (sat 4.5g, mono 9g, poly 3.5g); Protein 27.1g; Carb 10.1g; Fiber 1.5g; Chol 44mg; Iron 2.6mg; Sodium 462mg; Calc 133mg

✳ Cider Vinegar

Made from the juice of apples (or apple cider), cider vinegar is light brown in color. Although it's still quite sharp, it has a sweeter fruit flavor and is less acidic than most white wine vinegars. Cider vinegar is an excellent everyday vinegar to use when preparing salad dressings.

Blue Cheese Vinaigrette
POINTS value: 2

- ¼ cup (1 ounce) crumbled blue cheese
- ¼ cup cider vinegar
- 3 tablespoons canola oil
- ¼ teaspoon salt
- ⅛ teaspoon freshly ground black pepper

1. Combine all ingredients in a small bowl, stirring with a whisk. **YIELD: ½ CUP (SERVING SIZE: 1 TABLESPOON).**

PER SERVING: Calories 61; Fat 6.3g (sat 1g, mono 3.4g, poly 1.6g); Protein 0.8g; Carb 0.2g; Fiber 0g; Chol 3mg; Iron 0mg; Sodium 122mg; Calc 19mg

SOUTHWESTERN TACO SALAD
POINTS value: 8   (pictured on page 136)

PREP: 10 minutes ■ **COOK:** 14 minutes
■ **OTHER:** 10 minutes

Making homemade tortilla bowls is a fun and simple procedure. The bowls can be made ahead and yield a much healthier version than store-bought brands. You will need large custard cups for shaping the bowls.

- ½ pound flank steak, trimmed
- ½ teaspoon freshly ground black pepper
- ¼ teaspoon salt
- Cooking spray
- 4 (9¾-inch) low-carb whole-wheat tortillas (such as Mission)
- 2 teaspoons salt-free fiesta lime seasoning (such as Mrs. Dash)
- 5 cups torn romaine lettuce
- 1 (15-ounce) can reduced-sodium black beans (such as Bush's), rinsed and drained
- 1 small diced peeled avocado
- ½ cup frozen whole-kernel corn, thawed
- ¾ cup fresh salsa
- ¼ cup light sour cream
- ½ cup (2 ounces) reduced-fat shredded colby-Jack cheese

1. Prepare grill. Preheat oven to 375°.

2. Sprinkle flank steak with pepper and salt. Place steak on grill rack coated with cooking spray; grill 7 to 8 minutes on each side or until desired degree of doneness. Cut steak diagonally across grain into thin slices. Cover and keep warm.

3. While steak cooks, place 4 (10-ounce) custard cups, upside down, on a large baking sheet. Coat both sides of tortillas with cooking spray; sprinkle 1 side of tortillas evenly with seasoning. Place tortillas, seasoned sides down, over bottoms of custard cups. Gently press each tortilla down with another 10-ounce custard cup, leaving each tortilla sandwiched between 2 cups.

4. Bake at 375° for 10 minutes. Carefully remove top custard cups, using tongs and an oven mitt. Bake tortillas on custard cups an additional 4 to 5 minutes or until centers are barely toasted. Remove tortilla bowls from cups, and cool on a wire rack.

5. Combine lettuce and next 3 ingredients, tossing gently. Combine salsa and sour cream. Divide lettuce mixture evenly among tortilla bowls; top with steak strips and salsa mixture. Sprinkle each serving with cheese. **YIELD: 4 SERVINGS (SERVING SIZE: 2¼ CUPS LETTUCE MIXTURE, ABOUT 1½ OUNCES STEAK, ¼ CUP SALSA MIXTURE, AND 2 TABLESPOONS CHEESE).**

PER SERVING: Calories 398; Fat 14.5g (sat 4.2g, mono 1.2g, poly 0.2g); Protein 25.8g; Carb 42.9g; Fiber 8.5g; Chol 24mg; Iron 3.7mg; Sodium 810mg; Calc 544mg

Romaine

Romaine is the lettuce of choice for a traditional Caesar salad. The leaves grow in heads, ranging from dark green outer leaves to yellowish green leaves at the heart. Baby romaine leaves, which are available prewashed in packages, offer the same pleasing, slightly bitter flavor of regular romaine. However, for the signature crunch that comes from a romaine leaf's center vein, stick with the full-sized version.

QUICK CHICKEN CAESAR SALAD

POINTS value: 6

PREP: 12 minutes ▪ **COOK:** 6 minutes

Garnish each salad with ¼ cup Caesar-flavored croutons for a nice crunch. The **POINTS** value will be 7.

7 chicken breast tenders (about 1 pound)
¼ teaspoon salt
¼ teaspoon pepper
2 tablespoons fresh lemon juice
Cooking spray
2 heads hearts of romaine lettuce
2 tomatoes, cut into wedges
Caesar Dressing
1 cup gourmet-cut Caesar-flavored croutons (such as Cardini's, optional)

1. Prepare grill.
2. Sprinkle chicken with salt and pepper; brush with lemon juice. Place on grill rack coated with cooking spray. Grill 3 to 4 minutes on each side or until done. Cut chicken into ½-inch slices.
3. Cut root ends from lettuce; cut in half crosswise. Separate lettuce leaves; rinse with cold water, drain, and pat dry. Divide lettuce leaves evenly among 4 plates. Place 3 tomato wedges on each plate. Top evenly with chicken slices. Drizzle dressing evenly over each salad. Top each with ¼ cup croutons, if desired.
YIELD: 4 SERVINGS.

PER SERVING: Calories 273; Fat 13.5g (sat 2.7g, mono 1.2g, poly 0.7g); Protein 26g; Carb 11g; Fiber 2.2g; Chol 78mg; Iron 2.4mg; Sodium 600mg; Calc 98mg

Caesar Dressing
POINTS value: 1

½ teaspoon minced garlic
1 canned anchovy fillet in oil, rinsed and drained
½ cup light mayonnaise
2 tablespoons grated fresh Parmesan cheese
2 tablespoons water
2 teaspoons fresh lemon juice
2 teaspoons Dijon mustard
1 teaspoon Worcestershire sauce
Dash of freshly ground black pepper

1. Mash garlic and anchovy to a paste in a bowl, using a fork. Stir in mayonnaise and remaining ingredients.
YIELD: ⅔ CUP (SERVING SIZE: ABOUT 1 TABLESPOON).

PER SERVING: Calories 43; Fat 3.9g (sat 0.7g, mono 0.1g, poly 0g); Protein 0.5g; Carb 1.4g; Fiber 0g; Chol 5mg; Iron 0.1mg; Sodium 142mg; Calc 11mg

CHICKEN AND STRAWBERRY SALAD

POINTS value: 4   *(pictured on page 134)*

PREP: 5 minutes

Here's one of the prettiest salads of the season. Honey-roasted almonds add a crunchy sweet surprise topping.

2 cups chopped cooked chicken
1 cup sliced strawberries
⅓ cup (1.3 ounces) crumbled reduced-fat feta cheese
1 (11-ounce) can mandarin oranges in light syrup, drained
1 (6-ounce) package baby spinach
¼ cup fat-free poppy seed dressing (such as Maple Grove Farms)
6 tablespoons honey-roasted sliced almonds (such as Almond Accents)

1. Combine first 5 ingredients in a large bowl. Drizzle with dressing; toss well. Divide salad among 6 plates; sprinkle each serving with 1 tablespoon almonds.
YIELD: 6 SERVINGS.

PER SERVING: Calories 187; Fat 6.3g (sat 1.2g, mono 0.6g, poly 0.4g); Protein 18.4g; Carb 14g; Fiber 1.6g; Chol 42mg; Iron 1.7mg; Sodium 270mg; Calc 75mg

SOUTHEAST ASIAN CHICKEN SALAD CUPS

POINTS value: 4

PREP: 9 minutes ■ **COOK:** 17 minutes

This quick, refreshing salad tantalizes the palate with fragrant lemongrass and a tangy, sweet sauce. Find lemongrass paste in a tube located with fresh herbs in the produce section. Choose lettuce leaves that form a "bowl" for the chicken mixture.

½ cup fresh lime juice
2 tablespoons sweet chili sauce (such as Maggi)
1 tablespoon fish sauce
½ cup fat-free, less-sodium chicken broth
1 pound ground chicken
½ cup thinly sliced green onions
1 teaspoon lemongrass paste
½ teaspoon crushed red pepper
1 English cucumber, halved lengthwise, seeded, and sliced
½ cup sliced red onion
8 Boston lettuce leaves

1. Combine first 3 ingredients in a small bowl, and set aside.
2. Bring chicken broth to a boil in a large nonstick skillet; add chicken and next 3 ingredients. Reduce heat, and simmer, uncovered, 15 minutes. Drain.
3. Combine chicken mixture, cucumber, and onion; stir in lime juice mixture. Spoon evenly into lettuce cups. **YIELD: 4 SERVINGS (SERVING SIZE: 2 LETTUCE CUPS).**

PER SERVING: Calories 200; Fat 9.5g (sat 2.5g, mono 0.4g, poly 0.4g); Protein 19.9g; Carb 11.3g; Fiber 1.7g; Chol 75mg; Iron 0.7mg; Sodium 581mg; Calc 37mg

ASIAN CHICKEN SALAD

POINTS value: 5

PREP: 10 minutes

Crinkly napa (Chinese) cabbage adds extra crunch to this salad. Look for firm cabbages with crisp, bright green leaves.

⅓ cup light sesame-ginger dressing (such as Newman's Own)
2 navel oranges
4 cups chopped romaine lettuce
3 cups shredded cooked chicken breast
2 cups shredded napa (Chinese) cabbage
1 cup thinly sliced snow peas
½ cup matchstick-cut carrots
¼ cup sliced almonds, toasted (optional)

1. Place dressing in a large bowl. Grate rind from 1 orange to measure 1 teaspoon; stir into dressing. Peel oranges and cut in half lengthwise. Cut orange halves crosswise into ¼-inch-thick slices.
2. Add orange slices, lettuce, and next 4 ingredients to dressing; toss well. Sprinkle with almonds, if desired.
YIELD: 4 SERVINGS (SERVING SIZE: ABOUT 2¾ CUPS).

PER SERVING: Calories 259; Fat 5.1g (sat 1.1g, mono 1.3g, poly 0.9g); Protein 34.9g; Carb 18g; Fiber 4.2g; Chol 89mg; Iron 2.2mg; Sodium 350mg; Calc 88mg

NAPA CABBAGE NUTRITION

A cup of napa (Chinese) cabbage contains small amounts of calcium, fiber, and vitamin C. And, like other cabbage and cruciferous vegetables, napa cabbage contains compounds called indoles, which research suggests may help prevent some cancers.

DILL CHICKEN SALAD

POINTS value: 6

PREP: 6 minutes

Chicken salad is always a great way to use leftover roasted chicken, but this salad is so good, you may want to roast a chicken, or pick one up from the deli, just to make this recipe.

¼ cup light mayonnaise
1 tablespoon Dijon mustard
2 teaspoons finely chopped fresh dill
2 teaspoons chopped fresh chives
¼ teaspoon seasoned salt
2 cups chopped cooked chicken breast
⅔ cup red grape halves
¼ cup chopped pecans, toasted
Mixed greens (optional)
Whole-wheat bread (optional)

1. Combine first 5 ingredients in a medium bowl, stirring well with a spoon. Stir in chicken, grape halves, and pecans. Serve over mixed greens or as a sandwich filling, if desired. **YIELD: 4 SERVINGS (SERVING SIZE: ¾ CUP).**

PER SERVING: Calories 239; Fat 12.8g (sat 1.9g, mono 3.9g, poly 2.2g); Protein 22.7g; Carb 7.9g; Fiber 1g; Chol 65mg; Iron 1.1mg; Sodium 349mg; Calc 20mg

✳ Fresh vs. Dried Dill

This herb has been used for centuries. Its feathery leaves lend a fresh, sharp flavor to a variety of foods. This is an herb that maintains good flavor when it's dried, so if you don't have fresh dill, substitute 1 teaspoon of dried dill for each tablespoon of fresh called for in a recipe.

ROASTED ASPARAGUS–TURKEY SALAD WITH DIJON VINAIGRETTE

POINTS value: 3

PREP: 6 minutes ■ **COOK:** 8 minutes

Roasted asparagus teams with turkey and tomatoes in this fresh one-dish meal.

1 pound fresh asparagus spears
Olive oil–flavored cooking spray
¼ teaspoon salt, divided
3 tablespoons fresh lemon juice
3 tablespoons olive oil
1 teaspoon Dijon mustard
⅛ teaspoon freshly ground black pepper
1 (6.5-ounce) package sweet butter lettuce blend (such as Fresh Express)
12 ounces oven-roasted skinless turkey breast (such as Boar's Head Golden), coarsely chopped
1 cup thinly sliced red onion
1 cup cherry tomatoes, halved

1. Preheat oven to 450°.
2. Snap off tough ends of asparagus. Place asparagus on a baking sheet coated with cooking spray. Coat asparagus with cooking spray; sprinkle with ⅛ teaspoon salt. Bake at 450° for 8 minutes. Cut asparagus into 2-inch pieces.
3. While asparagus cooks, combine remaining ⅛ teaspoon salt, lemon juice, and next 3 ingredients in a large bowl, stirring with a whisk. Add lettuce and next 3 ingredients; toss well. Add asparagus, and toss gently. **YIELD: 6 SERVINGS (SERVING SIZE: 1⅔ CUPS).**

PER SERVING: Calories 161; Fat 8.2g (sat 1g, mono 4.9g, poly 0.8g); Protein 15.7g; Carb 7.6g; Fiber 2.6g; Chol 25mg; Iron 2.6mg; Sodium 467mg; Calc 36mg

sandwiches

Cobb Salad Panini, *page 126*

"PIMIENTO" CHEESE AND SPINACH QUESADILLAS

POINTS value: 6

PREP: 10 minutes ■ COOK: 9 minutes

Roasted red bell pepper stands in for the expected pimiento in this crispy spinach quesadilla oozing cheese.

- ½ cup drained bottled roasted red bell pepper, sliced
- 1 tablespoon low-fat mayonnaise
- 1 (8-ounce) package 50% reduced-fat jalapeño cheddar cheese (such as Cabot), shredded
- 4 (8-inch) 96% fat-free whole-wheat tortillas (such as Mission)
- 1 cup bagged fresh baby spinach
- Cooking spray
- ¼ cup fresh salsa (optional)

1. Combine first 3 ingredients in a medium bowl. Spread cheese mixture evenly on 1 side of each tortilla. Top each with ¼ cup spinach leaves. Fold each tortilla in half.
2. Heat a large nonstick skillet over medium-high heat. Coat pan with cooking spray. Place 2 tortillas, folded edges together, in pan. Coat tops of tortillas with cooking spray. Cook 2 to 3 minutes on each side or until lightly browned and cheese melts. Remove from pan, and keep warm. Repeat procedure with remaining tortillas. Cut each quesadilla in half; serve each quesadilla with 1 tablespoon salsa, if desired.

YIELD: 4 SERVINGS (SERVING SIZE: 1 QUESADILLA).

PER SERVING: Calories 282; Fat 11.4g (sat 6.1g, mono 0g, poly 1.1g); Protein 20.3g; Carb 28.7g; Fiber 3.1g; Chol 30mg; Iron 0.2mg; Sodium 807mg; Calc 411mg

THE HISTORY OF FALAFEL

Falafel is made from chickpeas (sometimes called garbanzo beans) and a variety of spices that gives it an intense flavor. It's then shaped into balls or patties and fried, although in this recipe we've pan-fried the patties to keep them light. Although it's been called "Israel's National Snack," falafel has an unclear origin. Citizens of Palestine, Israel, and Egypt claim to be the creators of the internationally known dish. Early Egyptians made falafel from fava beans, and later cooks substituted chickpeas for the beans.

FALAFEL SANDWICHES WITH TAHINI SAUCE

POINTS value: 7

PREP: 8 minutes ■ COOK: 28 minutes
■ OTHER: 30 minutes

Highly seasoned chickpea patties are nestled in pita halves, then drizzled with a sesame seed sauce. Pitas from a local bakery or Middle Eastern market will be fresher and easier to split than those found in the grocery store.

- 1½ tablespoons olive oil, divided
- 1 cup finely chopped onion (about 1 large)
- 3 garlic cloves, coarsely chopped
- 1 teaspoon ground cumin
- ½ teaspoon ground coriander
- 4 ounces white bread, torn into large pieces
- 2 tablespoons chopped fresh cilantro
- ¼ teaspoon salt
- ¼ teaspoon freshly ground black pepper
- 1 (16-ounce) can chickpeas (garbanzo beans), rinsed and drained
- 1 large egg
- Tahini Sauce
- Cooking spray
- 2 (6-inch) whole-wheat pitas, cut in half
- 4 romaine lettuce leaves
- 4 (¼-inch-thick) slices tomato
- 8 cucumber slices

1. Heat 1½ teaspoons oil in a large nonstick skillet over medium heat. Add onion, and sauté 4 minutes. Add garlic, and sauté 1 minute. Add cumin and coriander, and sauté 1 minute.

2. Place onion mixture, bread, and next 5 ingredients in a food processor; pulse 5 to 6 times until mixture is coarsely ground. Cover and chill at least 30 minutes.

3. While chickpea mixture chills, prepare Tahini Sauce.

4. Shape chickpea mixture into 8 (½-inch-thick) patties on a sheet of wax paper (mixture will be sticky). Heat 1½ teaspoons oil in a large nonstick skillet coated with cooking spray over medium-high heat. Add 4 patties, and cook 5 minutes on each side or until lightly browned. Remove patties from pan; keep warm. Repeat procedure with remaining 1½ teaspoons oil and remaining 4 patties.

5. Line each pita half with 1 lettuce leaf, 1 tomato slice, and 2 cucumber slices. Fill each pita half with 2 falafel patties; drizzle 2 tablespoons Tahini Sauce over each pita half. **YIELD: 4 SERVINGS (SERVING SIZE: 1 PITA HALF).**

PER SERVING: Calories 357; Fat 10.7g (sat 1.2g, mono 5.2g, poly 2.4g); Protein 13.4g; Carb 55.1g; Fiber 8.2g; Chol 53mg; Iron 3.7mg; Sodium 753mg; Calc 99mg

Tahini Sauce
POINTS value: 1

¼ **cup tahini (sesame seed paste)**
¼ **cup water**
2 **tablespoons chopped fresh parsley**
2 **tablespoons fresh lemon juice**
1 **teaspoon minced garlic**
¼ **teaspoon salt**
⅛ **teaspoon ground red pepper**

1. Combine all ingredients in a food processor; process until smooth. **YIELD: ½ CUP (SERVING SIZE: 1 TABLESPOON).**

PER SERVING: Calories 46; Fat 4g (sat 0.6g, mono 1.5g, poly 1.8g); Protein 1.4g; Carb 2.1g; Fiber 0.4g; Chol 0mg; Iron 0.4mg; Sodium 76mg; Calc 13mg

HOT OPEN-FACED ITALIAN TOMATO SANDWICHES
POINTS value: 4

PREP: 2 minutes ■ **COOK:** 13 minutes

Sprouted-grain breads are made from wheat berries that have just begun to sprout. When wheat sprouts, the grain changes nutritionally, so it's higher in protein, fiber, and certain vitamins and minerals. Look for this bread in the freezer section.

2 **(3-ounce) 7-sprouted-grains English muffins (such as Food for Life), split**
1 **cup arugula**
1 **medium heirloom tomato, cut into 4 slices**
¼ **cup chopped pitted kalamata olives**
4 **ounces fresh mozzarella cheese, cut into 4 slices**
2 **teaspoons balsamic vinegar**
Freshly ground black pepper (optional)

1. Preheat oven to 400°.

2. Place English muffin halves on a baking sheet. Bake at 400° for 7 minutes or until lightly browned.

3. Top each muffin half with ¼ cup arugula, 1 tomato slice, 1 tablespoon olives, and 1 slice cheese.

4. Bake at 400° for 6 minutes or until cheese melts. Remove from oven and sprinkle each sandwich with ½ teaspoon vinegar and black pepper, if desired. Serve immediately. **YIELD: 4 SERVINGS (SERVING SIZE: 1 OPEN-FACED SANDWICH).**

PER SERVING: Calories 198; Fat 9.5g (sat 4.4g, mono 1.8g, poly 0.3g); Protein 9.8g; Carb 19.9g; Fiber 3.7g; Chol 22mg; Iron 1.2mg; Sodium 309mg; Calc 178mg

✳ Heirloom Tomatoes
Heirloom tomatoes are some of the summer's most beautiful gems. They come in a variety of shades, such as purple, yellow, orange, and red. In addition to the array of colors these tomatoes bring to the table, they also come in an assortment of sizes, from grape-sized to hefty globes.

JALAPEÑO RANCH BURGERS

POINTS value: 7   *(pictured on page 138)*

PREP: 4 minutes ■ **COOK:** 15 minutes

This indulgent burger gets a subtle kick from jalapeños inside the patties, but melted cheese, cool ranch dressing, and smoky bacon take center stage. Serve with sweet potato fries or Baked Onion Rings on page 150.

  1 pound ground sirloin
  2 tablespoons minced pickled jalapeño pepper
  ½ teaspoon garlic powder
  Cooking spray
  4 (0.5-ounce) slices reduced-fat Monterey Jack cheese with jalapeño peppers
  ¼ cup refrigerated light ranch dressing (such as Naturally Fresh)
  4 (1.8-ounce) white wheat hamburger buns
  4 green leaf lettuce leaves
  4 tomato slices
  4 center-cut bacon slices, cooked

1. Prepare grill.
2. Combine first 3 ingredients in a large bowl; shape into 4 (½-inch-thick) patties. Place patties on grill rack coated with cooking spray. Grill 7 minutes on each side or until done. Top patties with cheese; cook 1 minute or until cheese melts.
3. Spread 1 tablespoon dressing on cut sides of bun tops. Place patties on bottom halves of buns; top with lettuce leaves, tomato slices, bacon slices, and bun tops. **YIELD: 4 SERVINGS (SERVING SIZE: 1 BURGER).**

PER SERVING: Calories 339; Fat 14.9g (sat 5g, mono 2g, poly 1.5g); Protein 32.8g; Carb 24.7g; Fiber 5.3g; Chol 80mg; Iron 1.9mg; Sodium 745mg; Calc 412mg

AVOIDING TEARS

Slicing onions doesn't have to bring you to tears. To avoid a major portion of tear-inducing gases, leave the root end of the onion intact until the very end of the slicing process. Also, be sure to chill the onion before you begin slicing. A cold onion gives off fewer gases than a room temperature one. First, slice off the top of the onion, and then remove the papery skin and slice the onion in half.

PATTY MELTS

POINTS value: 7   *(pictured on page 134)*

PREP: 5 minutes ■ **COOK:** 25 minutes

A traditional patty melt has a **POINTS** value of 23. In our version of this classic diner sandwich, we've shaved off a noticeable amount of fat and calories, but our version is just as tasty and comforting. Serve with fresh fruit.

  Cooking spray
  1½ cups thinly sliced sweet onion (about 1 small)
  ½ cup water
  1 pound ground sirloin
  1 tablespoon salt-free steak grilling blend (such as Mrs. Dash)
  ¼ teaspoon salt
  8 (0.9-ounce) slices white wheat bread
  2 tablespoons yogurt-based spread (such as Brummel & Brown)
  4 (0.6-ounce) slices 2% reduced-fat American cheese

1. Heat a large nonstick skillet over medium-high heat. Coat pan with cooking spray. Add onion, and cook 11 minutes or until golden and very tender, adding ½ cup water, 1 tablespoon at a time, as needed, to prevent sticking, stirring frequently.
2. While onion cooks, combine beef, grilling blend, and salt in a large bowl; shape mixture into 4 (½-inch-thick) patties.
3. Remove onion from pan; cover and keep warm. Coat pan with cooking spray. Add patties; cook 4 to 5 minutes on each side or until done. Remove patties from pan. Wipe pan dry with a paper towel.
4. Spread 1 side of bread slices evenly with yogurt-based spread. Place 1 slice of cheese on uncoated side of each of 4 bread slices; top each with ¼ cup onion and 1 patty. Top with remaining bread slices, uncoated sides down.
5. Heat pan over medium-high heat. Place sandwiches in pan; cook 2 minutes on each side or until bread is browned and cheese melts. **YIELD: 4 SERVINGS (SERVING SIZE: 1 SANDWICH).**

PER SERVING: Calories 354; Fat 11.6g (sat 4.7g, mono 2.5g, poly 2.2g); Protein 31.6g; Carb 33.1g; Fiber 3.4g; Chol 69mg; Iron 2mg; Sodium 736mg; Calc 232mg

MOO SHU PORK WRAPS

POINTS value: 4

PREP: 11 minutes ■ **COOK:** 10 minutes

Cooking spray
1 (¾-pound) pork tenderloin, cut diagonally
    into ¼-inch-thick slices
¼ teaspoon black pepper
1 (3.5-ounce) package shiitake mushrooms
5 tablespoons water, divided
2 large eggs
⅛ teaspoon salt
3 cups packaged cabbage-and-carrot
    coleslaw
2 tablespoons less-sodium soy sauce
2 teaspoons cornstarch
1 teaspoon dark sesame oil
2 tablespoons hoisin sauce (such as Dynasty)
6 (6-inch) low-carb, high-fiber flour tortillas
    (such as Mission)
3 tablespoons sliced green onions

1. Heat a large nonstick skillet over medium-high heat. Coat pan with cooking spray. Sprinkle pork with pepper. Add pork to pan, and cook 3 minutes or until pork is browned, stirring after 1 minute. Transfer pork to a plate; keep warm. Add mushrooms to pan; coat mushrooms with cooking spray, and cook 2 minutes without stirring. Stir in 2 tablespoons water, scraping pan to loosen browned bits; cook 1 minute or until liquid evaporates. Add mushrooms to pork; keep warm.

2. Combine eggs and salt, stirring with a whisk. Heat a small skillet over medium-high heat. Coat pan with cooking spray. Add egg mixture to pan, and cook 30 seconds or until scrambled, stirring constantly. Transfer scrambled egg to another plate.

3. Place pan over medium-high heat. Coat pan with cooking spray. Add coleslaw; cook 2 minutes or until slightly wilted, stirring frequently. Combine remaining 3 tablespoons water, soy sauce, cornstarch, and sesame oil in a small bowl, stirring with a whisk until smooth. Add soy sauce mixture to coleslaw. Stir in pork and mushrooms.

4. Spread hoisin sauce evenly on 1 side of each tortilla. Spoon pork mixture evenly over hoisin sauce; top evenly with scrambled egg and green onions. Fold tortilla over filling. **YIELD: 6 SERVINGS (SERVING SIZE: 1 WRAP).**

PER SERVING: Calories 228; Fat 6.1g (sat 1.3g, mono 1.5g, poly 0.5g); Protein 17g; Carb 23.4g; Fiber 2.9g; Chol 97mg; Iron 2.7mg; Sodium 594mg; Calc 90mg

STEAK SANDWICHES WITH HORSERADISH MAYONNAISE

POINTS value: 7

PREP: 3 minutes ■ **COOK:** 9 minutes

Prepared horseradish is made by preserving grated horseradish root in vinegar. It adds a pungent bite to the creamy sauce that smothers the juicy steak filling in this sandwich.

Cooking spray
¾ pound sirloin steak, thinly sliced
¼ teaspoon salt
¼ teaspoon freshly ground black pepper
½ cup thinly sliced red onion
1 garlic clove, minced
1 tablespoon Worcestershire sauce
¼ cup low-fat mayonnaise
3 tablespoons fat-free milk
1 tablespoon prepared horseradish
4 (4-ounce) onion hamburger buns (such as
    Cobblestone Mill)

1. Heat a large nonstick skillet over medium-high heat. Coat pan with cooking spray. Sprinkle steak evenly with salt and pepper. Add steak to pan. Cook 4 minutes or until browned, stirring frequently. Add onion; cook 3 minutes or until onion is tender, stirring frequently. Add garlic; cook 1 minute, stirring constantly. Stir in Worcestershire sauce. Remove pan from heat; cover and keep warm.

2. While steak cooks, combine mayonnaise, milk, and horseradish, stirring with a whisk. Spoon beef mixture evenly onto bottoms of buns; drizzle evenly with horseradish mayonnaise. Top with bun tops. **YIELD: 4 SERVINGS (SERVING SIZE: 1 SANDWICH).**

PER SERVING: Calories 322; Fat 8.7g (sat 2.8g, mono 3g, poly 1.7g); Protein 25g; Carb 36.5g; Fiber 1.4g; Chol 50mg; Iron 3.2mg; Sodium 674mg; Calc 211mg

STROMBOLI

POINTS value: 8

PREP: 6 minutes ■ **COOK:** 23 minutes

You can use any spaghetti sauce you may have on hand instead of the marinara sauce. Just drain it briefly in a colander lined with paper towels until it thickens.

> 1 (11-ounce) can refrigerated thin crust pizza dough (such as Pillsbury)
> Cooking spray
> ¼ pound thinly sliced less-sodium ham (such as Boar's Head)
> ⅓ cup turkey pepperoni slices (28 slices)
> ⅓ cup refrigerated presliced onion
> 4 ounces reduced-fat provolone cheese slices (6 slices)
> ½ cup loosely packed fresh basil leaves
> Marinara sauce (optional)

1. Preheat oven to 375°.
2. Roll dough into a 15 x 12–inch rectangle on a baking sheet coated with cooking spray. Arrange ham, pepperoni, onion, cheese, and basil over dough. Roll up dough, beginning at 1 short side. Pinch dough to seal. Position roll seam side down. Diagonally cut small slits in top of roll. Coat roll with cooking spray.
3. Bake at 375° for 23 to 30 minutes or until golden brown. Cut crosswise into 8 pieces. Serve with marinara sauce, if desired. **YIELD: 4 SERVINGS (SERVING SIZE: 2 PIECES).**

PER SERVING: Calories 357; Fat 11.5g (sat 3.6g, mono 3.6g, poly 1.6g); Protein 22.8g; Carb 39.5g; Fiber 1.6g; Chol 45mg; Iron 2.5mg; Sodium 993mg; Calc 266mg

STROMBOLI

The name of this dish reportedly derived from the 1950s Ingrid Bergman movie with the same title. This calzone-like creation seals calcium and protein into a single, doughy envelope that delivers a wonderful Italian taste. It offers a way to satisfy those cravings for tasty Italian food without sacrificing nutritional benefits. While the stromboli offered in a mall food court may be tempting, it can contain at least three times as many calories and four times as much fat as this healthful recipe.

COBB SALAD PANINI

POINTS value: 7   *(pictured on page 137)*

PREP: 7 minutes ■ **COOK:** 8 minutes

> ¼ cup refrigerated guacamole (such as Wholly)
> 8 (1-ounce) slices ciabatta
> ⅛ teaspoon freshly ground black pepper
> 1 hard-cooked egg, chopped
> 6 ounces very thinly sliced 42%-lower-sodium roast chicken breast (such as Boar's Head)
> 2 plum tomatoes, cut into 8 slices
> 4 precooked bacon slices
> ¼ cup (1 ounce) crumbled Roquefort cheese
> Olive oil–flavored cooking spray
> 1 cup shredded romaine lettuce

1. Preheat panini grill.
2. Spread 1 tablespoon guacamole over each of 4 bread slices; sprinkle evenly with pepper. Layer each evenly with chopped egg and next 4 ingredients. Top with remaining bread slices. Coat outsides of sandwiches with cooking spray. Place 2 sandwiches on panini grill; cook 4 minutes or until browned. Repeat procedure with remaining 2 sandwiches. Add ¼ cup lettuce to each sandwich. Serve immediately. **YIELD: 4 SERVINGS (SERVING SIZE: 1 SANDWICH).**

PER SERVING: Calories 309; Fat 11g (sat 4.4g, mono 3g, poly 0.6g); Protein 19.7g; Carb 35.3g; Fiber 1.6g; Chol 83mg; Iron 2.3mg; Sodium 990mg; Calc 59mg

CHICKEN CAPRESE MELTS

POINTS value: 8

PREP: 4 minutes ■ **COOK:** 6 minutes

> 8 (1.1-ounce) slices sourdough bread (such as Cobblestone Mill)
> Cooking spray
> 3 tablespoons reduced-fat commercial pesto (such as Buitoni)
> 2 cups sliced cooked chicken breast
> 1 large ripe tomato, cut into 8 slices
> ¼ teaspoon freshly ground black pepper
> 4 ounces fresh mozzarella cheese, cut into 4 slices
> 8 large fresh basil leaves

1. Preheat broiler.

2. Place bread slices on a large baking sheet coated with cooking spray. Broil 4 minutes or until bread is lightly toasted.

3. Spread pesto evenly on 1 side of each toasted bread slice. Top 4 bread slices evenly with chicken and tomato slices; sprinkle evenly with pepper. Cut mozzarella slices in half, and place on top of each tomato slice. Broil 2 minutes or until cheese is bubbly. Top cheese evenly with basil leaves and remaining bread slices. **YIELD: 4 SERVINGS (SERVING SIZE: 1 SANDWICH).**

PER SERVING: Calories 378; Fat 13.4g (sat 5.5g, mono 2.9g, poly 1.4g); Protein 34.8g; Carb 27.4g; Fiber 2.2g; Chol 78mg; Iron 2.4mg; Sodium 570mg; Calc 297mg

GRILLED SOUTHWESTERN CHICKEN WRAPS

POINTS value: 8

PREP: 3 minutes ■ COOK: 3 minutes

1½ cups sliced cooked chicken
4 (7-inch) flour tortillas
¼ cup refrigerated light ranch dressing (such as Naturally Fresh)
1 cup canned no-salt-added black beans, rinsed and drained
1½ cups (6 ounces) shredded 50%-less-fat sharp cheddar cheese (such as Cabot)
Cooking spray
½ cup fresh salsa

1. Preheat panini grill.

2. Arrange chicken evenly in center of tortillas; top evenly with ranch dressing, black beans, and cheese. Fold in opposite sides of tortillas toward centers and roll up. Coat grill with cooking spray. Place wraps, seam sides down, on grill; grill 3 to 4 minutes or until golden brown. Serve wraps with salsa. **YIELD: 4 SERVINGS (SERVING SIZE: 1 WRAP AND 2 TABLESPOONS SALSA).**

PER SERVING: Calories 366; Fat 13.6g (sat 5.6g, mono 0.7g, poly 0.4g); Protein 33.6g; Carb 27.1g; Fiber 3.6g; Chol 72mg; Iron 2.1mg; Sodium 725mg; Calc 396mg

GREEK TURKEY BURGERS

POINTS value: 7

PREP: 10 minutes ■ COOK: 8 minutes
■ OTHER: 30 minutes

The type of ground turkey we call for here includes a mix of white and dark meat, which gives these burgers a richer taste. You can substitute ground turkey breast if you'd like (the *POINTS* value per serving will be 6) but the meat mixture may be a bit more difficult to work with. Chill these patties for optimum results on the grill. Toast buns on the grill for 30 seconds, if desired.

1 pound ground turkey
¼ cup (1 ounce) crumbled feta cheese
1 tablespoon light mayonnaise
1 teaspoon Greek seasoning
Cooking spray
½ cup plain fat-free Greek yogurt
⅓ cup grated peeled cucumber
¼ teaspoon freshly ground black pepper
⅛ teaspoon salt
4 (1.5-ounce) whole-wheat hamburger buns
Toppings: green leaf lettuce leaves, red onion slices, tomato slices (optional)

1. Combine first 4 ingredients in a large bowl; shape mixture into 4 (4-inch) patties. Cover and chill 30 minutes.

2. While patties chill, prepare grill.

3. Place burgers on grill rack coated with cooking spray; grill 4 to 5 minutes on each side or until done.

4. While burgers grill, combine yogurt and next 3 ingredients.

5. Place a burger on bottom half of each bun. Top each with about 3 tablespoons yogurt mixture and, if desired, lettuce, onion, and tomato. Top with bun tops. **YIELD: 4 SERVINGS (SERVING SIZE: 1 BURGER).**

PER SERVING: Calories 330; Fat 14.1g (sat 4.2g, mono 4.4g, poly 3.2g); Protein 27.1g; Carb 23.8g; Fiber 3.3g; Chol 97mg; Iron 2.5mg; Sodium 522mg; Calc 116mg

TURKEY SANDWICHES WITH CHUTNEY AND PEARS

POINTS value: 4

PREP: 13 minutes

Watercress adds a peppery flavor, but you can substitute 1 cup fresh spinach.

- ¼ cup mango chutney
- 1 tablespoon Dijon mustard
- 1 (10-ounce) round loaf focaccia, split horizontally
- ¾ pound shaved smoked deli turkey breast
- 1 cup watercress sprigs
- 1 pear, cored and thinly sliced

1. Combine chutney and mustard in a small bowl; spread half of mixture over cut sides of bread.

2. Arrange turkey over chutney mixture on bottom half of bread; top with watercress. Spoon remaining half of chutney mixture over watercress, and top with pear slices. Replace top half of bread. Cut into 6 wedges.

YIELD: 6 SERVINGS (SERVING SIZE: 1 WEDGE).

PER SERVING: Calories 231; Fat 1.8g (sat 0.2g, mono 0.9g, poly 0.2g); Protein 17.5g; Carb 35.7g; Fiber 1.7g; Chol 25mg; Iron 1.9mg; Sodium 668mg; Calc 9mg

BUYING AND STORING PEARS

When buying pears, you can test for ripeness by using your thumb to apply light pressure near the pear's stem. If it's ripe, there will be a slight give to the flesh. If the pears aren't quite ripe, place them on a kitchen counter in a brown paper bag, and check them daily. It may take three to five days for them to fully ripen. Once ripe, store them in the refrigerator for three to five days.

TURKEY DOGS WITH FENNEL SLAW

POINTS value: 3   *(pictured on page 137)*

PREP: 5 minutes ▪ **COOK:** 8 minutes

You can make the slaw on these highly rated sandwiches ahead of time and store it in the refrigerator. The slaw will only be better since the flavors have had extra time to meld. You can grill the hot dogs, if you'd like.

- 4 (1.75-ounce) 98% fat-free turkey hot dogs (such as Oscar Mayer)
- 1 cup packaged coleslaw
- 1 cup thinly sliced fennel
- ¼ cup thinly sliced red onion
- ¼ cup light coleslaw dressing
- 1 tablespoon finely chopped fennel fronds
- 1 tablespoon fresh lemon juice
- 4 (0.7-ounce) white wheat hot dog buns, toasted

1. Heat hot dogs according to package directions. Keep warm.

2. While hot dogs heat, combine coleslaw and next 5 ingredients. Place hot dogs in buns; top evenly with slaw. YIELD: 4 SERVINGS (SERVING SIZE: 1 SANDWICH).

PER SERVING: Calories 139; Fat 4.2g (sat 0.5g, mono 0g, poly 0.4g); Protein 8.7g; Carb 21.2g; Fiber 2.9g; Chol 27mg; Iron 1.8mg; Sodium 814mg; Calc 129mg

Italian Pinwheel
Steaks, *page 90*

Grilled Pork Chops with
Warm Apple Chutney,
page 93

Horseradish-Crusted Beef Tenderloin
Steaks with Fresh Citrus Salad,
page 89

Chicken and Vegetable Pad Thai,
page 102

Braised Chicken with Plum Tomatoes and Feta, *page 98*

Sweet and Spicy Oven-Barbecued Chicken Thighs, *page 103*

132

Turkey Florentine
Skillet Lasagna,
page 109

133

Chicken and Strawberry Salad, *page 118*

Patty Melts, *page 124*

Grilled Vegetable
Panzanella, *page 112*

Southwestern Taco Salad, *page 117*

Cobb Salad
Panini,
page 126

Turkey Dogs with
Fennel Slaw,
page 128

Jalapeño Ranch Burgers, *page 124*

Baked Onion
Rings, *page 150*

"Fried" Apples and
Onions, *page 146*

Spicy Chipotle Roasted
Corn, *page 148*

140

Shrimp Noodle Bowl,
page 160

Tomato-Fennel Soup with Feta, *page 158*

Fudgy Chocolate Peppermint
Brownies, *page 169*

Watercress and Sweet Pea
Salad, *page 172*

side dishes

Spicy Chipotle Roasted Corn, *page 148*

WATERMELON AND CANTALOUPE COMPOTE

POINTS value: 1

PREP: 7 minutes

Serve this refreshing side during the summer when the melons are at their peak of sweetness.

1½ cups watermelon chunks
1½ cups cantaloupe chunks
1½ tablespoons fresh lime juice
2 tablespoons minced fresh mint
1 tablespoon honey

1. Combine all ingredients in a medium bowl, tossing gently. Cover and chill until ready to serve. YIELD: 4 SERVINGS (SERVING SIZE: ¾ CUP).

PER SERVING: Calories 56; Fat 0.2g (sat 0g, mono 0g, poly 0.1g); Protein 0.9g; Carb 14.2g; Fiber 0.3g; Chol 0mg; Iron 0.3mg; Sodium 11mg; Calc 13mg

"FRIED" APPLES AND ONIONS

POINTS value: 1

(pictured on page 139)

PREP: 6 minutes ■ COOK: 15 minutes

Vidalia onions and brown sugar sweeten tart apples in this delicious side that earned our Test Kitchens' highest rating. It's a wonderful year-round complement to pork chops or any roasted meat or poultry. To save time, peel, core, and slice the apples while the onion cooks.

2 teaspoons light butter
1 large Vidalia or other sweet onion, vertically sliced
2 large Granny Smith apples, peeled and sliced
½ cup water
2 tablespoons dark brown sugar
½ teaspoon ground cinnamon
¼ teaspoon salt

1. Melt butter in a large nonstick skillet over medium-high heat. Add onion; cook 7 to 8 minutes or until tender, stirring occasionally.

2. Add apple and remaining ingredients; cover and cook 5 minutes or until apple is tender, stirring occasionally. Uncover and cook 2 minutes or until liquid almost evaporates. YIELD: 6 SERVINGS (SERVING SIZE: ABOUT ⅔ CUP).

PER SERVING: Calories 70; Fat 0.9g (sat 0.5g, mono 0.2g, poly 0g); Protein 0.9g; Carb 16g; Fiber 1.6g; Chol 2mg; Iron 0.4mg; Sodium 108mg; Calc 24mg

ASPARAGUS WITH TANGY LEMON SAUCE

POINTS value: 1

PREP: 3 minutes ■ COOK: 8 minutes

Look for asparagus spears of even thickness so all the spears will cook in the same amount of time. We tested with ½-inch-thick spears.

1 pound fresh asparagus spears (about 20 spears)
¼ teaspoon salt
¼ teaspoon freshly ground black pepper
2 tablespoons low-fat mayonnaise
2 tablespoons light sour cream
2 tablespoons fresh lemon juice
2 tablespoons water
1 tablespoon butter, melted
½ teaspoon Dijon mustard
⅛ teaspoon ground red pepper

1. Pour water to a depth of ½ inch in a large skillet; bring to a boil.
2. While water boils, snap off tough ends of asparagus. Add asparagus to boiling water. Cover and cook 5 minutes or until crisp-tender. Drain asparagus and place on a serving platter; sprinkle with salt and pepper.
3. While asparagus cooks, combine mayonnaise and next 6 ingredients in a small bowl, stirring with a whisk. Spoon sauce over asparagus. YIELD: 4 SERVINGS (SERVING SIZE: ABOUT 5 ASPARAGUS SPEARS AND 2 TABLE-SPOONS SAUCE).

PER SERVING: Calories 65; Fat 3.9g (sat 2.2g, mono 0.7g, poly 0.1g); Protein 1.7g; Carb 6.2g; Fiber 1.3g; Chol 10mg; Iron 1.3mg; Sodium 259mg; Calc 26mg

ROASTED ASPARAGUS WITH FETA

POINTS value: 1

PREP: 1 minute ■ **COOK:** 8 minutes

By roasting asparagus, you're ensured that it will cook evenly and without your attention. A topping of melted feta makes this recipe all the more special.

> 1 pound asparagus spears (about 20 spears)
> Cooking spray
> 1/8 teaspoon kosher salt
> 1/8 teaspoon freshly ground black pepper
> 1/2 cup (2 ounces) crumbled feta cheese
> 1 teaspoon extra-virgin olive oil (optional)

1. Preheat oven to 450°.
2. Snap off tough ends of asparagus. Arrange asparagus on a large baking sheet coated with cooking spray. Coat asparagus with cooking spray; sprinkle with salt and pepper.
3. Bake at 450° for 7 minutes or until crisp-tender. Sprinkle with cheese, and bake 1 minute or until cheese softens. Drizzle with olive oil, if desired. Serve immediately. **YIELD: 4 SERVINGS (SERVING SIZE: 5 ASPARAGUS SPEARS).**

PER SERVING: Calories 76; Fat 4.3g (sat 2.3g, mono 1.6g, poly 0.3g); Protein 4.5g; Carb 5g; Fiber 2.4g; Chol 13mg; Iron 2.5mg; Sodium 220mg; Calc 97mg

SAUTÉED GREEN BEANS AND CHERRY TOMATOES

POINTS value: 0

PREP: 2 minutes ■ **COOK:** 8 minutes

A simple technique gently coaxes the tomato essence out of the plump fruit as it cooks, and it becomes a wonderful tomato gravy to coat the beans. A double serving of this side has a ***POINTS*** value of 1.

> 1 (12-ounce) package trimmed green beans
> 1 tablespoon light butter
> 8 cherry tomatoes, halved
> 1/4 teaspoon salt
> 1 tablespoon chopped fresh basil
> 1/8 teaspoon freshly ground black pepper

1. Microwave green beans according to package directions; drain.
2. While green beans cook, melt butter in a large nonstick skillet over medium-high heat. Add tomatoes and salt; sauté 4 minutes or until tomatoes are tender, pressing tomatoes against the pan with a wide spatula to release juices.
3. Add beans; sauté 1 minute or until thoroughly heated. Stir in basil and pepper. **YIELD: 4 SERVINGS (SERVING SIZE: ABOUT 2/3 CUP).**

PER SERVING: Calories 44; Fat 1.9g (sat 1.1g, mono 0.5g, poly 0.1g); Protein 1.5g; Carb 6.8g; Fiber 3.5g; Chol 3mg; Iron 0.6mg; Sodium 163mg; Calc 46mg

SAUTÉED MIXED VEGETABLES

POINTS value: 1

PREP: 12 minutes ■ **COOK:** 5 minutes

This fresh, quick, and easy stir-fry is the perfect side for your next dinner inspired by Asian cuisine.

> Cooking spray
> 2 cups broccoli slaw
> 2 baby bok choy (about 9 ounces), trimmed and thinly sliced
> 1 (8-ounce) package sliced fresh mushrooms
> 1 red bell pepper, thinly sliced
> 3 tablespoons less-sodium soy sauce
> 1 teaspoon dark sesame oil

1. Heat a large nonstick skillet over medium heat. Coat pan with cooking spray. Add broccoli slaw and next 3 ingredients to pan; cook 4 minutes or until crisp-tender. Stir in soy sauce and oil. Serve immediately. **YIELD: 4 SERVINGS (SERVING SIZE: 1 CUP).**

PER SERVING: Calories 56; Fat 1.5g (sat 0.2g, mono 0.5g, poly 0.7g); Protein 4.6g; Carb 7.2g; Fiber 2.6g; Chol 0mg; Iron 1.3mg; Sodium 489mg; Calc 69mg

BOK CHOY NUTRITION

Also known as Chinese cabbage and pak choi, bok choy has been grown in China for over 6,000 years. It's low in sodium, an excellent source of vitamins A and C, and a good source of folate.

SWEET APPLE CABBAGE

POINTS value: 1

PREP: 10 minutes ■ COOK: 24 minutes

 1 tablespoon canola oil
 ¾ cup chopped red onion
 ⅓ cup apple cider
 2½ tablespoons cider vinegar
 2 tablespoons light brown sugar
 ½ teaspoon salt
 ½ teaspoon freshly ground black pepper
 6 cups shredded red cabbage
 2 cups chopped Braeburn apple (1 large)
 ½ teaspoon caraway seeds (optional)

1. Heat oil in a Dutch oven over medium heat. Add onion, and sauté 8 minutes. Stir in cider and next 4 ingredients. Add cabbage and apple, stirring until well blended. Cover and cook 15 to 20 minutes or until desired degree of doneness, stirring often. Stir in caraway seeds, if desired. **YIELD: 8 SERVINGS (SERVING SIZE: ½ CUP).**

PER SERVING: Calories 70; Fat 1.9g (sat 0.2g, mono 1g, poly 0.5g); Protein 1g; Carb 13.7g; Fiber 2.4g; Chol 0mg; Iron 0.4mg; Sodium 160mg; Calc 30mg

BROCCOLI CASSEROLE

POINTS value: 4

PREP: 4 minutes ■ COOK: 45 minutes

We've lightened this creamy classic, but the only things sacrificed were calories and fat.

 2 (10-ounce) packages frozen chopped broccoli
 1 (10¾-ounce) can condensed 45% less-sodium, 98% fat-free cream of mushroom soup, undiluted
 ¾ cup light mayonnaise
 ½ cup (2 ounces) reduced-fat shredded extra-sharp cheddar cheese
 ½ cup egg substitute
 Butter-flavored cooking spray
 24 reduced-fat round buttery crackers (such as Ritz), crushed

1. Preheat oven to 350°.
2. Place broccoli in a wire mesh strainer; rinse with cold water until thawed. Drain well. Combine broccoli, soup, and next 3 ingredients in a large bowl. Spoon mixture into a 2-quart baking dish coated with cooking spray.
3. Bake at 350° for 40 minutes or until bubbly and golden brown. Top with cracker crumbs, coat crumbs with cooking spray, and bake an additional 5 minutes or until crumbs are golden. **YIELD: 8 SERVINGS (SERVING SIZE: ⅛ OF CASSEROLE).**

PER SERVING: Calories 192; Fat 11.6g (sat 2.5g, mono 0.3g, poly 0.7g); Protein 7.1g; Carb 15.4g; Fiber 2.5g; Chol 15mg; Iron 1.4mg; Sodium 455mg; Calc 115mg

SPICY CHIPOTLE ROASTED CORN

POINTS value: 2   *(pictured on page 140)*

PREP: 6 minutes ■ COOK: 25 minutes

Next time you're grilling steak or chicken, throw the corn for this spicy side dish alongside instead of baking it.

 ¼ cup yogurt-based spread (such as Brummel & Brown)
 1 tablespoon chopped fresh chives
 1 tablespoon chopped chipotle chile, canned in adobo sauce
 ¼ teaspoon ground red pepper
 ¼ teaspoon salt
 4 small ears shucked yellow corn

1. Preheat oven to 475°.
2. Combine first 5 ingredients in a small bowl; spread mixture evenly over corn. Wrap corn in foil, and place on a rimmed baking sheet.
3. Bake at 475° for 25 minutes or until tender. **YIELD: 4 SERVINGS (SERVING SIZE: 1 EAR).**

PER SERVING: Calories 125; Fat 6.2g (sat 1.2g, mono 1.3g, poly 3g); Protein 3g; Carb 17.7g; Fiber 2.9g; Chol 0mg; Iron 0.6mg; Sodium 290mg; Calc 3mg

FRESH CORN FRITTERS

POINTS value: 2

PREP: 7 minutes ■ COOK: 14 minutes

Sweet corn gets a kick of cayenne in this buttery, straight-from-the-county-fair treat.

>   2 cups fresh corn kernels (about 4 small ears)
>   1 large egg, lightly beaten
>   ¼ cup all-purpose flour
>   ½ teaspoon baking powder
>   ¼ teaspoon salt
>   ⅛ teaspoon ground red pepper
>   2 tablespoons butter, divided
>   Cooking spray

1. Combine first 6 ingredients in a large bowl, stirring with a whisk.
2. Melt 1 tablespoon butter in a large nonstick skillet coated with cooking spray over medium-high heat. Spoon 4 (¼-cup) batter mounds onto pan. Cook 3 minutes on each side or until lightly browned. Remove fritters from pan; drain on paper towels. Repeat procedure with remaining 1 tablespoon butter and ¾ cup batter. **YIELD: 7 SERVINGS (SERVING SIZE: 1 FRITTER).**

PER SERVING: Calories 91; Fat 4.5g (sat 2.4g, mono 1.3g, poly 0.5g); Protein 2.7g; Carb 11.5g; Fiber 1.3g; Chol 39mg; Iron 0.6mg; Sodium 148mg; Calc 31mg

CORN, ZUCCHINI, AND TOMATO SÁUTE

POINTS value: 2

PREP: 9 minutes ■ COOK: 6 minutes

Cook up summer's sweetest offerings from the field in less than 15 minutes.

>   1 tablespoon butter
>   1¾ cups fresh corn kernels (about 4 ears)
>   1 medium zucchini, sliced
>   1 teaspoon Greek seasoning (such as Cavender's)
>   1 cup grape tomatoes, halved

1. Melt butter in a large nonstick skillet over medium-high heat. Add corn, zucchini, and seasoning; sauté 4 minutes. Add tomato; sauté 1 minute or until thoroughly heated. **YIELD: 6 SERVINGS (SERVING SIZE: ½ CUP).**

PER SERVING: Calories 87; Fat 3.7g (sat 1.2g, mono 0.5g, poly 0.1g); Protein 3.3g; Carb 14.3g; Fiber 2g; Chol 5mg; Iron 0.5mg; Sodium 180mg; Calc 7mg

ROASTED EGGPLANT WITH BALSAMIC GLAZE

POINTS value: 1

PREP: 6 minutes ■ COOK: 25 minutes

Smaller eggplants, weighing around 1 pound each, have thin skins and the best texture for this recipe.

>   2 (1-pound) eggplants, cut into 1-inch cubes
>   1 tablespoon olive oil
>   ¼ teaspoon salt
>   ¼ teaspoon freshly ground black pepper
>   Cooking spray
>   2 teaspoons chopped fresh rosemary
>   1 large shallot, minced
>   ⅓ cup balsamic vinegar

1. Preheat oven to 450°.
2. Combine first 4 ingredients on a large rimmed baking sheet coated with cooking spray. Bake at 450° for 25 minutes or until roasted, stirring rosemary into vegetables during the last 5 minutes of cook time.
3. While eggplant roasts, heat a medium saucepan over medium-high heat. Coat pan with cooking spray. Add shallots; sauté 1 minute or until tender. Stir in balsamic vinegar; bring to a boil. Boil 3 to 4 minutes or until mixture is reduced to 2 tablespoons. Spoon eggplant into a serving bowl; drizzle with balsamic glaze, and toss well. **YIELD: 6 SERVINGS (SERVING SIZE: ⅔ CUP).**

PER SERVING: Calories 68; Fat 2.6g (sat 0.4g, mono 1.7g, poly 0.4g); Protein 1.6g; Carb 11g; Fiber 5.2g; Chol 0mg; Iron 0.4mg; Sodium 105mg; Calc 16mg

SWEET ONION GRATIN
POINTS value: 1

PREP: 5 minutes ■ **COOK:** 14 minutes

    4 cups (1-inch) sweet onion pieces (about 2 large)
    ½ teaspoon freshly ground black pepper
    ¼ teaspoon salt
    ⅓ cup 1% low-fat milk
    2 teaspoons all-purpose flour
    ¼ cup (1 ounce) shredded Swiss cheese
    1 tablespoon light butter
      Cooking spray
    ¼ cup (1 ounce) shredded Parmigiano-Reggiano
      cheese

1. Preheat broiler.
2. Place first 3 ingredients in a large microwave-safe bowl; cover bowl with plastic wrap, and vent. Microwave at HIGH 8 minutes or until onion is tender, stirring once.
3. While onion cooks, combine milk and flour in a small saucepan, stirring with a whisk until blended. Cook, stirring constantly, over medium heat 3 minutes or until thickened and bubbly. Stir in Swiss cheese and butter; cook 1 minute or until cheese melts.
4. Stir cheese sauce into onion mixture. Pour onion mixture into an 11 x 7–inch baking dish coated with cooking spray. Sprinkle with Parmigiano-Reggiano cheese. Broil 6 minutes or until bubbly and top is lightly browned. **YIELD: 8 SERVINGS (SERVING SIZE: ½ CUP).**

PER SERVING: Calories 70; Fat 3g (sat 1.9g, mono 0.9g, poly 0.1g); Protein 3.5g; Carb 7.6g; Fiber 0.8g; Chol 8mg; Iron 0.3mg; Sodium 161mg; Calc 109mg

✳ Parmigiano-Reggiano
Parmesan cheese is perhaps the most widely used hard cheese, and Parmigiano-Reggiano is considered the finest of Parmesans. It has an appealing grainy texture and a rich, strong, nutty flavor that makes it a great addition to vegetable side dishes, soups, salads, and pasta dishes.

BAKED ONION RINGS
POINTS value: 3   *(pictured on page 139)*

PREP: 6 minutes ■ **COOK:** 16 minutes

You can enjoy crunchy onion rings without all the fat. Serve them as an appetizer or alongside your favorite burger.

    1 large Vidalia or other sweet onion, sliced and
      separated into rings
      Cooking spray
    ¼ cup all-purpose flour
    ¼ teaspoon ground red pepper
    3 large egg whites
    2 tablespoons water
    1¾ cups panko (Japanese breadcrumbs)
    ¼ teaspoon salt

1. Preheat oven to 475°.
2. Place a large baking sheet in oven while it preheats. Coat onion rings with cooking spray. Combine flour and ground red pepper in a large heavy-duty zip-top plastic bag. Add onion; shake to coat.
3. Combine egg whites and 2 tablespoons water in a shallow bowl, stirring with a whisk. Place panko in a food processor; process into fine crumbs. Place crumbs in another shallow dish.
4. Dip onion rings in egg white mixture; dredge in crumbs. Remove hot baking sheet from oven; coat pan with cooking spray. Arrange onion rings in a single layer on pan. Coat onion rings with cooking spray.
5. Bake at 475° for 16 minutes or until browned and crisp. Sprinkle hot onion rings evenly with salt; serve immediately. **YIELD: 4 SERVINGS (SERVING SIZE: ¼ OF ONION RINGS).**

PER SERVING: Calories 176; Fat 1.1g (sat 0.1g, mono 0g, poly 0.1g); Protein 8.1g; Carb 32.6g; Fiber 2.8g; Chol 0mg; Iron 0.6mg; Sodium 265mg; Calc 25mg

POTATO-CHEESE SOUFFLÉS

POINTS value: 3

PREP: 13 minutes ■ **COOK:** 30 minutes

Who knew soufflés could be so easy? No one will know that you started with refrigerated mashed potatoes.

> Cooking spray
> 2½ tablespoons dry breadcrumbs
> 1 (24-ounce) package refrigerated mashed potatoes (such as Simply Potatoes)
> 1 large egg yolk
> ¼ cup fat-free milk
> ¼ teaspoon black pepper
> ¾ cup (3 ounces) shredded Gruyère cheese, divided
> 5 large egg whites

1. Preheat oven to 425°.
2. Coat 8 (6-ounce) soufflé dishes with cooking spray; sprinkle evenly with breadcrumbs. Place dishes on a baking sheet, and set aside.
3. Place mashed potatoes and next 3 ingredients in a food processor; pulse 3 to 4 times or until smooth. Add 6 tablespoons cheese; pulse 2 times or just until combined. Transfer potato mixture to a bowl.
4. Beat egg whites with a mixer at high speed until stiff peaks form. Gently fold one-fourth of egg whites into potato mixture; gently fold in remaining three-fourths of egg whites. Divide potato mixture evenly among prepared soufflé dishes; sprinkle with remaining 6 tablespoons cheese.
5. Bake at 425° for 30 minutes or until puffed and golden brown. **YIELD: 8 SERVINGS (SERVING SIZE: 1 SOUFFLÉ).**

PER SERVING: Calories 133; Fat 5.1g (sat 2.3g, mono 1.3g, poly 0.3g); Protein 7.6g; Carb 14.3g; Fiber 1.3g; Chol 37mg; Iron 0.3mg; Sodium 314mg; Calc 132mg

✳ Gruyère Cheese

A member of the Swiss cheese family, Gruyère cheese has a rich, nutty taste and is commonly seen as the top layer of French onion soup. The name "Gruyère" comes from the Swiss town in which it was created. Since it melts easily and smoothly, this type of cheese is perfect for a delicate soufflé.

SAVORY TWICE-BAKED SWEET POTATOES

POINTS value: 2

PREP: 8 minutes ■ **COOK:** 18 minutes

The combination of apples, rosemary, bacon, and Parmesan cheese creates a dish bursting with flavors, including sweet, tart, salty, and savory.

> 2 (8-ounce) sweet potatoes
> 2 center-cut bacon slices
> 1 cup chopped peeled Gala apple (about 1)
> ¼ cup (1 ounce) shredded Parmigiano-Reggiano cheese
> 1 teaspoon chopped fresh rosemary
> ¼ teaspoon salt
> ¼ teaspoon freshly ground black pepper
> Cooking spray

1. Preheat oven to 450°.
2. Scrub potatoes, and place in a single layer in a microwave-safe bowl (do not pierce potatoes with a fork). Cover bowl with plastic wrap (do not allow plastic wrap to touch food); vent. Microwave at HIGH 8 minutes or until tender.
3. While potatoes bake, cook bacon in a large non-stick skillet over medium-high heat until crisp. Remove bacon from pan, reserving 1 tablespoon drippings in pan; drain bacon and set aside. Add apple to drippings in pan; sauté 3 to 4 minutes. Remove from heat.
4. Cut potatoes in half lengthwise. Scoop out pulp, leaving about a ¼-inch-thick shell. Stir potato into apple mixture. Stir in reserved bacon, cheese, and next 3 ingredients. Divide potato mixture evenly into potato shells.
5. Place stuffed potatoes on a baking sheet coated with cooking spray. Bake at 450° for 10 minutes or until cheese melts and potatoes are thoroughly heated. **YIELD: 4 SERVINGS (SERVING SIZE: 1 POTATO HALF).**

PER SERVING: Calories 141; Fat 2.7g (sat 1.4g, mono 0g, poly 0g); Protein 5.1g; Carb 24.6g; Fiber 4g; Chol 9mg; Iron 0.7mg; Sodium 350mg; Calc 96mg

Spinach offers a variety of nutrition benefits. The dark green leaves are a rich source of vitamins A, C, and K; calcium; iron; and potassium. However, its nutritional value is somewhat inhibited by the oxalic acid it contains, which may curtail the absorption of calcium and iron. While this doesn't affect calcium absorption from other foods cooked with spinach, you may want to get your calcium from other sources.

BAKED CREAMED SPINACH

POINTS value: 3

PREP: 2 minutes ■ **COOK:** 19 minutes

This recipe, which received our Test Kitchens' highest rating, proves a small number of ingredients can yield an indulgent and satisfying side.

- 2 **teaspoons butter**
- 2 **(6-ounce) packages fresh baby spinach**
- 1 **(8-ounce) package ⅓-less-fat cream cheese**
- ¼ **cup 1% low-fat milk**
- ¼ **teaspoon salt**
- ¼ **teaspoon freshly ground black pepper**
  Cooking spray
- ½ **cup fat-free herb-seasoned croutons**

1. Preheat oven to 400°.
2. Melt butter in a large Dutch oven over medium-high heat; add spinach. Cook 3 minutes or until spinach wilts, stirring often.
3. Beat cream cheese and next 3 ingredients with a mixer at medium speed until creamy. Stir cream cheese mixture into spinach mixture until blended. Spoon spinach mixture into an 11 x 7–inch baking dish coated with cooking spray.
4. Place croutons in a food processor; process until crumbly. Sprinkle crumbs over spinach mixture. Coat crumbs with cooking spray. Bake at 400° for 15 minutes or until thoroughly heated. **YIELD: 6 SERVINGS (SERVING SIZE: ⅙ OF CASSEROLE).**

PER SERVING: Calories 140; Fat 9.5g (sat 6.3g, mono 0.4g, poly 0.1g); Protein 6.3g; Carb 6.6g; Fiber 1.4g; Chol 31mg; Iron 1.8mg; Sodium 372mg; Calc 94mg

SAUTÉED SPINACH WITH GARLIC

POINTS value: 1

PREP: 1 minute ■ **COOK:** 4 minutes

Add the spinach gradually to the skillet and turn it with tongs. This allows the first batch to wilt, making room for more as it cooks.

- 2 **teaspoons olive oil**
- 2 **garlic cloves, pressed**
- 2 **(6-ounce) packages fresh baby spinach**
- ¼ **teaspoon crushed red pepper**
- 1 **tablespoon lemon juice**
- ⅛ **teaspoon salt**

1. Heat oil in a large skillet over medium heat. Add garlic; sauté 30 seconds. Add spinach and crushed red pepper; cook 2 to 3 minutes or until spinach wilts, turning with tongs. Drizzle spinach with lemon juice; sprinkle with salt. Serve immediately. **YIELD: 4 SERVINGS (SERVING SIZE: ½ CUP).**

PER SERVING: Calories 58; Fat 2.3g (sat 0.3g, mono 1.6g, poly 0.3g); Protein 2.1g; Carb 9.9g; Fiber 4.1g; Chol 0mg; Iron 2.8mg; Sodium 208mg; Calc 63mg

ITALIAN ZUCCHINI AND TOMATOES

POINTS value: 2

PREP: 4 minutes ■ **COOK:** 11 minutes

This versatile side is delicious with chicken or spooned over rice or polenta and sprinkled with Parmesan cheese.

- 2 **medium zucchini**
- 2 **teaspoons olive oil**
- 1 **cup refrigerated presliced onion, cut in half**
- 2 **garlic cloves, minced**
- 1 **(14.5-ounce) can diced tomatoes with basil, garlic, and oregano, undrained**

1. Cut zucchini in half lengthwise; cut crosswise into ¼-inch-thick slices.
2. Heat oil in a large nonstick skillet over medium-high heat. Add zucchini, onion, and garlic; sauté

8 minutes or until tender. Add tomato; cook 2 minutes or until thoroughly heated, stirring occasionally. **YIELD: 4 SERVINGS (SERVING SIZE: ¾ CUP).**

PER SERVING: Calories 90; Fat 2.5g (sat 0.4g, mono 1.7g, poly 0.3g); Protein 2.5g; Carb 15.5g; Fiber 2.3g; Chol 0mg; Iron 1.1mg; Sodium 437mg; Calc 78mg

CILANTRO ORZO WITH FETA
POINTS value: 3

PREP: 5 minutes ■ **COOK:** 19 minutes

Melty feta adds a tangy punch of flavor to this side dish.

> **2** teaspoons olive oil
> **1** garlic clove, minced
> **⅛** teaspoon crushed red pepper
> **⅔** cup uncooked orzo (rice-shaped pasta)
> **1** cup fat-free, less-sodium chicken broth
> **3** tablespoons dry white wine
> **⅓** cup chopped fresh cilantro
> **2** tablespoons crumbled feta cheese
> **¼** teaspoon salt

1. Heat oil in a large saucepan over medium-high heat. Add garlic and red pepper; sauté 30 seconds. Add orzo, stirring to coat. Stir in chicken broth and wine. Bring to a boil; reduce heat, and simmer, covered, 13 minutes or until liquid is nearly absorbed.
2. Remove pan from heat. Add cilantro, cheese, and salt, stirring until cheese melts. **YIELD: 4 SERVINGS (SERVING SIZE: ABOUT ⅓ CUP).**

PER SERVING: Calories 144; Fat 3.9g (sat 1g, mono 1.9g, poly 0.3g); Protein 4.6g; Carb 22.1g; Fiber 1.1g; Chol 4mg; Iron 0.1mg; Sodium 337mg; Calc 26mg

Orzo
While often mistaken for rice, orzo is actually a small, rice-shaped pasta. However, unlike rice, orzo is denser and keeps its shape during cooking. Soup dishes frequently use orzo rather than rice because the pasta will remain intact.

Thyme
This herb pairs well with many other herbs, including rosemary, parsley, sage, and oregano. Because the leaves are so small, they often don't require much chopping. Add thyme during cooking; its powerful taste develops best at high temperatures.

CARAMELIZED ONION–MUSHROOM PILAF
POINTS value: 2

PREP: 8 minutes ■ **COOK:** 25 minutes

To save some time, you can sauté the mushrooms in a separate pan while caramelizing the onion.

> **1** tablespoon butter, divided
> **1½** cups thinly vertically sliced sweet onion (1 large onion)
> **¼** cup water
> **1** (8-ounce) package sliced fresh mushrooms
> **1** (8.5-ounce) package 7-whole-grain pilaf (such as Seeds of Change)
> **1** tablespoon chopped fresh thyme
> **¼** teaspoon salt
> **⅛** teaspoon black pepper

1. Melt 1½ teaspoons butter in a large nonstick skillet over medium-high heat. Add onion; cook 15 minutes or until golden, adding ¼ cup water, 1 tablespoon at a time, as necessary to prevent sticking, stirring occasionally.
2. Remove onion from pan. Melt remaining 1½ teaspoons butter in pan. Add mushrooms; cook 8 to 10 minutes or until tender, stirring twice.
3. While mushrooms cook, microwave pilaf according to package directions. Place rice in a medium bowl; add onion, mushrooms, thyme, salt, and black pepper. Toss well. **YIELD: 6 SERVINGS (SERVING SIZE: ABOUT ½ CUP).**

PER SERVING: Calories 107; Fat 3.1g (sat 1.3g, mono 0.5g, poly 0.1g); Protein 4.1g; Carb 18.6g; Fiber 3g; Chol 5mg; Iron 0.4mg; Sodium 122mg; Calc 13mg

COCONUT-PINEAPPLE RICE PILAF

POINTS value: 3

PREP: 1 minute ■ **COOK:** 20 minutes

Fragrant jasmine rice gets a tropical spin with sweet pineapple, coconut, and almonds.

> 1 cup uncooked jasmine rice
> 1 (13.5-ounce) can light coconut milk
> ¼ teaspoon salt
> ¼ teaspoon freshly ground black pepper
> Cooking spray
> 1 cup diced fresh pineapple
> ¼ cup sliced almonds, toasted
> ¼ cup sliced green onions

1. Cook rice according to package directions, using coconut milk instead of water and stirring in salt and black pepper. Fluff rice with a fork.
2. While rice cooks, heat a small nonstick skillet over medium-high heat. Coat pan with cooking spray. Add pineapple, and sauté 4 minutes or until golden brown. Add pineapple, almonds, and green onions to rice mixture; toss well. **YIELD: 6 SERVINGS (SERVING SIZE: ½ CUP).**

PER SERVING: Calories 132; Fat 5.7g (sat 3.4g, mono 1.5g, poly 0.6g); Protein 3g; Carb 19.1g; Fiber 1.2g; Chol 0mg; Iron 0.8mg; Sodium 115mg; Calc 18mg

Jasmine Rice

Jasmine rice is an aromatic rice, which is apparent the moment it begins to cook. It's grown primarily in Thailand, but you'll find it served with Thai and Chinese dishes. Jasmine rice is readily available in most grocery stores and should be stored in a cool, dry place and used within six months of purchase. If stored too long, the aromatic scent will diminish and eventually disappear entirely.

ALMOND-GINGER RICE

POINTS value: 3

PREP: 1 minute ■ **COOK:** 20 minutes

While the rice cooks, you can toast the almonds in a 350° oven for 5 to 6 minutes or just until lightly browned. Serve this easy accompaniment alongside fish, chicken, or tofu dishes. It pairs well with Pan-Seared Chicken with Fresh Plum Sauce on page 99.

> 1 cup water
> 2 teaspoons grated peeled fresh ginger
> ¼ teaspoon salt
> 1 (14-ounce) can fat-free, less-sodium chicken broth
> 1 cup long-grain parboiled rice (such as Uncle Ben's)
> ¼ cup slivered almonds, toasted
> ¼ cup sliced green onions

1. Bring first 4 ingredients to a boil in a medium saucepan. Stir in rice; reduce heat, and simmer, covered, 18 minutes or until rice is tender and liquid is absorbed. Fluff with a fork. Stir in almonds and green onions. **YIELD: 6 SERVINGS (SERVING SIZE: ½ CUP).**

PER SERVING: Calories 169; Fat 2.9g (sat 0.3g, mono 1.5g, poly 0.7g); Protein 4.5g; Carb 30.4g; Fiber 1.7g; Chol 0mg; Iron 2.3mg; Sodium 285mg; Calc 36mg

soups & stews

Shrimp Noodle Bowl, *page 160*

CHILLED AVOCADO AND CUCUMBER SOUP

POINTS value: 5

PREP: 10 minutes

This cold, creamy soup is the perfect light meal for a hot summer evening, or chill your thermos and take it for lunch.

>   1 cup coarsely chopped English cucumber (½ large)
>   1 cup water
>   ½ cup fresh cilantro leaves
>   ½ cup nonfat buttermilk
>   3 tablespoons fresh lime juice
>   ½ teaspoon salt
>   2 ripe peeled avocados, coarsely chopped
>   Spicy Shrimp Pico de Gallo

1. Place first 7 ingredients in a blender; process until smooth. Pour soup evenly into each of 4 bowls; top evenly with Spicy Shrimp Pico de Gallo. **YIELD: 4 SERVINGS (SERVING SIZE: ABOUT ¾ CUP SOUP AND ABOUT ⅔ CUP PICO DE GALLO).**

PER SERVING: Calories 229; Fat 14.6g (sat 2.3g, mono 9.3g, poly 1.9g); Protein 15.1g; Carb 11.9g; Fiber 4.4g; Chol 111mg; Iron 2.7mg; Sodium 604mg; Calc 85mg

Spicy Shrimp Pico de Gallo

POINTS value: 2

>   1½ cups coarsely chopped cooked peeled shrimp (8 ounces)
>   1 cup refrigerated prechopped tomato, bell pepper, and onion mix
>   1 tablespoon fresh lime juice
>   1 tablespoon extra-virgin olive oil
>   ¼ teaspoon salt
>   ¼ teaspoon freshly ground black pepper
>   2 garlic cloves, minced
>   1 jalapeño pepper, seeded and minced

1. Combine all ingredients in a bowl. **YIELD: 2½ CUPS (SERVING SIZE: ABOUT ⅔ CUP).**

PER SERVING: Calories 102; Fat 4.2g (sat 0.7g, mono 2.8g, poly 0.6g); Protein 12.4g; Carb 3.4g; Fiber 0.7g; Chol 111mg; Iron 1.9mg; Sodium 274mg; Calc 32mg

Avocados

If you love the creamy rich taste of avocados but are concerned about the fat and calories, you shouldn't worry. While it's true avocados are high in fat, the majority of it is the heart-healthy mono- and polyunsaturated kind. And one-fifth of a medium-sized avocado contains about 50 calories, which isn't many considering that this fruit contains nearly 20 vitamins and minerals. Just use moderation as your guide.

EGG AND GARLIC SOUP

POINTS value: 2

PREP: 2 minutes ■ **COOK:** 13 minutes

Prepare this simple soup as a meal starter or add a salad and bread for a light supper.

>   6 cups fat-free, less-sodium chicken broth
>   6 fresh sage leaves
>   6 large garlic cloves, minced
>   3 large eggs, lightly beaten
>   ⅛ teaspoon freshly ground black pepper
>   ¼ cup thinly sliced green onions

1. Combine chicken broth and sage in a large saucepan. Bring to a boil; remove and discard sage leaves. Stir garlic into broth; reduce heat, and simmer, uncovered, 5 minutes.
2. While stirring broth mixture, pour eggs into broth in a slow, steady stream; remove from heat. Ladle soup into bowls. Sprinkle evenly with pepper and green onions. **YIELD: 4 SERVINGS (SERVING SIZE: 1¼ CUPS).**

PER SERVING: Calories 101; Fat 3.2g (sat 0.9g, mono 1.4g, poly 0.6g); Protein 11.2g; Carb 5.5g; Fiber 1g; Chol 135mg; Iron 1.3mg; Sodium 821mg; Calc 54mg

CAULIFLOWER NUTRITION

While many (both adults and children alike) profess a strong dislike for cauliflower, you shouldn't shy away from the pale vegetable. Cauliflower is a great source of vitamins C and K, and scientific research shows that the compounds in this vegetable may assist in preventing a variety of cancers. When purchasing cauliflower, be sure that the tops are their traditional off-white color with no brown patches.

ROASTED CAULIFLOWER SOUP

POINTS value: 1

PREP: 5 minutes ■ **COOK:** 32 minutes

The small amount of full-fat half-and-half we've added to this soup imparts richness without adding a significant amount of calories.

- 8 cups cauliflower florets (about 1 large head)
- 1 large sweet onion, cut into wedges
- 1 tablespoon olive oil
- ½ teaspoon curry powder
- ¼ teaspoon salt
- ¼ teaspoon freshly ground black pepper
- 1 (32-ounce) container fat-free, less-sodium chicken broth
- ½ cup half-and-half

1. Preheat oven to 450°.
2. Combine first 3 ingredients on a large rimmed baking sheet; toss well to coat. Combine curry powder, salt, and pepper; sprinkle over vegetables. Bake at 450° for 30 minutes or until cauliflower is tender and browned.
3. Place half of vegetable mixture, half of chicken broth, and ¼ cup half-and-half in a blender; process until smooth. Pour into a large bowl. Repeat procedure with remaining vegetables, broth, and half-and-half. Pour soup into a Dutch oven. Cook over medium-high heat 2 minutes or until thoroughly heated. **YIELD: 8 SERVINGS (SERVING SIZE: ABOUT 1 CUP).**

PER SERVING: Calories 82; Fat 3.8g (sat 1.3g, mono 1.8g, poly 0.3g); Protein 3.4g; Carb 10g; Fiber 3.1g; Chol 6mg; Iron 0.6mg; Sodium 389mg; Calc 48mg

CHEESY POTATO BROCCOLI SOUP

POINTS value: 4

PREP: 2 minutes ■ **COOK:** 20 minutes

Frozen steam-and-mash potatoes provide the thickening base for this comforting soup.

- 1 (12-ounce) package fresh broccoli florets
- 3 cups frozen steam-and-mash cut red potatoes (such as Ore-Ida Steam n' Mash)
- 2 cups 1% low-fat milk
- 4 ounces light processed cheese, cubed (such as Velveeta Light)
- 1 teaspoon Worcestershire sauce
- ¼ teaspoon salt
- ⅛ teaspoon dry mustard
- ⅛ teaspoon ground red pepper

1. Microwave broccoli according to package directions. Remove bag from microwave, and set aside.
2. Place potatoes in a medium microwave–safe bowl, and microwave at HIGH 9 minutes or until tender.
3. While potatoes cook, heat milk in a large saucepan over low heat, stirring frequently.
4. When potatoes are done, stir in ½ cup hot milk and cheese. Beat with a mixer at high speed until smooth. Stir potato mixture into remaining hot milk in pan. Stir in broccoli, Worcestershire sauce, and remaining ingredients. Cook 7 minutes or until thoroughly heated. **YIELD: 4 SERVINGS (SERVING SIZE: ABOUT 1⅓ CUPS).**

PER SERVING: Calories 207; Fat 1.6g (sat 0.9g, mono 0.4g, poly 0.2g); Protein 13.6g; Carb 29.7g; Fiber 3.5g; Chol 5mg; Iron 0.9mg; Sodium 939mg; Calc 375mg

Worcestershire Sauce

Pronounced WOOS-tur-shur, this sauce is the perfect addition to meats and seafood, as well as this delicious soup recipe. Its tangy, spicy flavor comes from a blend of soy sauce, vinegar, garlic, lime, tamarind, onions, anchovies, and molasses. While this is the most basic recipe, over the years other spices have found their way into the mix.

TOMATO-FENNEL SOUP WITH FETA

POINTS value: 2   *(pictured on page 142)*

PREP: 5 minutes ■ COOK: 16 minutes
■ OTHER: 10 minutes

This tasty soup is just as delicious even if you don't
have time to puree it. Use plain feta instead of flavored,
if desired.

  1 **fennel bulb with stalks (10 ounces)**
  1 **tablespoon olive oil**
  2 **garlic cloves, minced**
2½ **cups fat-free, less-sodium chicken broth**
  1 **tablespoon fresh lemon juice**
  ¼ **teaspoon freshly ground black pepper**
  2 **(14.5-ounce) cans organic diced tomatoes**
    (such as Muir Glen), undrained
  1 **tablespoon chopped fresh dill**
  ½ **cup (2 ounces) crumbled feta cheese with**
    basil and sun-dried tomatoes
    Fresh dill sprigs (optional)

1. Remove and discard stalks from fennel bulb. Cut
bulb in half lengthwise; discard core. Cut halves into
⅛-inch-thick vertical slices.
2. Heat oil in a Dutch oven over medium heat. Add
fennel; sauté 6 minutes. Add garlic; sauté 2 minutes or
until fennel is tender. Stir in broth and next 3 ingredients. Bring mixture to a boil; reduce heat, and simmer, uncovered, 5 minutes. Stir in dill. Remove from
heat, and cool 10 minutes.
3. Place half of tomato mixture in a blender. Remove
center piece of blender lid (to allow steam to escape);
secure blender lid on blender. Place a clean towel over
opening in blender lid (to avoid splatters). Process
until smooth. Pour soup into a large bowl. Repeat
procedure with remaining half of mixture. Ladle
soup evenly into each of 6 bowls. Top with cheese
and dill sprigs, if desired. **YIELD: 6 SERVINGS (SERVING
SIZE: 1 CUP).**

PER SERVING: Calories 99; Fat 4.7g (sat 1.6g, mono 1.6g, poly 0.2g);
Protein 4.6g; Carb 9.6g; Fiber 2.9g; Chol 8mg; Iron 1.3mg;
Sodium 393mg; Calc 59mg

ITALIAN WEDDING SOUP

POINTS value: 5

PREP: 1 minute ■ COOK: 15 minutes

Our meatballs come together in just the time it takes to
bring the broth to a boil.

  1 **(32-ounce) container fat-free, less-sodium**
    beef broth
1½ **cups water**
  ½ **teaspoon salt, divided**
  8 **ounces lean ground beef**
  2 **tablespoons Italian-seasoned panko**
    (Japanese breadcrumbs)
  ½ **teaspoon garlic powder**
  ¼ **teaspoon freshly ground black pepper**
  1 **large egg**
  3 **cups chopped kale**
  1 **cup uncooked orzo (rice-shaped pasta)**
  5 **tablespoons shredded fresh Parmigiano-**
    Reggiano cheese

1. Combine broth, 1½ cups water, and ¼ teaspoon salt
in a large saucepan. Bring to a boil.
2. While broth mixture comes to a boil, combine
remaining ¼ teaspoon salt, beef, and next 4 ingredients in a bowl. Shape mixture into 32 (¾-inch) balls.
Add meatballs, kale, and orzo to boiling broth; reduce
heat, and simmer, uncovered, 9 minutes or until orzo
is tender. Ladle soup into 5 bowls; sprinkle evenly
with cheese. **YIELD: 5 SERVINGS (SERVING SIZE: 1⅓ CUPS
SOUP AND 1 TABLESPOON CHEESE).**

PER SERVING: Calories 264; Fat 6.8g (sat 2.8g, mono 2.4g, poly 0.5g);
Protein 19.1g; Carb 31.7g; Fiber 2.3g; Chol 64mg; Iron 2mg;
Sodium 743mg; Calc 123mg

THE HISTORY OF A "WEDDING"

The name of this soup doesn't come from a long-
standing tradition of the dish Italians serve at weddings.
Instead, the "wedding" portion of the title refers to how
deliciously the meats and greens go together within the
soup. "Minestra maritata" was the original name for
the soup, but through a mistranslation, the title changed.
On top of this, most food historians believe that the
soup came from Spain, not Italy.

TORTELLONI SOUP WITH SPINACH AND MUSHROOMS

POINTS value: 3

PREP: 3 minutes ▪ **COOK:** 13 minutes

Substitute smaller-shaped cheese tortellini if tortelloni aren't available.

> 3½ **cups fat-free, less-sodium chicken broth**
> 1½ **cups water**
> 1 **(9-ounce) package refrigerated cheese and roasted garlic tortelloni (such as Buitoni)**
> **Cooking spray**
> 3 **garlic cloves, minced**
> 1 **(8-ounce) package sliced fresh mushrooms**
> 1 **(6-ounce) package fresh baby spinach**
> ½ **teaspoon freshly ground black pepper**
> ⅛ **teaspoon salt**

1. Bring chicken broth and 1½ cups water to a boil in a Dutch oven. Stir in tortelloni, and cook according to package directions. Do not drain.

2. While pasta cooks, heat a large nonstick skillet over medium-high heat. Coat pan with cooking spray. Add garlic and mushrooms. Cook 5 minutes; stir, and cook 1 minute.

3. Stir mushroom mixture into tortelloni mixture. Bring to a boil over high heat; add spinach, pepper, and salt. Cook 1 minute or just until spinach wilts. Serve immediately. **YIELD: 6 SERVINGS (SERVING SIZE: ABOUT 1 CUP).**

PER SERVING: Calories 161; Fat 4.2g (sat 1.9g, mono 0g, poly 0g); Protein 7.8g; Carb 22.5g; Fiber 2.7g; Chol 17mg; Iron 1.7mg; Sodium 564mg; Calc 102mg

SODIUM RECOMMENDATIONS

The American Heart Association and the United States Department of Agriculture's Dietary Guidelines recommend limiting your daily sodium intake to 2,300 milligrams or less for healthy adults. The recommendation for those who are salt sensitive—typically individuals who have high blood pressure, are 40 years of age or older, or who are African-American—is 1,500 milligrams a day. Consider this: One teaspoon of table salt contains about 2,300 milligrams of sodium, so you may want to reconsider when you pick up the salt shaker to add a little extra to your dish. One way to keep your sodium intake in check is by using fresh or frozen foods instead of canned, but make sure you choose frozen foods that don't contain added salty seasonings. When you need to buy canned, select products labeled "no salt added," "low sodium," or "less sodium."

SHRIMP NOODLE BOWL

POINTS value: 6   *(pictured on page 141)*

PREP: 2 minutes ■ COOK: 15 minutes

Multitasking is the key to preparing this recipe in record time, so cut up the peas and onions while the shrimp cook.

    4 ounces uncooked linguine, broken in half
    2 cups pretrimmed snow peas, cut diagonally in half
    2 teaspoons dark sesame oil
  1¼ pounds peeled and deveined medium shrimp
    Cooking spray
   ½ (8-ounce) package sliced fresh mushrooms
    1 tablespoon cornstarch
    2 cups fat-free, less-sodium chicken broth (such as Swanson's), divided
    1 tablespoon less-sodium soy sauce
    1 teaspoon chili sauce with garlic (such as Hokan)
   ¼ cup diagonally sliced green onions
    Freshly ground black pepper (optional)

1. Cook pasta in a 5-quart Dutch oven according to package directions, omitting salt and fat. Add snow peas to boiling pasta water during the last 2 minutes of cooking; drain well, and set pan aside.

2. While pasta cooks, heat sesame oil in a large non-stick skillet over medium–high heat. Add shrimp, and cook 2 minutes or until shrimp are done, stirring frequently. Remove shrimp from pan; cover and keep warm. Heavily coat pan with cooking spray. Add mushrooms; cook over medium–high heat 4 minutes, stirring frequently. Remove from heat.

3. Place cornstarch in a 1-cup glass measure or small bowl. Gradually add ½ cup broth, stirring with a whisk. Pour cornstarch mixture into pasta pan. Add remaining 1½ cups broth, soy sauce, and chili sauce, stirring with a whisk. Bring to a boil; cook 1 minute or until slightly thickened, stirring constantly. Stir in pasta, snow peas, shrimp, mushrooms, and green onions. Serve immediately. Sprinkle with pepper, if desired.
YIELD: 4 SERVINGS (SERVING SIZE: 1½ CUPS).

PER SERVING: Calories 333; Fat 5.4g (sat 1g, mono 0.4g, poly 1.1g); Protein 37.9g; Carb 31.9g; Fiber 3.6g; Chol 215mg; Iron 6mg; Sodium 614mg; Calc 119mg

---

✳ **Light vs. Dark Sesame Oil**
When buying sesame oil, you'll find two varieties: light and dark. Light sesame oil has a subtle flavor and high smoke point that makes it ideal for cooking methods like stir-frying that cook foods at high temperatures. Dark sesame oil has a nutty flavor and aroma and is typically used when an ingredient doesn't have to cook for long, or when the oil is added at the end to finish a dish or used as a dipping sauce.

BACON AND BEAN SOUP

POINTS value: 6

PREP: 1 minute ■ COOK: 1 hour and 45 minutes
■ OTHER: 8 hours

You can discard the seasoning packet from the bean mix, or save it for another use. The bacon supplies plenty of smoky flavor in this soup without excessive sodium.

    2 cups dried 15-bean soup mix
    4 center-cut bacon slices
    1 cup refrigerated prechopped celery, onion, and green bell pepper mix
    1 (14.5-ounce) can diced tomatoes with basil, garlic, and oregano, undrained
    2 cups fat-free, less-sodium chicken broth
    2 cups water
    Shredded fresh Parmigiano-Reggiano cheese (optional)

1. Sort and wash beans; place in a large Dutch oven. Cover with water to 2 inches above beans; cover and let stand 8 hours. Drain beans.

2. Cook bacon in a large Dutch oven over medium heat 4 minutes or until crisp. Remove bacon from pan; crumble. Add celery mix to drippings in pan; sauté 4 minutes or until tender. Add crumbled bacon, beans, tomatoes, broth, and 2 cups water. Bring to a boil; cover, reduce heat, and simmer 1½ to 2 hours or until beans are tender. Ladle soup into bowls. Garnish with cheese, if desired. **YIELD: 6 SERVINGS (SERVING SIZE: 1½ CUPS).**

PER SERVING: Calories 314; Fat 3.4g (sat 0.3g, mono 0g, poly 0g); Protein 21.2g; Carb 55.6g; Fiber 0.9g; Chol 3mg; Iron 7.2mg; Sodium 612mg; Calc 95mg

CHICKEN ORZO SOUP

POINTS value: 3

PREP: 5 minutes ■ **COOK:** 18 minutes

Orzo replaces noodles in this twist on homemade chicken noodle soup. The addition of lime juice gives it a fresh, light tang. Be sure to use freshly squeezed lime juice for the best flavor.

- 6 cups fat-free, less-sodium chicken broth (such as Swanson's), divided
- 1 cup baby carrots, thinly sliced
- ½ cup uncooked orzo (rice-shaped pasta)
- Cooking spray
- ½ cup refrigerated prechopped celery, onion, and green bell pepper mix
- 1 tablespoon water
- 2 cups chopped cooked chicken breast
- ¼ cup fresh lime juice
- ¼ teaspoon salt
- ¼ teaspoon freshly ground black pepper
- Chopped fresh parsley (optional)

1. Combine 4 cups broth and carrots in a Dutch oven. Cover and bring to a boil. Stir in orzo, and cook, uncovered, 8 minutes or until pasta is tender. Do not drain pasta.

2. While orzo cooks, heat a large nonstick skillet over medium-high heat. Coat pan with cooking spray. Add celery mixture, and cook 5 minutes or until tender, stirring often, adding 1 tablespoon water after 2 minutes, if necessary, to keep from sticking. Stir celery mixture, remaining 2 cups broth, chicken, and next 3 ingredients into orzo mixture. Cook over medium-high heat 1 to 2 minutes or until thoroughly heated. Garnish with parsley, if desired. **YIELD: 6 SERVINGS (SERVING SIZE: 1⅓ CUPS).**

PER SERVING: Calories 165; Fat 2g (sat 0.5g, mono 0.6g, poly 0.4g); Protein 20.6g; Carb 15.3g; Fiber 1.5g; Chol 40mg; Iron 0.8mg; Sodium 664mg; Calc 20mg

COCONUT CHICKEN SOUP

POINTS value: 7

PREP: 3 minutes ■ **COOK:** 10 minutes

You can add the rice directly to the soup without microwaving it. The heat from the soup will warm it.

- 1 tablespoon olive oil
- 2 garlic cloves, minced
- 1½ tablespoons minced peeled fresh ginger
- 1 tablespoon lemongrass paste (such as Gourmet Garden)
- 3 cups fat-free, less-sodium chicken broth
- 3 cups shredded cooked chicken
- 1 (13.5-ounce) can light coconut milk
- 2 tablespoons fish sauce
- 1 tablespoon fresh lime juice
- 1 tablespoon chopped fresh cilantro
- 1 (8.8-ounce) package precooked jasmine rice (such as Uncle Ben's Ready Rice)
- Fresh cilantro leaves (optional)

1. Heat oil in a large Dutch oven over medium-high heat. Add garlic, ginger, and lemongrass paste; sauté 1 minute or until tender. Stir in broth and next 5 ingredients. Bring to a boil; cover, reduce heat, and simmer 5 minutes or until thoroughly heated. Add rice, stirring until thoroughly heated. Sprinkle with cilantro leaves, if desired. **YIELD: 6 SERVINGS (SERVING SIZE: ABOUT 1 CUP).**

PER SERVING: Calories 330; Fat 9.1g (sat 4.2g, mono 2.5g, poly 0.8g); Protein 26.3g; Carb 37.8g; Fiber 0.1g; Chol 60mg; Iron 2.4mg; Sodium 791mg; Calc 13mg

* Fish Sauce

Made of anchovies, fish sauce is low in calories but high in sodium, so it's best to use it sparingly. The good news is that a little goes a long way.

KALE, LENTIL, AND SAUSAGE SOUP

POINTS value: 3

PREP: 4 minutes ■ **COOK:** 19 minutes

You'll benefit from the many nutrients found in kale when you enjoy this quick-cooking hearty soup.

Cooking spray
1 cup chopped onion
2 garlic cloves, minced
6 ounces reduced-fat chicken sweet Italian sausage (such as Applegate Farms), cut into ¼-inch slices
4 cups fat-free, less-sodium chicken broth
3 cups coarsely chopped kale
1 cup coarsely chopped seeded tomato (about 1 medium)
⅛ teaspoon freshly ground black pepper
1 (15-ounce) can lentils, rinsed and drained
2 tablespoons chopped fresh basil (optional)

1. Heat a 4-quart saucepan or Dutch oven over medium-high heat. Coat pan with cooking spray. Add onion and garlic to pan. Sauté 2 minutes or until lightly browned. Add sausage; sauté 2 minutes.
2. Stir in chicken broth and next 4 ingredients. Bring to a boil; cover, reduce heat, and simmer 12 minutes. Remove from heat, and stir in basil, if desired. Ladle into bowls. **YIELD: 4 SERVINGS (SERVING SIZE: ABOUT 1⅓ CUPS).**

PER SERVING: Calories 185; Fat 4.5g (sat 1.1g, mono 0.1g, poly 0.2g); Protein 15.4g; Carb 22.1g; Fiber 7.6g; Chol 35mg; Iron 4.2mg; Sodium 873mg; Calc 105mg

BUYING AND STORING KALE

When buying this winter green, look for a deep blue-green color and choose small bunches that don't have any signs of wilting or discoloration. When storing fresh kale, wash it as soon as you get home from the grocery store, then pat dry, wrap in damp paper towels, and store in an unsealed plastic bag in the refrigerator. It will stay fresh for three to five days.

ITALIAN SAUSAGE AND CABBAGE SOUP

POINTS value: 3

PREP: 15 minutes ■ **COOK:** 43 minutes

If you prefer a little less spice, opt for regular turkey Italian sausage.

¾ pound hot turkey Italian sausage
Cooking spray
2 cups frozen vegetable seasoning blend
2 garlic cloves, minced
4 cups coarsely chopped green cabbage
3 cups fat-free, less-sodium chicken broth
1 (14.5-ounce) can diced tomatoes with basil, garlic, and oregano (such as Hunt's), undrained
1 cup chopped carrot
1 cup water
½ teaspoon freshly ground black pepper
1 (15.5-ounce) can cannellini beans, rinsed and drained

1. Remove and discard casings from sausage. Heat a Dutch oven over medium-high heat. Coat pan with cooking spray. Add sausage, seasoning blend, and garlic to pan; cook 8 minutes or until browned, stirring to crumble sausage. Add cabbage and next 5 ingredients.
2. Mash ½ cup beans with a fork; stir mashed beans and remaining beans into soup. Bring to a boil; cover, reduce heat, and simmer 30 minutes. **YIELD: 8 SERVINGS (SERVING SIZE: 1¼ CUPS).**

PER SERVING: Calories 167; Fat 5.2g (sat 0.1g, mono 0.1g, poly 0.2g); Protein 10.4g; Carb 20g; Fiber 3.6g; Chol 25mg; Iron 1.5mg; Sodium 737mg; Calc 36mg

seasonal menus

Fudgy Chocolate Peppermint Brownies, *page 169*

Fall Harvest Menu

Serves 8

Total **POINTS** value per serving: 16

Orange-and-Herb–Roasted Turkey Breast

Cranberry-Almond Couscous Pilaf

Roasted Sweet Potato Halves with Rosemary and Garlic

Roasted Green Beans and Shallots

White Chocolate–Drizzled Cranberry-Oatmeal Cookies

GAME PLAN:

1. **One day in advance:**
   - Trim green beans for **Roasted Green Beans and Shallots.**
   - Prepare **White Chocolate–Drizzled Cranberry-Oatmeal Cookies.**

2. **About 1½ hours before the meal:**
   - Prepare **Orange-and-Herb–Roasted Turkey Breast.**

3. **While turkey cooks:**
   - Prepare **Sweet Potato Halves with Rosemary and Garlic,** and place in oven during last 30 minutes of cook time for the turkey.

4. **While turkey and sweet potato halves cook:**
   - Prepare **Cranberry-Almond Couscous Pilaf.**
   - Prepare ingredients for **Roasted Green Beans and Shallots.**

5. **While turkey stands:**
   - Increase oven temperature to 450°, and cook **Roasted Green Beans and Shallots.**
   - Prepare gravy.

ORANGE-AND-HERB–ROASTED TURKEY BREAST

POINTS value: 7

PREP: 5 minutes ■ **COOK:** 1 hour and 16 minutes
■ **OTHER:** 10 minutes

We used an herb blend of fresh rosemary, marjoram, sage, and thyme to avoid purchasing packages of individual herbs. These blends are usually available in the supermarket during the holidays.

> 1 navel orange
> 2 tablespoons chopped fresh mixed herbs
> ¼ cup butter, softened
> 2 garlic cloves, minced
> ¼ teaspoon salt
> ¼ teaspoon freshly ground black pepper
> 1 (5- to 5½-pound) whole turkey breast
> Cooking spray
> 3 tablespoons all-purpose flour
> ¾ cup fat-free, less-sodium chicken broth
> Orange wedges (optional)
> Chopped fresh mixed herbs (optional)

1. Preheat oven to 400°.
2. Grate 1 tablespoon rind and squeeze ⅓ cup juice from orange. Combine rind, herbs, and next 4 ingredients in a small bowl.
3. Rinse turkey breast with cold water; pat dry. Trim excess fat. Starting at neck cavity, loosen skin from breast by inserting fingers, gently pushing between skin and meat. Do not completely detach skin. Rub herb butter under loosened skin.
4. Place turkey breast, skin side up, on a rack coated with cooking spray. Place rack in roasting pan. Pour orange juice over turkey. Insert meat thermometer into meaty part of breast, making sure not to touch bone. Bake at 400° for 1 hour and 10 minutes or until thermometer registers 170°, basting occasionally. Let stand 10 minutes.
5. While turkey stands, pour pan drippings through a sieve into a saucepan. Add flour, stirring with a whisk until smooth. Add chicken broth, stirring with a whisk until smooth. Bring to a boil; reduce heat, and simmer 4 to 5 minutes or until thickened.

6. Remove and discard skin from turkey. Cut turkey into thin slices; garnish with orange wedges and mixed herbs, if desired. Serve with gravy. **YIELD: 8 SERVINGS (SERVING SIZE: 3 OUNCES TURKEY AND 3½ TABLESPOONS GRAVY).**

PER SERVING: Calories 308; Fat 7.1g (sat 4g, mono 1.7g, poly 0.6g); Protein 53.8g; Carb 3.9g; Fiber 0.2g; Chol 162mg; Iron 2.9mg; Sodium 257mg; Calc 28mg

CRANBERRY-ALMOND COUSCOUS PILAF

POINTS value: 3

PREP: 4 minutes ■ **COOK:** 6 minutes
■ **OTHER:** 5 minutes

Transform this side dish into a salad simply by tossing leftover turkey or chopped cooked chicken and your favorite fat-free vinaigrette into the cooled couscous.

> 1 tablespoon olive oil
> 3 tablespoons minced shallots (1 large shallot)
> 1¼ cups water
> ¼ teaspoon salt
> ¼ teaspoon freshly ground black pepper
> 1 cup uncooked couscous
> ⅓ cup chopped sweetened dried cranberries
> 2 teaspoons grated lemon rind
> ¼ cup sliced almonds, toasted
> 1 tablespoon chopped fresh parsley

1. Heat oil in a medium saucepan over medium–high heat. Add shallots; sauté 2 minutes or until tender. Add 1¼ cups water, salt, and pepper. Bring to a boil; stir in couscous, cranberries, and rind. Remove from heat. Cover and let stand 5 minutes or until liquid is absorbed.
2. Add almonds and parsley; fluff with a fork. **YIELD: 8 SERVINGS (SERVING SIZE: ½ CUP).**

PER SERVING: Calories 132; Fat 3.4g (sat 0.4g, mono 2.2g, poly 0.6g); Protein 3.5g; Carb 22.3g; Fiber 1.8g; Chol 0mg; Iron 0.5mg; Sodium 76mg; Calc 16mg

ROASTED SWEET POTATO HALVES WITH ROSEMARY AND GARLIC

POINTS value: 2

PREP: 13 minutes ■ **COOK:** 25 minutes

Small sweet potatoes work best for this recipe.

- **2 tablespoons olive oil**
- **8 small sweet potatoes (about 3½ pounds), halved lengthwise**
- **½ teaspoon salt**
- **½ teaspoon freshly ground black pepper**
- **2 garlic cloves, minced**
- **4 teaspoons chopped fresh rosemary**

1. Preheat oven to 400°.
2. Brush oil evenly over cut sides of potatoes; sprinkle with salt and pepper. Place potatoes, cut sides down, on a foil-lined baking sheet.
3. Bake at 400° for 15 minutes. Turn potatoes; sprinkle with garlic and rosemary, and bake an additional 10 minutes or until tender. **YIELD: 8 SERVINGS (SERVING SIZE: 2 HALVES).**

PER SERVING: Calories 141; Fat 3.6g (sat 0.5g, mono 2.5g, poly 0.4g); Protein 2.5g; Carb 25.4g; Fiber 4.1g; Chol 0mg; Iron 0.9mg; Sodium 189mg; Calc 49mg

ROASTED GREEN BEANS AND SHALLOTS

POINTS value: 1

PREP: 13 minutes ■ **COOK:** 15 minutes

Packaged trimmed green beans are available now and will save you time if you're in a rush.

- **2 pounds fresh green beans, trimmed**
- **½ cup thinly sliced shallots (about 3 large)**
- **1½ tablespoons olive oil**
- **½ teaspoon salt**
- **½ teaspoon freshly ground black pepper**
- **Cooking spray**
- **1 tablespoon white balsamic vinegar**

1. Preheat oven to 450°.
2. Combine first 5 ingredients on a large rimmed baking sheet coated with cooking spray. Bake at 450°

for 15 to 20 minutes or until green beans are tender and shallots begin to caramelize. Drizzle balsamic vinegar over bean mixture; toss well. **YIELD: 8 SERVINGS (SERVING SIZE: ABOUT 1 CUP).**

PER SERVING: Calories 63; Fat 2.7g (sat 0.4g, mono 1.9g, poly 0.3g); Protein 2.1g; Carb 9.2g; Fiber 3.5g; Chol 0mg; Iron 1.2mg; Sodium 153mg; Calc 42mg

WHITE CHOCOLATE–DRIZZLED CRANBERRY-OATMEAL COOKIES

POINTS value: 3   *(pictured on page 8)*

PREP: 9 minutes ■ **COOK:** 11 minutes
■ **OTHER:** 1 hour and 20 minutes

Substitute regular-flavored dried cranberries, if desired. Chill cookies briefly to firm up the white chocolate if you're in a hurry.

- **½ cup light butter, softened**
- **2 large egg whites**
- **1 (17.5-ounce) package oatmeal cookie mix (such as Betty Crocker)**
- **½ cup orange-flavored sweetened dried cranberries (such as Craisins)**
- **2 ounces premium white baking chocolate (such as Ghirardelli)**

1. Preheat oven to 375°.
2. Place butter in a bowl. Beat with a mixer at medium speed until creamy; beat in egg whites. Add cookie mix, and beat until combined. Stir in cranberries.
3. Drop dough by rounded tablespoonfuls onto baking sheets lined with parchment paper. Bake at 375° for 11 minutes or until golden. Let cool on pans 5 minutes, and transfer cookies to wire racks. Cool completely.
4. While cookies cool, place white chocolate in a small microwave-safe bowl. Microwave at MEDIUM (50% power) 1 minute; stir until smooth. Drizzle chocolate over cookies with a fork; let stand 1 hour or until white chocolate is firm. **YIELD: 24 SERVINGS (SERVING SIZE: 1 COOKIE).**

PER SERVING: Calories 121; Fat 4g (sat 2g, mono 0.7g, poly 0.1g); Protein 2.1g; Carb 20.3g; Fiber 0.9g; Chol 5mg; Iron 0.4mg; Sodium 107mg; Calc 9mg

Hearty Winter Menu

Serves 6

Total **POINTS** value per serving: 10

Beef Burgundy Stew

White Cheddar–Rosemary Skillet Cornbread

Radicchio and Brussels Sprouts Salad

Fudgy Chocolate Peppermint Brownies

GAME PLAN:

1. One day in advance:

- Prepare **Beef Burgundy Stew.**
- Prepare dressing and chop radicchio and Brussels sprouts for **Radicchio and Brussels Sprouts Salad;** store each separately in an airtight container in the refrigerator.

2. About 1½ hours before the meal:

- Prepare **Fudgy Chocolate Peppermint Brownies.**

3. While brownies cool:

- Prepare **White Cheddar–Rosemary Skillet Cornbread.**

4. While cornbread bakes:

- Reheat stew.
- Toast the hazelnuts, and assemble salad.

BEEF BURGUNDY STEW

POINTS value: 4

PREP: 2 minutes ■ **COOK:** 1 hour and 7 minutes

Burgundy wines are dry and robust in flavor and are traditionally made from pinot noir grapes. If you can't find a high-quality Burgundy wine, substitute cabernet sauvignon.

   3 cups frozen stew vegetables (such as McKenzie's)
   2 center-cut bacon slices
1½ pounds beef sirloin, cut into 1-inch pieces
   ½ teaspoon salt
   ½ teaspoon freshly ground black pepper
   2 tablespoons water
   1 (8-ounce) package sliced mushrooms
   2 tablespoons all-purpose flour
   1 cup water
1½ cups Burgundy or other dry red wine

1. Place vegetables in a colander; rinse with cold water until thawed. Drain well.
2. While vegetables drain, cook bacon in a Dutch oven over medium-high heat until crisp. Remove bacon from pan, reserving drippings in pan; set bacon aside.
3. Sprinkle beef with salt and pepper; add to drippings in pan. Sauté 8 minutes or until browned. Remove beef from pan; keep warm. Stir in 2 tablespoons water and mushrooms, scraping pan to loosen browned bits. Cook 4 minutes or until mushrooms are browned, stirring often.
4. Return bacon and beef to pan. Gradually stir in flour; add vegetables, 1 cup water, and wine. Bring to a boil; cover, reduce heat, and simmer 45 minutes or until stew is thickened and vegetables are tender. **YIELD: 6 SERVINGS (SERVING SIZE: 1 CUP).**

PER SERVING: Calories 201; Fat 5g (sat 1.9g, mono 1.8g, poly 0.2g); Protein 25.3g; Carb 12.5g; Fiber 0.9g; Chol 43mg; Iron 2mg; Sodium 313mg; Calc 21mg

WHITE CHEDDAR–ROSEMARY SKILLET CORNBREAD

POINTS value: 3

PREP: 4 minutes ■ **COOK:** 16 minutes

Invert this Southern favorite on a serving plate to show off its crusty brown bottom. Store the other two wedges in an airtight container to reheat and serve with soup or salad for a quick lunch.

   1 large egg, lightly beaten
   2 cups nonfat buttermilk
1¾ cups self-rising cornmeal mix
   ½ cup (2 ounces) reduced-fat shredded sharp white cheddar cheese (such as Cabot)
   1 tablespoon chopped fresh rosemary
Cooking spray

1. Preheat oven to 450°.
2. Place a 10-inch cast-iron skillet in oven while it preheats.
3. Combine first 5 ingredients in a medium bowl, stirring well with a whisk.
4. Remove hot pan from oven. Coat pan with cooking spray. Pour batter into pan. Bake at 450° for 16 minutes or until bread is brown around edges and pulls away from sides of pan. Invert onto a wire rack. Cut into 8 wedges. **YIELD: 8 SERVINGS (SERVING SIZE: 1 WEDGE).**

PER SERVING: Calories 142; Fat 2.9g (sat 1.2g, mono 0.2g, poly 0.1g); Protein 6.5g; Carb 23.2g; Fiber 1.8g; Chol 28mg; Iron 1.1mg; Sodium 505mg; Calc 164mg

RADICCHIO AND BRUSSELS SPROUTS SALAD

POINTS value: 2

PREP: 11 minutes ■ **COOK:** 5 minutes

Mild sherry vinegar and honey create a sweet and sour flavor profile that mellows out the bitterness of the radicchio and complements the Brussels sprouts in this high-fiber, antioxidant-rich pairing.

    2 tablespoons sherry vinegar
    1 tablespoon finely chopped shallots (1 shallot)
    1 tablespoon water
    1 tablespoon extra-virgin olive oil
    1 tablespoon honey
    ¼ teaspoon salt
    ¼ teaspoon freshly ground black pepper
    2½ cups coarsely chopped radicchio
    2 cups shredded trimmed Brussels sprouts (about
       8 ounces)
    ⅓ cup coarsely chopped hazelnuts, toasted
    2 tablespoons (0.5 ounce) shaved Parmigiano-
       Reggiano cheese

1. Combine first 7 ingredients in a medium bowl. Add radicchio and Brussels sprouts; toss well. Divide salad evenly among 6 plates. Top evenly with hazelnuts and cheese. **YIELD: 6 SERVINGS (SERVING SIZE: ¾ CUP SALAD, 2½ TEASPOONS HAZELNUTS, AND 1 TEASPOON CHEESE).**

PER SERVING: Calories 99; Fat 6.8g (sat 0.9g, mono 4.9g, poly 0.8g); Protein 2.9g; Carb 7.8g; Fiber 1.9g; Chol 1mg; Iron 0.9mg; Sodium 134mg; Calc 42mg

FUDGY CHOCOLATE PEPPERMINT BROWNIES

POINTS value: 1   *(pictured on page 143)*

PREP: 7 minutes ■ **COOK:** 25 minutes
■ **OTHER:** 30 minutes

These decadent brownies earned our Test Kitchens' highest rating. For a **POINTS** value of 2, try topping each serving with ¼ cup light ice cream.

    1 cup self-rising flour
    1 cup "measures like sugar" reduced-calorie
       baking blend (such as Splenda Sugar Blend)
    3 tablespoons Dutch process cocoa
    3 large egg whites
    1 tablespoon vegetable oil
    1 teaspoon peppermint extract
    ⅓ cup semisweet chocolate chunks
    Cooking spray

1. Preheat oven to 350°.
2. Lightly spoon flour into a dry measuring cup; level with a knife. Combine flour, baking blend, and cocoa in a large bowl. Add egg whites, oil, and peppermint extract; stir until blended. Stir in chocolate chunks.
3. Spread batter into an 8-inch square pan coated with cooking spray. Bake at 350° for 25 minutes. Cool completely in pan on a wire rack. Cut into 16 squares. **YIELD: 16 SERVINGS (SERVING SIZE: 1 SQUARE).**

PER SERVING: Calories 57; Fat 2.1g (sat 0.8g, mono 0.8g, poly 0.4g); Protein 1.8g; Carb 8.6g; Fiber 0.7g; Chol 0mg; Iron 0.7mg; Sodium 110mg; Calc 29mg

Celebrating Spring Menu

Serves 8

Total **POINTS** value per serving: 15

Creamy Asparagus Soup

Herb-Roasted Leg of Lamb

Horseradish Mashed Potatoes

Watercress and Sweet Pea Salad

Vanilla Bean Bread Pudding with Mixed Berries

GAME PLAN:

1. One day in advance:
- Prepare **Creamy Asparagus Soup,** reserving fresh dill, lemon juice, salt, and pepper. Store in an airtight container in refrigerator.
- Prepare **Vanilla Bean Bread Pudding.** Store, covered, in the refrigerator.
- Prepare marinade for **Herb-Roasted Leg of Lamb,** and marinate lamb overnight.

2. About 1½ hours before the meal:
- Cook Herb-Roasted Leg of Lamb.

3. While lamb cooks:
- Prepare **Watercress and Sweet Pea Salad.**
- Prepare **Horseradish Mashed Potatoes.**
- Reheat **Creamy Asparagus Soup.**
- Prepare **Mixed Berries.**

4. While lamb stands:
- Decrease oven temperature to 350°, and reheat **Vanilla Bean Bread Pudding.**
- Prepare pan jus.
- Stir fresh dill, lemon juice, salt, and pepper into **Creamy Asparagus Soup.**

5. Top bread pudding with berries just before serving.

CREAMY ASPARAGUS SOUP

POINTS value: 1

PREP: 6 minutes ■ **COOK:** 11 minutes

Reserve some of the cooked asparagus tips and a few sprigs of dill for a festive garnish.

- 1 tablespoon olive oil
- 1½ cups chopped onion
- 2 garlic cloves, minced
- 1 pound asparagus spears
- 1 tablespoon water
- 2 cups fat-free, less-sodium chicken broth
- 2 cups fat-free milk
- 1 cup refrigerated country-style mashed potatoes (such as Simply Potatoes)
- 1 tablespoon chopped fresh dill
- 2 tablespoons fresh lemon juice
- ¼ teaspoon salt
- ¼ teaspoon black pepper

1. Heat oil in a large Dutch oven over medium-high heat. Add onion and garlic; cook 4 minutes or until tender, stirring often.

2. While onion mixture cooks, break off tough ends of asparagus, and cut spears into 2-inch pieces. Place asparagus and 1 tablespoon water in a microwave-safe bowl. Cover with plastic wrap; vent. Microwave at HIGH 5 minutes or until almost tender.

3. Add asparagus, broth, milk, and potatoes to onion mixture in pan. Cover and cook over medium-high heat 5 minutes or until thoroughly heated. Place one-third of soup in a blender. Remove center piece of blender lid (to allow steam to escape); secure blender lid on blender. Place a clean towel over opening in blender lid (to avoid splatters). Blend until smooth. Pour into a large bowl. Repeat procedure with remaining soup. Return soup to pan. Stir in dill and remaining ingredients just before serving. **YIELD: 8 SERVINGS (SERVING SIZE: ABOUT 1 CUP).**

PER SERVING: Calories 86; Fat 2.1g (sat 0.3g, mono 1.2g, poly 0.2g); Protein 4.5g; Carb 13.1g; Fiber 2.2g; Chol 1mg; Iron 0.4mg; Sodium 313mg; Calc 87mg

HERB-ROASTED LEG OF LAMB

POINTS value: 8

PREP: 13 minutes ■ **COOK:** 1 hour and 18 minutes
■ **OTHER:** 8 hours and 10 minutes

Look for a rolled lamb leg with an even thickness for even cooking. You can roll and tie your own with kitchen string if your market doesn't carry them.

- 1 large lemon
- 3 tablespoons chopped fresh mint
- 2 tablespoons chopped fresh rosemary
- 2 tablespoons olive oil
- 3 garlic cloves, minced
- 1 (4-pound) rolled boneless leg of lamb
- Cooking spray
- ½ teaspoon salt
- ½ teaspoon freshly ground black pepper
- 1 tablespoon all-purpose flour
- 1 cup fat-free, less-sodium beef broth

1. Grate 1 teaspoon rind and squeeze 3 tablespoons juice from lemon. Combine rind, juice, mint, and next 3 ingredients in a large heavy-duty zip-top plastic bag. Add lamb, and seal bag, turning to coat. Refrigerate 8 hours.

2. Preheat oven to 425°.

3. Remove lamb from marinade, discarding marinade. Place lamb in bottom of a broiler pan coated with cooking spray. Sprinkle with salt and pepper. Bake at 425° for 1 hour and 5 minutes or until a thermometer registers 145° (medium-rare) to 160° (medium). Let roast stand 10 minutes before slicing. Place pan drippings in a saucepan. Add flour, stirring with a whisk until smooth. Gradually add broth, stirring with a whisk. Bring to a boil; reduce heat, and simmer, uncovered, 5 minutes or until slightly thickened, stirring often. Serve lamb with herbed pan jus. **YIELD: 8 SERVINGS (SERVING SIZE: 3 OUNCES LAMB AND 2 TABLESPOONS PAN JUS).**

PER SERVING: Calories 356; Fat 16.4g (sat 5.8g, mono 7.9g, poly 1g); Protein 47.2g; Carb 1.9g; Fiber 0.3g; Chol 150mg; Iron 3.8mg; Sodium 316mg; Calc 23mg

HORSERADISH MASHED POTATOES

POINTS value: 2

PREP: 3 minutes ■ **COOK:** 8 minutes

2 pounds Yukon Gold potatoes, unpeeled and cut into 1-inch cubes
¾ cup 1% low-fat milk
¼ cup light sour cream
2 tablespoons prepared horseradish
1 tablespoon butter
½ teaspoon salt
½ teaspoon freshly ground black pepper

1. Place potato in a microwave-safe bowl. Cover bowl with plastic wrap (do not allow plastic wrap to touch food); vent. Microwave at HIGH 8 minutes or until tender. Carefully remove plastic wrap.
2. Mash potato with a potato masher. Add milk and remaining ingredients; mash with potato masher to desired consistency. **YIELD: 8 SERVINGS (SERVING SIZE: ABOUT ⅔ CUP).**

PER SERVING: Calories 110; Fat 2.2g (sat 1.4g, mono 0.4g, poly 0.1g); Protein 4.1g; Carb 22.5g; Fiber 2.5g; Chol 7mg; Iron 0.9mg; Sodium 186mg; Calc 47mg

WATERCRESS AND SWEET PEA SALAD

POINTS value: 1

(pictured on page 144)

PREP: 10 minutes

1 tablespoon fresh lemon juice
1 tablespoon water
1 tablespoon extra-virgin olive oil
2 teaspoons Dijon mustard
½ teaspoon freshly ground black pepper
¼ teaspoon salt
2 small carrots
1 cup frozen petite green peas, thawed
¼ cup mint leaves
2 (4-ounce) packages watercress

1. Combine first 6 ingredients in a large bowl, stirring with a whisk.
2. Cut carrots into thin ribbons using a vegetable peeler to measure 1 cup. Add carrot ribbons, peas,

mint, and watercress to dressing in bowl; toss well.
YIELD: 8 SERVINGS (SERVING SIZE: ABOUT 1 CUP).

PER SERVING: Calories 37; Fat 1.8g (sat 0.3g, mono 1.4g, poly 0.2g); Protein 1.6g; Carb 4.4g; Fiber 1.4g; Chol 0mg; Iron 0.4mg; Sodium 150mg; Calc 46mg

VANILLA BEAN BREAD PUDDING WITH MIXED BERRIES

POINTS value: 3

PREP: 8 minutes ■ **COOK:** 46 minutes

Melted vanilla bean ice cream is the secret ingredient for this light, fluffy dessert topped with juicy, sweet berries. We used 1 cup each of strawberries, blueberries, and raspberries, but you can use any combination you prefer.

4 large egg whites
1 large egg
5 cups vanilla bean low-fat ice cream
8 cups (1-inch) French bread cubes (about 10 ounces)
Butter-flavored cooking spray
3 cups mixed fresh berries
1 tablespoon sugar
1 tablespoon water
Mint sprigs (optional)

1. Preheat oven to 350°.
2. Combine egg whites and egg in a large bowl, stirring with a whisk. Place ice cream in a microwave-safe bowl. Microwave at HIGH 1 minute; stir with a whisk until smooth and melted. Add ice cream to egg, stirring with a whisk. Add bread cubes, stirring until coated with egg mixture.
3. Spoon bread mixture into an 8-inch square pan coated with cooking spray.
4. Bake at 350° for 45 minutes or until pudding is puffed and a knife inserted in center comes out clean.
5. While pudding bakes, combine berries, sugar, and 1 tablespoon water; cover and let stand. Top warm pudding with berry mixture. Garnish with mint sprigs, if desired. **YIELD: 12 SERVINGS (SERVING SIZE: ¹⁄₁₂ OF PUDDING AND ¼ CUP BERRY MIXTURE).**

PER SERVING: Calories 189; Fat 2.9g (sat 0.9g, mono 0.2g, poly 0.6g); Protein 6.7g; Carb 33.5g; Fiber 2.8g; Chol 19mg; Iron 1mg; Sodium 172mg; Calc 110mg

Summer Mexican Fiesta Menu

Serves 8

Total **POINTS** value per serving: 11

Kiwi-Watermelon Agua Fresca

Roasted Tomatillo and Tomato Salsa

Seven-Layer Mexican Salad

Chicken Enchiladas

Caramel Flans

GAME PLAN:

1. One day in advance:
- Prepare **Roasted Tomatillo and Tomato Salsa;** store in an airtight container in refrigerator.
- Prepare **Kiwi-Watermelon Agua Fresca;** chill until ready to serve.
- Prepare **Caramel Flans;** cover and chill overnight.

2. About 1 hour before the meal:
- Prepare **Chicken Enchiladas.**

3. While enchiladas bake:
- Prepare **Seven-Layer Mexican Salad.**

4. Pour agua fresca, and invert custards onto plates just before serving.

KIWI-WATERMELON AGUA FRESCA

POINTS value: 1

PREP: 6 minutes

- 8 ripe kiwifruit, peeled and halved
- 6 cups cubed watermelon
- 4 cups water
- ⅔ cup "measures-like-sugar" calorie-free sweetener (such as Splenda)
- ¼ cup fresh lime juice

1. Place one-third of kiwifruit, 2 cups watermelon, and 1⅓ cups water in a blender; process until smooth. Pour pureed mixture through a sieve into a pitcher; discard solids. Repeat procedure twice with remaining kiwifruit, watermelon, and water. Stir in sweetener and lime juice. Chill until ready to serve. **YIELD: 8 SERVINGS (SERVING SIZE: 1 CUP).**

PER SERVING: Calories 81; Fat 0.6g (sat 0g, mono 0.1g, poly 0.3g); Protein 1.6g; Carb 19.9g; Fiber 2.7g; Chol 0mg; Iron 0.5mg; Sodium 3mg; Calc 34mg

ROASTED TOMATILLO AND TOMATO SALSA

POINTS value: 0

PREP: 3 minutes ■ **COOK:** 10 minutes

Serve this salsa with your Chicken Enchiladas or atop the Seven-Layer Mexican Salad. You can also pair it with baked tortilla chips—a serving of 8 light baked tortilla chips has a **POINTS** value of 1. If you prefer, cover and refrigerate the salsa 2 hours or until thoroughly chilled. A ½-cup serving has a **POINTS** value of 1.

- 4 medium tomatillos
- 4 plum tomatoes, halved
- Cooking spray
- 1 large garlic clove
- 1 large jalapeño pepper, seeded and halved
- ½ cup fresh cilantro leaves
- 2 tablespoons fresh lime juice
- 2 teaspoons olive oil
- ¼ teaspoon salt
- ¼ teaspoon freshly ground black pepper

1. Preheat broiler.
2. Discard husks and stems from tomatillos; cut tomatillos in half. Place tomatillos and tomatoes, skin sides up, on a large rimmed baking sheet coated with cooking spray. Broil 10 minutes or until vegetables begin to blister and are lightly browned.
3. Drop garlic through food chute with processor on. Process until minced. Add jalapeño pepper and cilantro; process until chopped. Add roasted vegetables, lime juice, and remaining ingredients. Process until chopped. **YIELD: 8 SERVINGS (SERVING SIZE: ¼ CUP).**

PER SERVING: Calories 24; Fat 1.4g (sat 0.2g, mono 0.9g, poly 0.2g); Protein 0.5g; Carb 3.1g; Fiber 0.8g; Chol 0mg; Iron 0.3mg; Sodium 76mg; Calc 5mg

SEVEN-LAYER MEXICAN SALAD

POINTS value: 3

PREP: 6 minutes

This colorful, easy-to-assemble salad earned our Test Kitchens' highest rating. Show off the layers of this salad by serving it in a trifle dish.

- 1¼ cups frozen whole-kernel corn
- 4 cups chopped romaine lettuce
- 1 (15-ounce) can no-salt-added black beans, rinsed and drained
- 1 large ripe tomato, chopped
- ½ cup refrigerated light ranch dressing (such as Naturally Fresh)
- 1 tablespoon 40%-less-sodium taco seasoning (such as Old El Paso)
- ½ cup (2 ounces) reduced-fat shredded sharp cheddar cheese
- ⅓ cup sliced green onions

1. Place frozen corn in a colander; rinse with cold water until thawed. Drain well.
2. Spread lettuce on bottom of a 2-quart trifle dish. Layer black beans, corn, and tomato over lettuce.
3. Combine ranch dressing and taco seasoning; spread evenly over tomatoes. Sprinkle with cheese and green onions. **YIELD: 8 SERVINGS (SERVING SIZE: 1 CUP).**

PER SERVING: Calories 142; Fat 6.4g (sat 1.9g, mono 0.1g, poly 0.2g); Protein 5.3g; Carb 17.2g; Fiber 3.1g; Chol 5mg; Iron 1mg; Sodium 242mg; Calc 78mg

CHICKEN ENCHILADAS

POINTS value: 4

PREP: 8 minutes ■ **COOK:** 20 minutes

These cheesy, slightly spicy chicken enchiladas are destined to become a family favorite.

1½ cups (12 ounces) chopped cooked chicken
1 (8-ounce) package fat-free cream cheese
1 (4-ounce) can chopped green chiles, undrained
1 teaspoon ground cumin
8 (7-inch) flour tortillas
Cooking spray
1 (10-ounce) can enchilada sauce
½ cup (2 ounces) reduced-fat shredded sharp cheddar cheese

1. Preheat oven to 400°.
2. Combine first 4 ingredients in a large bowl. Spoon chicken mixture evenly down center of tortillas. Roll jelly-roll style, and place filled tortillas, seam sides down, in an 11 x 7–inch baking dish coated with cooking spray.
3. Pour enchilada sauce over filled tortillas; sprinkle with cheese. Bake at 400° for 20 minutes or until bubbly.
YIELD: 8 SERVINGS (SERVING SIZE: 1 ENCHILADA).

PER SERVING: Calories 209; Fat 5.5g (sat 1.8g, mono 0.5g, poly 0.3g); Protein 21.3g; Carb 17.6g; Fiber 1.2g; Chol 45mg; Iron 1.6mg; Sodium 565mg; Calc 193mg

CARAMEL FLANS

POINTS value: 3

PREP: 4 minutes ■ **COOK:** 56 minutes
■ **OTHER:** 8 hours and 5 minutes

Coffee creamer and a cinnamon stick lend a delicate cinnamon flavor to these creamy custards.

2 cups 1% low-fat milk
1 cup cinnamon-vanilla–flavored fat-free coffee creamer (such as Coffeemate)
⅛ teaspoon salt
1 (3-inch) cinnamon stick
½ cup sugar
6 large egg whites
2 large egg yolks

1. Preheat oven to 325°.
2. Combine first 4 ingredients in a medium saucepan. Bring to a simmer over medium heat, stirring occasionally; remove from heat. Cover and let steep 5 minutes. Remove cinnamon stick.
3. While milk mixture steeps, place sugar in a small heavy skillet over medium-high heat; cook 4 to 5 minutes until sugar melts evenly and turns golden (do not stir), shaking pan occasionally. Immediately pour sugar mixture into 8 (6-ounce) custard cups, tipping quickly to coat bottoms of cups. Set cups in 2 (8-inch) square baking dishes.
4. Combine egg whites and egg yolks in a large bowl, stirring with a whisk until blended. Gradually add milk mixture, stirring constantly with a whisk. Ladle egg mixture evenly into prepared cups. Add hot water to baking dishes to a depth of 1 inch; cover baking dishes with foil.
5. Bake at 325° for 50 minutes or until a knife inserted in center of custards comes out clean. Remove cups from pan; cool completely on a wire rack. Cover and chill at least 8 hours.
6. Loosen edges of custards with a knife or rubber spatula. Place a plate, upside down, on top of each cup, and invert custards onto plates. Drizzle any remaining caramelized syrup over each custard. **YIELD: 8 SERVINGS (SERVING SIZE: 1 CUSTARD).**

PER SERVING: Calories 151; Fat 1.9g (sat 0.8g, mono 0.7g, poly 0.2g); Protein 5.4g; Carb 25.9g; Fiber 0.2g; Chol 55mg; Iron 0.4mg; Sodium 112mg; Calc 87mg

	MONDAY	TUESDAY	WEDNESDAY	THURSDAY
BREAKFAST	**Weight Watchers bagel,** 1 toasted **light or whipped cream cheese,** 2 tablespoons **strawberries,** 1½ cups **light orange juice,** 1 cup	**egg,** 1 scrambled **Cheese and Turkey Bagel** (Place 1 ounce deli turkey on the cut side of half of a Weight Watchers bagel. Top turkey with 1 slice reduced-fat cheddar cheese; broil until melted - **POINTS value: 4.**) **banana,** 1 small	**oatmeal,** 1 cup cooked **blueberries,** 1 cup **light orange juice,** 1 cup	**Weight Watchers bagel,** 1 toasted **peanut butter,** 1 tablespoon **peach,** 1 medium **fat-free milk,** 1 cup
LUNCH	**Balsamic Chicken Salad Sandwich** (Toss together ½ cup shredded skinless rotisserie chicken breast, ¼ cup halved grapes, and 1 tablespoon chopped pecans; whisk together 2 tablespoons each of light balsamic vinaigrette and low-fat mayonnaise. Add to chicken mixture, tossing to combine. Gently spoon on 1 slice toasted high-fiber bread; top with lettuce leaf and another slice toasted bread - **POINTS value: 7.**) **blueberries,** 1 cup **baby carrots,** 1 cup	**Fresh Mozzarella and Arugula Salad with Prosciutto, page 113,** 1 serving **peach,** 1 medium **warm pita bread,** ½ of a round **fat-free milk,** 1 cup	**Roast Beef Submarine Sandwich,** 1 (6-inch) on wheat bread with lettuce and tomato **baked potato chips,** 1 ounce **white chocolate–raspberry light fat-free yogurt,** 1 (6-ounce) carton	**Chicken Orzo Soup, page 161,** 1 serving **saltine crackers,** 6 **orange sections,** 1 cup **fat-free milk,** 1 cup
DINNER	**Italian Pinwheel Steaks, page 90,** 1 serving **mashed potatoes,** ½ cup **steamed asparagus,** 12 spears **fat-free milk,** 1 cup	**baked turkey tenderloin,** 4 ounces **Garlic Roasted Potato Wedges** (Cut 2 [4-ounce] small red potatoes into ½-inch cubes. Toss with 1 teaspoon olive oil, ½ teaspoon garlic powder, and ⅛ teaspoon salt. Roast potato cubes at 450° for 30 minutes or until crisp, stirring occasionally - **POINTS value: 3.**) **Greek Slaw, page 114,** 1 serving	**Salmon Cakes with Corn and Dill Cream, page 70,** 1 serving **mixed salad greens,** 2 cups **light balsamic vinaigrette,** 2 tablespoons	**Quick Cassoulet, page 95,** 1 serving **steamed green beans,** 1 cup **pear,** 1 medium
SNACK	**black cherry light fat-free yogurt,** 1 (6-ounce) carton **light microwave popcorn,** 3 cups	**Whole-Grain Toffee Scones, page 30,** 1 serving **pear,** 1 medium **fat-free milk,** 1 cup	**Raspberry Upside-Down Cupcakes, page 36,** 1 serving **fat-free milk,** 1 cup	**hummus,** ¼ cup **baby carrots and cucumber slices,** 1 cup
POINTS VALUE	**POINTS** value for the day: 27	**POINTS** value for the day: 28	**POINTS** value for the day: 25	**POINTS** value for the day: 23

One day's menu provides at least two servings of dairy and at least five servings of fruits and/or vegetables.

	FRIDAY	SATURDAY	SUNDAY
BREAKFAST	**Ham and Cheese Omelet** (Whisk together 1 large egg, 3 large egg whites, and a dash each of salt and pepper. Pour into a small skillet coated with cooking spray, and cook over medium heat 1 minute or until almost set. Top with ¼ cup each of reduced-fat sharp cheddar cheese and chopped lean ham; fold in half. Cook just until egg is set and cheese begins to melt - **POINTS** value: 5.) strawberries, 1½ cups	**oatmeal,** 1 cup cooked **brown sugar,** 1 tablespoon **raisins,** 2 tablespoons **fat-free milk,** 1 cup	**Weight Watchers bagel,** 1 toasted **light or whipped cream cheese,** 2 tablespoons **strawberry light fat-free yogurt,** 1 (6-ounce) carton
LUNCH	**cheese and meatball sandwich,** 1 low-fat frozen pocket **blueberries,** 1 cup **Key lime pie light fat-free yogurt,** 1 (6-ounce) carton	**Steak Caesar Salad** (Toss together 2 cups torn romaine lettuce leaves, 6 halved cherry tomatoes, ¼ cup fat-free croutons, and 2 tablespoons shredded Parmesan cheese. Top with 3 ounces lean cooked and trimmed flank steak; drizzle with 2 tablespoons light Caesar dressing, tossing to combine - **POINTS** value: 8.) **whole-wheat French bread roll,** 1	**macaroni and cheese,** 1 low-fat frozen entrée **cucumber slices,** 1 cup **peach,** 1 medium
DINNER	**Bacon Ranch Chicken Pasta, page 106,** 1 serving **mixed salad greens,** 2 cups **light Italian dressing,** 2 tablespoons **watermelon,** 1 cup **fat-free milk,** 1 cup	**grilled vegetable burger,** 1 patty **lite wheat hamburger bun,** 1 **tomato slice and lettuce leaf,** 1 each **Baked Onion Rings, page 150,** 1 serving **grapes,** 1 cup	**Scallop Kebabs with Salsa Verde, page 75,** 1 serving **Quick Spinach Salad** (Combine 2 cups baby spinach leaves; ⅓ cup chopped tomato; 1 piece cooked turkey bacon, crumbled; and 2 tablespoons shredded Parmesan cheese. Top with 2 tablespoons light balsamic vinaigrette - **POINTS** value: 3.)
SNACK	**light microwave popcorn,** 3 cups **cocoa-dusted almonds,** 1 (100-calorie) package	**part-skim mozzarella string cheese,** 1 **peach light fat-free yogurt,** 1 (6-ounce) carton	**apple,** 1 medium **peanut butter,** 1 tablespoon **fat-free milk,** 1 cup
POINTS VALUE	**POINTS** value for the day: 26	**POINTS** value for the day: 26	**POINTS** value for the day: 26

WEEK 1

	MONDAY	TUESDAY	WEDNESDAY	THURSDAY
BREAKFAST	**raisin bran,** 1 cup **fat-free milk,** 1 cup **honeydew,** 1 cup	**Raspberry-Granola Parfait** (Spoon ½ of a 6-ounce carton of raspberry light fat-free yogurt into a parfait glass or bowl; top with ½ cup raspberries and ¼ cup low-fat granola. Repeat layers - **POINTS** value: 5.)	**low-fat multigrain waffles,** 2 frozen **light maple syrup,** 2 tablespoons **fat-free milk,** 1 cup	**raisin bran,** 1 cup **fat-free milk,** 1 cup
LUNCH	**Tuna Melt** (Combine 2 ounces chunk light tuna; 2 tablespoons each chopped celery and light mayonnaise; and a dash each of salt, pepper, and lemon juice. Mix well. Top 1 slice toasted high-fiber bread with tuna mixture and 1 slice reduced-fat Swiss cheese; broil until melted. Top cheese with lettuce leaf, tomato slice, and additional slice toasted bread - **POINTS value:** 6.) **pear,** 1 medium **blackberry light fat-free yogurt,** 1 (6-ounce) carton	**canned tomato-basil soup,** 1 cup **Cheesy Pita Toasts** (Split half of a pita round in half; cut into triangles. Coat triangles with olive oil–flavored cooking spray; sprinkle wth 2 tablespoons grated Parmesan cheese. Place on a baking sheet; bake at 400° for 5 minutes or until lightly toasted - **POINTS** value: 2.) **grapes,** 1 cup	**Chicken Caprese Melts, page 126,** 1 serving **celery sticks and baby carrots,** 1 cup **light blue cheese dressing,** 2 tablespoons **plum,** 1 medium	**hamburger,** 1 small fast food **lettuce leaf and tomato slice,** 1 each **apple,** 1 medium **fat-free milk,** 1 cup
DINNER	**Greek Lemon-Artichoke Chicken, page 98,** 1 serving **brown rice,** ½ cup **steamed broccoli and carrots,** 1 cup	**Peanutty Beef Pasta, page 90,** 1 serving **steamed sugar snap peas,** 1 cup **fat-free milk,** 1 cup	**grilled or baked tilapia (or other white fish),** 6 ounces cooked **Wild Mushroom Flatbread, page 34,** 1 serving **Roasted Asparagus with Feta, page 147,** 1 serving	**Zucchini-Tomato-Rice Frittata, page 83,** 1 serving **mixed salad greens,** 2 cups **light ranch dressing,** 2 tablespoons **lemon chiffon light fat-free yogurt,** 1 (6-ounce) carton
SNACK	**Key Lime Cheesecake Parfaits, page 40,** 1 serving **orange,** 1 medium	**fat-free sugar-free chocolate pudding,** 1 cup **cherries,** 1 cup	**Strawberry-Banana Smoothie** (Combine 1 cup each of light orange juice and sliced strawberries, 1 [6-ounce] carton strawberry light fat-free yogurt, and ½ cup ice in a blender; process until smooth - **POINTS** value: 3.)	**Quick Cheese Quesadilla** (Top half of an 8-inch low-fat whole-wheat tortilla with ⅓ cup preshredded reduced-fat Mexican blend cheese; fold other half over cheese. Cook folded tortilla over medium heat in pan coated with cooking spray until lightly browned - **POINTS** value: 4.) **Poblano–Roasted Corn Salsa, page 18,** 1 serving
POINTS VALUE	**POINTS** value for the day: 25	**POINTS** value for the day: 24	**POINTS** value for the day: 27	**POINTS** value for the day: 26

One day's menu provides at least two servings of dairy and at least five servings of fruits and/or vegetables.

	FRIDAY	SATURDAY	SUNDAY
BREAKFAST	**Banana-Nut Muffins with Peanut Butter–Honey Drizzle, page 28,** 1 serving **vanilla light fat-free yogurt,** 1 (6-ounce) carton **light orange juice,** 1 cup	**raisin bran,** 1 cup **fat-free milk,** 1 cup **cantaloupe,** 1 cup	**Waffles with Berries** (Toast 2 low-fat multigrain waffles; top with 1 cup mixed berries and 2 tablespoons light maple syrup. Sprinkle with 2 teaspoons powdered sugar - **POINTS value: 6.)** **fat-free milk,** 1 cup
LUNCH	**White Bean and Bulgur Salad, page 115,** 1 serving **tomato,** 2 slices **warm pita bread,** ½ of a round **hummus,** ¼ cup **grapes,** 1 cup	**pepperoni pizza,** 1 low-fat frozen entrée **baby carrots,** 1 cup **plum,** 1 medium	**Fruit and Gorgonzola Salad** (Top 2 cups mixed salad greens with ⅓ cup each of sliced strawberries and chopped pear, and 2 tablespoons each of crumbled Gorgonzola cheese and light balsamic vinaigrette; toss to combine - **POINTS value: 5.)** **whole-wheat crackers,** 4 **grapes,** 1 cup
DINNER	**baked teriyaki pork tenderloin,** 3 ounces **Savory Twice-Baked Sweet Potatoes, page 151,** 1 serving **steamed green beans,** 1 cup	**Shrimp and Asparagus Risotto, page 76,** 1 serving **baby spinach leaves,** 2 cups **light balsamic vinaigrette,** 2 tablespoons **raspberries,** 1 cup **fat-free milk,** 1 cup	**Lamb Chops with Herbed-Feta Orzo, page 91,** 1 serving **sauteed zucchini,** 1 cup
SNACK	**blueberries,** 1 cup **reduced-fat vanilla wafers,** 6 **fat-free milk,** 1 cup	**light cookies and cream ice cream,** ¾ cup	**orange mango light fat-free yogurt,** 1 (6-ounce) carton **reduced-fat vanilla wafers,** 6
POINTS VALUE	**POINTS** value for the day: 23	**POINTS** value for the day: 25	**POINTS** value for the day: 27

7-Day Menu Planner

WEEK 2

	MONDAY	TUESDAY	WEDNESDAY	THURSDAY
BREAKFAST	**whole-wheat English muffin,** 1 split and toasted **light butter,** 1 tablespoon **lemon chiffon light fat-free yogurt,** 1 (6-ounce) carton	**Kiwi-Blueberry Smoothie** (Combine 2 small chopped peeled kiwifruit, 1 small frozen banana, and 1 [6-ounce] carton blueberry light fat-free yogurt in a blender; process until smooth - **POINTS** value: 3.) **part-skim mozzarella stick,** 1	**grits,** 1 cup **turkey bacon,** 3 slices **grapefruit sections,** 1 cup	**Honey–Peanut Butter Muffin-wich** (Split and toast 1 whole-wheat English muffin. Evenly spread 2 tablespoons peanut butter over cut sides of muffin. Slice 1 small banana; top peanut butter with banana slices, and drizzle with 1 tablespoon honey. Serve muffin open-faced - **POINTS** value: 8.) **fat-free milk,** 1 cup
LUNCH	**Spicy Ham and Cheese Melt** (Toast 2 slices high-fiber whole-wheat bread. Spread 2 tea-spoons each of light mayonnaise and Dijon mustard over 1 side of bread; top with 2 ounces lean deli ham and 1 slice reduced-fat pepper-Jack cheese. Broil until cheese melts; top cheese with lettuce leaf, tomato slice, and remaining bread slice - **POINTS** value: 6.) **cucumber slices,** 1 cup **peach,** 1 large	**barbecue boneless chicken breast,** 3 ounces with skin removed **blackeyed peas,** ½ cup **tomato slices,** 2 **cornbread,** 1 [2-inch] square	**Tomato-Fennel Soup with Feta,** page 158, 2 servings **whole-wheat crackers,** 4 **clementines,** 2 small	**shrimp marinara with linguine,** 1 low-fat frozen entrée **steamed green beans,** 1 cup **cherry vanilla light fat-free yogurt,** 1 (6-ounce) carton
DINNER	**Orange-Basil Grouper,** page 67, 1 serving **Parmesan couscous,** ½ cup **steamed asparagus,** 12 spears	**Sausage, Sage, and Butternut Squash–Stuffed Shells,** page 95, 1 serving **baby spinach leaves,** 2 cups **light Italian dressing,** 2 tablespoons	**Chicken and Vegetable Pad Thai,** page 102, 1 serving **pineapple chunks,** 1 cup **fat-free milk,** 1 cup	**grilled or baked center-cut boneless pork chop,** 3 ounces **wild rice,** ½ cup **Broccoli Casserole,** page 148, 1 serving
SNACK	**apple,** 1 medium **peanut butter,** 1 tablespoon **fat-free milk,** 1 cup	**Weight Watchers chocolate cake,** 1 **fat-free milk,** 1 cup	**strawberry light yogurt smoothie,** 1 (7-ounce) container **whole-wheat crackers,** 4 **Swiss cheese,** 1 ounce	**hummus,** ¼ cup **baby carrots and celery sticks,** 1 cup **warm pita bread,** ½ of a round
POINTS VALUE	**POINTS** value for the day: 24	**POINTS** value for the day: 26	**POINTS** value for the day: 26	**POINTS** value for the day: 26

One day's menu provides at least two servings of dairy and at least five servings of fruits and/or vegetables.

FRIDAY	SATURDAY	SUNDAY	BREAKFAST
Egg, Cheese, and Bacon Sandwich (Whisk together 1 large egg, 2 large egg whites, and a dash each of salt and pepper. Scramble egg mixture until done; place eggs on 1 half of a toasted whole-wheat English muffin. Top eggs with 1 slice cooked turkey bacon, halved; 1 slice reduced-fat cheddar cheese; and remaining toasted muffin half - **POINTS** value: 6.) **grapefruit sections,** 1 cup	**grits,** 1 cup **egg,** 1 scrambled **peach,** 1 medium	**Blueberry-Cornmeal Pancakes, page 32,** 1 serving **light maple syrup,** 2 tablespoons **vanilla light fat-free yogurt,** 1 (6-ounce) carton **light orange juice,** 1 cup	
Chicken and Strawberry Salad, page 118, 1 serving **whole-wheat crackers,** 4 **peach light fat-free yogurt,** 1 (6-ounce) carton	**bean burrito,** 1 small fast food **blueberries,** 1 cup **cucumber and celery slices,** 1 cup **fat-free milk,** 1 cup	**Southwest Turkey Spud** (Top 1 large [7-ounce] baked potato with 2 ounces chopped deli turkey breast, ¼ cup preshredded reduced-fat Mexican blend cheese, ¼ cup chopped tomatoes, 2 tablespoons reduced-fat sour cream, and 1 tablespoon chopped green onions - **POINTS** value: 8.) **mixed salad greens,** 2 cups **light Italian dressing,** 2 tablespoons	LUNCH
grilled or baked salmon, 6 ounces **Caramelized Onion–Mushroom Pilaf, page 153,** 1 serving **steamed snow peas,** 1 cup	**Seared Beef Fillets with "Melted" Tomatoes and Green Onions, page 88,** 1 serving **Basil-Parmesan Pasta** (Toss 1 cup hot cooked whole-wheat spaghetti with 1 teaspoon olive oil and ⅛ teaspoon salt; gently stir in 2 tablespoons each of chopped basil and grated Parmesan cheese - **POINTS** value: 5.) **sautéed spinach,** 1 cup	**baked marinated turkey tenderloin,** 4 ounces cooked **mashed potatoes,** ½ cup **Italian Zucchini and Tomatoes, page 152,** 1 serving	DINNER
Frozen Peanut Butter–Banana Pops, page 45, 1 serving **fat-free milk,** 1 cup	**fat-free cottage cheese,** 1 cup **pineapple chunks,** 1 cup	**orange,** 1 medium **blueberry light yogurt smoothie,** 1 (7-ounce) container	SNACK
POINTS value for the day: 28	**POINTS** value for the day: 28	**POINTS** value for the day: 23	POINTS VALUE

7-Day Menu Planner

WEEK 3

	MONDAY	TUESDAY	WEDNESDAY	THURSDAY
BREAKFAST	**bran flakes,** 1 cup **banana,** 1 small **fat-free milk,** 1 cup	**Cheese Muffins** (Split 1 whole-wheat English muffin; top each cut side of muffin halves with 1 slice reduced-fat provolone cheese. Broil until cheese melts - **POINTS** value: 6.) cantaloupe, 1 cup	**Weight Watchers blueberry muffin,** 1 **peach light fat-free yogurt,** 1 (6-ounce) carton	**bran flakes,** 1 cup **blueberries,** 1 cup **fat-free milk,** 1 cup **light orange juice,** 1 cup
LUNCH	**chicken and rice soup,** 1½ cups **whole-wheat crackers,** 4 **strawberries,** 1½ cups **lemon chiffon light fat-free yogurt,** 1 (6-ounce) carton	**Southwestern Taco Salad,** page 117, 1 serving **watermelon,** 1 cup **fat-free milk,** 1 cup	**grilled chicken sandwich,** 1 fast food with no mayonnaise **lettuce leaf and tomato slice,** 1 each **unsweetened mandarin oranges,** 1 cup **carrot and celery sticks,** 1 cup	**Beef and Cheese Sandwich with Roasted Bell Peppers** (Toast 2 slices high-fiber whole-wheat bread. Stir together 2 teaspoons each of light mayonnaise and pesto; spread over 1 slice bread. Top with ¼ cup chopped roasted red bell peppers, 2 ounces lean deli roast beef, and 1 slice reduced-fat provolone cheese. Broil until cheese melts; top cheese with 2 lettuce leaves and remaining slice toasted bread - **POINTS** value: 6.) **baked potato chips,** 1 ounce **fat-free milk,** 1 cup
DINNER	**Turkey Florentine Skillet Lasagna,** page 109, 1 serving **steamed carrots,** 1 cup	**steamed shrimp,** 6 ounces cooked and shelled **whole-wheat French bread,** 1 ounce **Blue Cheese–Bacon Slaw,** page 114, 1 serving	**Honey Balsamic–Glazed Pork Tenderloin,** page 92, 1 serving **whole-wheat couscous,** 1 cup **Baked Creamed Spinach,** page 152, 1 serving	**Asian Chicken Salad,** page 119, 1 serving **pear,** 1 medium
SNACK	**Honey Frozen Yogurt with Fresh Figs and Gingersnap Crumble,** page 41, 1 serving	**fat-free cottage cheese,** 1 cup **mixed fruit,** 1 cup	**clementines,** 2 small **mixed berry light yogurt smoothie,** 1 (7-ounce) container	**cocoa-dusted almonds,** 1 (100-calorie) package **fat-free milk,** 1 cup
POINTS VALUE	**POINTS** value for the day: 23	**POINTS** value for the day: 28	**POINTS** value for the day: 25	**POINTS** value for the day: 26

One day's menu provides at least two servings of dairy and at least five servings of fruits and/or vegetables.

	FRIDAY	SATURDAY	SUNDAY	
BREAKFAST	Weight Watchers blueberry muffin, 1 turkey bacon, 3 slices fat-free milk, 1 cup	bran flakes, 1 cup dried cranberries, 2 tablespoons fat-free milk, 1 cup light orange juice, 1 cup	Stuffed French Toast, page 31, 1 serving light maple syrup, 2 tablespoons fat-free milk, 1 cup blueberries, 1 cup	
LUNCH	roasted vegetable pizza, 1 low-fat frozen entrée side salad, 1 fast food light Italian dressing, 2 tablespoons	Blueberry-Feta Chicken Salad (Top 2 cups mixed greens with ½ cup shredded skinless rotisserie chicken breast, ¼ cup blueberries, 2 tablespoons each of feta cheese and light balsamic vinaigrette, and 1 tablespoon toasted sliced almonds; toss gently - *POINTS* value: 5.) whole-wheat breadstick, 1	Turkey Dogs with Fennel Slaw, page 128, 1 serving baked potato chips, 1 ounce grapes, 1 cup	
DINNER	Baja Fish Soft Tacos, page 73, 1 serving unsweetened mandarin oranges, 1 cup	Grilled Polenta and Summer Vegetables, page 79, 1 serving fat-free milk, 1 cup	rotisserie chicken, 3 ounces white meat with skin removed Almond-Ginger Rice, page 154, 1 serving steamed green beans, 1 cup watermelon, 1 cup	
SNACK	honey wheat pretzel sticks, 8 strawberries, 1½ cups Key lime pie light fat-free yogurt, 1 (6-ounce) carton	part-skim mozzarella string cheese, 1 mango, 1 cup	low-fat graham crackers, 1 sheet peanut butter, 1 tablespoon fat-free milk, 1 cup	
POINTS VALUE	*POINTS* value for the day: 26	*POINTS* value for the day: 24	*POINTS* value for the day: 28	

7-Day Menu Planner

WEEK 4

GENERAL RECIPE INDEX

POINTS® Value Index

10 SIMPLE SIDE DISHES

Vegetable	Servings	Preparation	Cooking Instructions
Asparagus	3 to 4 per pound	Snap off tough ends. Remove scales, if desired.	To steam: Cook, covered, on a rack above boiling water 2 to 3 minutes. To boil: Cook, covered, in a small amount of boiling water 2 to 3 minutes or until crisp-tender.
Broccoli	3 to 4 per pound	Remove outer leaves and tough ends of lower stalks. Wash; cut into spears.	To steam: Cook, covered, on a rack above boiling water 5 to 7 minutes or until crisp-tender.
Carrots	4 per pound	Scrape; remove ends, and rinse. Leave tiny carrots whole; slice large carrots.	To steam: Cook, covered, on a rack above boiling water 8 to 10 minutes or until crisp-tender. To boil: Cook, covered, in a small amount of boiling water 8 to 10 minutes or until crisp-tender.
Cauliflower	4 per medium head	Remove outer leaves and stalk. Wash. Break into florets.	To steam: Cook, covered, on a rack above boiling water 5 to 7 minutes or until crisp-tender.
Corn	4 per 4 large ears	Remove husks and silks. Leave corn on the cob, or cut off kernels.	To boil: Cook, covered, in boiling water to cover 8 to 10 minutes (on cob) or in a small amount of boiling water 4 to 6 minutes (kernels).
Green beans	4 per pound	Wash; trim ends, and remove strings. Cut into 1½-inch pieces.	To steam: Cook, covered, on a rack above boiling water 5 to 7 minutes. To boil: Cook, covered, in a small amount of boiling water 5 to 7 minutes or until crisp-tender.
Potatoes	3 to 4 per pound	Scrub; peel, if desired. Leave whole, slice, or cut into chunks.	To boil: Cook, covered, in boiling water to cover 30 to 40 minutes (whole) or 15 to 20 minutes (slices or chunks). To bake: Bake at 400° for 1 hour or until done.
Snow peas	4 per pound	Wash; trim ends, and remove tough strings.	To steam: Cook, covered, on a rack above boiling water 2 to 3 minutes. Or sauté in cooking spray or 1 teaspoon oil over medium-high heat 3 to 4 minutes or until crisp-tender.
Squash, summer	3 to 4 per pound	Wash; trim ends, and slice or chop.	To steam: Cook, covered, on a rack above boiling water 6 to 8 minutes. To boil: Cook, covered, in a small amount of boiling water 6 to 8 minutes or until crisp-tender.
Squash, winter (including acorn, butternut, and buttercup)	2 per pound	Rinse; cut in half, and remove all seeds. Leave in halves to bake, or peel and cube to boil.	To boil: Cook cubes, covered, in boiling water 20 to 25 minutes. To bake: Place halves, cut sides down, in a shallow baking dish; add ½ inch water. Bake, uncovered, at 375° for 30 minutes. Turn and season, or fill; bake an additional 20 to 30 minutes or until tender.